TAMING
THE TIGER

ALSO BY WITOLD RYBCZYNSKI

Paper Heroes:
A Review of Appropriate Technology

**WITOLD
RYBCZYNSKI**

TAMING
THE TIGER

THE STRUGGLE TO CONTROL
TECHNOLOGY

THE VIKING PRESS   NEW YORK

Library of Congress Cataloging in Publication Data
Rybczynski, Witold.
Taming the tiger.
Bibliography: p.
Includes index.
1. Technology.   I. Title.
T49.5.R93   1983   303.4'83   82-42732
ISBN 0-670-69359-6

Printed in the United States of America
Set in Video Gael

FOR SHIRLEY

FOREWORD

We must learn to live with the machine; we have little other choice. Historians of technology remind us that the machine is not new, and that the origins of our technology are in devices that were invented many hundreds of years before the European Industrial Revolution. Although our forebears may have used technology, their societies could hardly be called technological. The overwhelming presence of machines in virtually every sphere of modern life, on the other hand, is a new phenomenon, and one that has led more than one writer to refer to ours as a "Technological Society" or a "Machine Age." There may be little comfort gained in attaching labels, but it is a start.

There was a time when we did love the machine, but that celebration of technology was short-lived and occurred during a period that now seems quaintly untechnological. The machines that inspired poets, writers, and painters at the beginning of the twentieth century consisted of flimsy, canvas-covered airplanes and large, but not very fast, automobiles. The dirigible and the ocean liner were celebrated as the harbingers of a new epoch; they turned out to be the swan song of an old one. The cavalier biplane aviator, who even in wartime was a "knight of the air," was replaced by the faceless Stuka pilot. The wealthy enthusiasts who took part in the Paris-Berlin car races, carrying their own mechanics, spare parts, and champagne, could not imagine that in forty years they would be replaced by throngs of inexpensive Citroëns and Volkswagens. The technology that was celebrated in the early 1900s was still the technology of an élite, of the Right People. The democratizing potential of the machine was not yet understood.

Although few would care to admit it, many of the problems associated with technology are the result of the use of the machine by the masses. Environmental pollution, the breakdown of society, and many of the stresses felt by both institutions and individuals are due to the *personal* use of the automobile, the aerosol can, or the handgun—of the machine. A technological society, after all, is one in which everyone has access to technology. It is the almost universal availability of technology, not just its presence, that distinguishes the rich countries from the poor.

Although the simple fact that so many individuals have access to so many machines has created many difficulties, it hardly accounts for all the unpleasant effects of technology. The use of automation in the workplace, for example, is the result of a choice made by organizations. The effects of television are due partly to individuals' decisions of what to watch, but also to corporate choices of which programs to distribute. The momentous decision to develop atomic technology was made by a very small group of people.

It is difficult to love something you do not understand, and it sometimes seems that it is lack of understanding above all that has resulted in a general feeling that technology is out of human control. Whether or not mankind is once again at a crossroads, it does seem appropriate to speak of a need for mechanisms that will alter our relationship to the machine and restore a sense of mastery instead of the current feeling of servitude. Part of the nostalgia that affects us when we look back at earlier periods is a sense of loss for a time when we were not controlled by the machine. If this happier relationship is to be re-established, something will have to change. Will it be our machines, or ourselves?

The British historian Arnold J. Toynbee once wrote to the effect that since the future is unknown, the only way we can hope to illuminate it is by looking at the past. This is by way of warning the reader that this book "looks at the past" a great deal. Since I am not a historian, I must acknowledge a debt to those whose works I have used, and I have done so not with interminable footnotes, but with a lengthy bibliography which I refer to in the text by citing either the author's name or the title of his work. I have not included page references; I assume that interested readers will want to read the relevant books and form their own conclusions, which may be different from my own.

I must also acknowledge the useful comments and criticisms of two historians—Reyner Banham and John Lukacs—whose friendly assistance to an amateur is appreciated. My friend and colleague Martin Pawley was also kind enough to review the manuscript.

Special thanks are due to Elaine Koss for her work in copy editing, and to my editor, William Strachan, whose suggestions and encouragement pushed this book along during its protracted writing, sandwiched as it was between bouts of teaching, traveling, and house construction.

W.R.
Hemmingford, Québec
October 1982

CONTENTS

PART I

THE SHOCK OF
THE MACHINE

CHAPTER 1

THE PROSTHETIC GOD

Man has, as it were, become a kind of prosthetic god. When he puts on all his auxiliary organs he is truly magnificent; but those organs have not grown on to him and they still give him much trouble at times.
—Sigmund Freud, *Civilization and Its Discontents*

Consider man, the prosthetic god. Not being able to run very fast or for very long, he has grafted on to himself additional feet, until he can travel farther and faster than any other animal, and not only on land but also on and under water and in the air. He can reinforce his eyes with glasses, telescopes, and microscopes. Thanks to orbiting satellites, he can, without displacing himself, count wildebeest in the African veldt, or missile silos outside Novosibirsk. Lacking the dolphin's ability to communicate great distances, he amplifies his voice with the aid of radio waves. In addition to his genetic code, which he shares with all other living things, he has acquired a perpetually growing communal memory in the shape of the written word, the photograph, and the recording. Everything we know now, we know forever.

These auxiliary parts not only extend man's natural abilities but change them beyond recognition. The book extends not only our memory, but also, says Argentine author Jorge Luis Borges, our imagination. The brain is supercharged by the computer; perhaps, one day, the two may become indistinguishable. Thanks also to the computer, all the books of the world can be assembled into one great Alexandrian library—no bigger than a small bedroom—through which a person may stroll, so to speak, finding in five minutes the one book he previously could not have found in a lifetime's searching. What is more, these extensions are detachable. The prosthetic eyes and ears can be sent far into the solar system to look at the other side of the moon, or on a deep interior voyage to see something even more marvelous, the human embryo.

Technology, as Freud drolly observed, is really a set of artificial organs, extensions of our natural ones. He understood, as many still do not, that the relationship between ourselves and our tools is often blurred, and frequently intimate.

Tools are not unique to the human; a number of animals and birds use tools both in hunting and in nest building. Whether man thinks because he uses tools, or vice versa, the fact remains that from the beginning of recorded history tools and technology have been part and parcel of man's essence. The prehistoric men and women who killed with a club, instead of with bare hands, or who, lacking protective pelts, covered themselves with animal skins, may have been imitating the sea otter, which cracks clams on a stone it picks up from the seabed, or the squirrel, which burrows under a pile of leaves to hibernate. It is even possible that the first projectile may not have been thrown by a man but by an ape. But it is the evolution and invention of improved tools that distinguish men from animals. It is human logic that leads from the projectile to the slingshot, from the Roman catapult to the ancient ballista, and, with the invention of gunpowder, to the cannon, which is, after all, merely a device to throw a stone a still greater distance.

But using technology to overcome man's biological limitations has not been altogether a painless experience. The artificial limbs, to continue Freud's metaphor, itch. Sometimes the scar will not heal; inflammation and infection set in. Occasionally the body rejects the implanted organ, and, if it is not quickly removed, serious damage can result. The patient barely recovers before another *assemblage* is attempted. The surgeons—the scientists and engineers—frequently neglect to tell the patient what the new organ is for, which is sometimes unpleasant and sometimes terrifying. Unmentioned also, until too late, are the accompanying side effects of this hazardous prosthesis. And always that itch.

Little wonder that the patient sometimes rebels. Do the surgeons really know what they are doing? he asks. Will the new appurtenance be compatible with the rest of the anatomy? Is it really needed, or will it do more harm than good? It is easy to overextend a metaphor, but it is a fact that growing numbers of people are beginning to question the wisdom of continued technological progress. Perhaps it would be better to remain where we are, or even backtrack a little. Much of this growing distrust of technology is based on the belief that technological development is ungovernable and ultimately outside of human control.

If the invention of fire represents one of the first instances of man's control over the forces of nature, as Friedrich Engels claimed, then the first man-caused forest fire must surely be one of the earliest examples of technology out of control. One can imagine that even then, in the murky shadows of prehistory, our ancestors must have had a lively discussion about the propriety of the continued use of this new discovery, so wonderful yet so awesome. The optimists obviously won out, as optimists usually do.

That technology has almost always had unintended side effects has often been cited by critics as a symptom of man's inability to control his inventions. Yet paradoxically, it is precisely the unpredictability of technology that has proved to be its most endearing characteristic. For instance, when John Gorrie, a Florida doctor, patented an ice-making machine in 1851, he intended it as a device to cool the rooms of his yellow fever patients. Like many doctors at the time, Gorrie mistakenly believed that yellow fever was due to miasma, or "bad air." His ice-making machine thus had little effect on curing this disease, but it was a very important contribution to the development of quite another technology—refrigeration.

The popular story of the absent-minded scientist who confusedly mixes two chemicals to produce an important discovery is not uncommon. The unpredictability of technological invention is illustrated by the case of Henri Moissan, a French chemist who was trying to manufacture artificial diamonds. In the process, he discovered, quite accidentally, the compound calcium carbide. Calcium carbide did not make diamonds, but when combined with water it did produce a burnable gas—acetylene—which became the most common form of domestic lighting until the invention of the electric light bulb. The accidents continued. A German chemist, Fritz Klatte, took up Moissan's invention and tried to develop an aircraft dope using acetylene. In 1912, one of the many unsuccessful combinations he tried turned out to be the world's first plastic—vinyl chloride.

In 1886, an Atlanta pharmacist concocted a compound which he claimed would whiten teeth, cleanse the mouth, harden and beautify the gums and relieve mental and physical exhaustion. John Styth Pemberton was the unrenowned inventor of Globe of Flower Cough Syrup, Triplex Liver Pills, and Indian Queen Hair Dye, and his latest patent medicine was equally unsuccessful. He sold it to another druggist, who marketed the odd mixture of coca leaves and cola nuts as a soft drink, under the same name that Pemberton had given it—Coca-Cola. Thus are the foundations for multinational corporations laid.

Of course the *negative* unforeseen effects of technological innovation can be frightening. One of the most notorious contemporary examples concerns the Aswan High Dam in Egypt, the enormous Soviet-aided irrigation and hydroelectric project that was to be the linchpin of Egyptian rural development. Instead, it is turning out to have the opposite effect. The dam, which is located in the extreme south of the country, prevents nutrient-rich silt from the Upper Nile from reaching the lower-river areas in the north. As a result, the seasonal cycle of fertilization, which has been the mainstay of Egyptian agriculture for centuries, has been interrupted. Although flooding still occurs, the level of nutrients in the otherwise sandy soil has dropped drastically, and the reduction in food production, coupled with Egypt's rising population, has created severe food shortages. Another ecological megadisaster may occur in Brazil, where, some scientists believe, the large-scale lumber industry could denude the jungle to the point that the reduction in vegetation, and hence in oxygen production, will affect the biosphere on a global scale.

These two examples give the impression that it is the scale of technology that is at fault; but even "small" technological innovations can have a large environmental impact. The innocuous flush toilet is a case in point. The first American urban sewerage system was built in Brooklyn in 1857, and represented at the time a hygienic and effective solution to the unsanitary cesspools and drainage ditches that had come to characterize the urban environment in the nineteenth century. Today the city of New York dumps five million tons of sewage sludge about twelve miles offshore in the Atlantic Ocean. The liquid residue that is left after so-called sewage treatment contains vast quantities of bacteria and concentrations of various heavy metals, such as zinc, chromium, and lead. In the last five years, New Jersey and Long Island beaches have been periodically shut down as the "foreign substance" (actually very American) washes ashore. The effect on marine life will take longer to be felt but could be more serious than it is on human life.

It sometimes seems that every step forward in technological development is (potentially, at least) accompanied by one step backward in terms of environmental or personal safety. The aerosol, for instance, turns out to emit fluorocarbons whose increased presence in the atmosphere depletes the ozone layer and may have severe long-term effects on the quantity of ultraviolet rays that reach the surface of the earth. Similarly, asbestos, a life-saving, fireproof material, is also a vicious carcinogen. DDT, which was developed to control malarial mosquitoes, is turning up in the food chain in dangerous concentrations, and as a result it has been banned in many countries.

It is technological "errors" such as these that give rise to the nagging feeling that the proud locomotive of progress is really an ominous juggernaut, and that our imminent demise, like that of the followers of the god Jagannath, who threw themselves beneath the wheels of his great ceremonial chariot, will be equally poignant for being self-inflicted.

Our fear of the machine is heightened by the feeling that the twentieth century is the first to experience the unintended side effects of technology. It may be a consolation to learn that humanity has experienced the impact of technological change no less mordantly in earlier times. The historian Lynn White, Jr., has documented in *Medieval Religion and Technology* how the adoption of the fireplace and chimney disturbed everyday life. Until the eleventh century, heating had been provided by open fireplaces. There were no mantels or even chimneys, and smoke was simply allowed to filter out through the thatch or shingles of the roof. Thus the entire household—lord, freeman, and servant—lived, ate, and slept (in curtained compartments) in the great hall, gathering for warmth around the central, open, cooking fire. With the development of the fireplace and chimney, it became possible to heat individual rooms on different floors throughout the house. As a result, the forced egalitarianism of the early Middle Ages began to give way to a more individual way of living. White quotes an eleventh-century observer, who wrote, "Now every rich man eats by himself in a private parlor to be rid of poor men, or in a chamber with a chimney, and leaves the great hall." Thus the chimney contributed in no small part to the upstairs-downstairs stratification that would last into the twentieth century.

White also describes the origin of another invention of the Middle Ages: the national flag. He traces it to the pennons that knights affixed to their lances. These heraldic colors, which in the case of the king became the national colors, had a utilitarian purpose quite apart from their symbolic function. They were intended to prevent the lance from transfixing a foe during a mounted charge, for if the lance became embedded too deeply in the body of one's unfortunate opponent, there was a danger that one might not be able to pull it out and would be left weaponless on the field of battle. The cloth pennon also had the advantage that, unlike a solid crosspiece, it could not get caught in the enemy's armor but could always be ripped free. These "grimly functional rags" were first used by the mounted soldiers of Central Asia, who simply tied a piece of cloth or horsehair to the ends of their spears. The barbarian invaders worried about piercing their opponents because they used a device unknown to the Europeans—the stirrup. The stirrup, which was quickly adopted by the Franks, transmitted the entire weight of both horse and rider to the lance point, giving the term "shock combat" its true meaning.

I should hasten to point out that White is no technological determinist. His point is that technology creates the opportunity for social change, not that it is always invented in response to specific problems. Indeed, sometimes innovation seems haphazard or simply accidental. The technology of artillery, for instance, was introduced into Europe in the thirteenth century. The first cannon were made out of bronze, and the expansion of their manufacture relied on a highly developed bronze-casting industry. This industry happened to be present in Europe at the time, although it had been perfected in producing a very dissimilar article—bronze church bells.

While technological developments have often pursued their own, sometimes random, logic, they have always been accompanied by overt attempts at exercising human control. In 1139, Pope Innocent II banned the crossbow as too cruel a weapon (though its use against the Moors—infidels—was permitted). The ban was not successful, in part, one guesses, because its aim was as much political as humanitarian, since it attempted to redress the balance between the mounted aristocrat and the commoner crossbowman. In another vein, Edward III of England, in order to promote the use of the Welsh longbow (the most devastating weapon of its day), prohibited on pain of death the practice of all sports *except* archery.

There are many examples of technological control in the workplace. In 1559, Queen Elizabeth I of England refused to grant a royal patent for a knitting machine on the grounds that it would deprive too many of her subjects of employment. Charles II, acting in the same spirit, gave a charter to the hosiers' guild which would protect them against mechanization until the nineteenth century.

Not all technological control was exercised by benign monarchs. Frequently workers who have felt themselves threatened by technical innovation have agitated for these innovations to be curtailed. Often this agitation has taken the form of violence directed against the guilty machine. In the nineteenth century, Belgian weavers took to "accidentally" dropping their heavy wooden clogs (or *sabots*) into the delicate mechanism of the loom, giving rise to the expression "sabotage." Probably the most well-known example of machine-wrecking in the workplace occurred during the Luddite rebellion in England (see Chapter 2). Although Luddism was by no means unique, it has become a generic description for all violent reactions to mechanization.

It may seem surprising that the issue of technology control should lead to violence. On the one hand, the choice of a technology is the choice of a particular set of values, and thus the debate about nuclear energy, or small-scale industry, or chemical agriculture, is really a debate about human values masquerading as a discussion of technical options. On the other hand, as history shows us, technology frequently contains the seeds of disruptive and threatening change. Did the medieval homeowner realize what he was getting into when he started building fireplaces? Not that we have more foresight today, but we are probably more skeptical about the side effects of technological innovation.

What distinguishes the current debate about controlling technology is that the two sides are so far apart. It seems to be less a question of what to do, than of whether to do anything at all. Instead of a discussion of how to control technology there is polarization. On the one hand are the "Boosters," for whom all technological change represents progress, and who see any attempt to control the technical future as a loss of nerve. On the other hand are the "Obstructionists," for whom *any* technical innovation is a threat, and for whom controlling technology means gradually reducing it, or at least doing so whenever possible. While the Boosters reflect a nineteenth-century optimism about the machine, the Obstructionists represent a more recent, and more novel view whose origins are worth exploring.

The Obstructionists' view of technology as a violent, animal force is widespread and, in popular culture at least, no longer needs justification. Charlie Chaplin devastatingly portrayed the carnivorous machine in his film *Modern Times,* which set if not the content at least the tone of the ensuing discussion. The French director Jacques Tati satirized the domestic world gone haywire in *Mon Oncle,* which showed the protagonist victimized by a series of rebellious household gadgets. Other filmmakers, such as Stanley Kubrick in *2001: A Space Odyssey*

or Woody Allen in *Sleeper,* have envisaged a future characterized by a combination of humanoid machines and dehuman-
ized persons. The image they have helped to create, that of a
largely malevolent machine environment, has become a widely
accepted cliché.

Renaissance humanists such as Leonardo da Vinci saw no
contradiction between culture and technology, and moved easily from the pursuit of one to the pursuit of the other. Confidence in the ability to control technology was part of a general
belief in progress that historians such as White have documented as originating much earlier, in the Middle Ages. It is not
just that the foundation for most of the industrial crafts was laid
during this period, but that it was the beginning of an unbridled
optimism about technology and science in general, and about
their ability to help man understand and exploit his environment.

What distinguishes the Middle Ages from earlier periods is
not only the technologies themselves—metallurgy, optics, mechanics, hydrology—but the development of a religious ideology that encouraged these processes. The Gothic cathedral, to
pick one of that period's most visible accomplishments, cannot
be explained simply as a functional response; there was no need
to build such tall buildings. Instead it is as if the creation of this
extravagant structure itself became an act of worship. Technology did not replace the deity, as is sometimes the case in secular
societies, but it became a means to an end, and was hence seen
as something positive and humane.

Historians of the Middle Ages, such as Lynn White or the
Frenchman Jean Gimpel, have suggested that it is this period,
rather than the eighteenth and nineteenth centuries, which
deserves to be called our first Industrial Revolution. It was during the Middle Ages that Gutenberg promoted printing, which
together with another medieval device, eyeglasses, made mass
literacy possible. Lenses resulted in the invention of microscopes and telescopes. This period also saw the development of

a number of power technologies such as the windmill, the watermill, and even the harnessing of tidal power (near Bayonne, in the twelfth century). The horizontal loom revolutionized clothmaking. In agriculture, the use of the horse, the development of improved harnesses, the invention of the deep plow, and the discovery of three-field crop rotation enabled the medieval farmer to more than double his production. The importance of these innovations can be judged by the fact that agricultural yields would not increase again until mechanization arrived some five hundred years later.

A catalog of medieval innovations would also include the clock, the compass, the sternpost rudder, mining machinery (including lifts and pumps), medical surgery, and international banking. There was a virtual explosion in the number of inventions whose effects were experienced, and hence obvious to all. It is not surprising that these people, better fed and housed, were optimistic about technology.

The origin of the idea that technology could be a *threat* to society is not easy to trace, but the modern censure of the effects of the machine on society probably stems from the Industrial Revolution of the late eighteenth century. One of the first to criticize the violent effects of industrialization, and to link these effects to the machine, was the German socialist Friedrich Engels, who was able to observe these effects firsthand in Manchester, where he had been sent to work in his father's cotton mill. His experience led directly to his first book, *The Condition of the Working Class in England,* written in 1844, in which he described the living and working conditions of the rural and urban proletariat, the misery of the sweatshop, the squalor of the tenement, and the effect of the industrial environment on the physical and moral well-being of the English worker.

Engels's tough-minded book lapsed into sentimentalism only once—when he described the pre-Industrial Revolution craftsman. "Righteous, God-fearing and honest," according to the German observer, he did not work "excessive hours" and raised his children in "idyllic simplicity and in happy intimacy with their playmates." Engels, however, did not advocate a return to this cheery past, and mocked those like John Ruskin who preached a "romantic feudalism." Nevertheless, he did help to promote the fiction that preindustrial England was a happy place, and furthermore, that it was so largely because of an absence of technology. To be sure, the stern socialist could not endorse the feudal system that enslaved these happy yeomen; but on the whole he painted a rosy picture of rustic charm, in sharp contrast to the hellhole that was Manchester in the 1840s.

Sympathy for the middle class was notably absent from Engels's book. The bourgeoisie, according to him, "was quite incapable of salvation," and his main purpose was to show that armed conflict was not only inevitable but imminent. To do this he assembled a large body of evidence to show the corrosive effects on society of industrialization. Although the predicted uprising did not occur, many of the very real ills he described (pollution, unsanitary housing, dangerous working conditions, child labor) were eventually eliminated through the efforts of like-minded reformers, but by legislation rather than by revolution.*

Engels, and his later collaborator, Karl Marx, are best remembered for their theory of class struggle, a theory in which technology plays a relatively passive role. But the reader of *The Condition of the Working Class in England* has the distinct impression that although the main villain is the middle class, much of the blame for the social and environmental effects of industrialization falls on technology itself. "The speed of technical innovation has increased to such an extent that the workers

---

*The first House of Commons legislation against woman and child labor was actually passed before Engels's book was written; the minimum work age was set at nine years old.

are unable to keep up with it," he wrote. "Every new machine brings with it unemployment, want and suffering."

The important point here is not so much Engels's condemnation of the machine, though he certainly fueled *that* debate, but the fact that he identified technology as having independent, and important, social and economic effects. History could no longer be thought of as simply the story of generals and statesmen. After Engels, technology moved from the background to the foreground, and it would not take historians long to consider anew the relationship between culture and technology, why certain machines evolved, and the effect that their use had on society.

The neglect that the history of technology had received until then is much to blame for the general ignorance of the role that machines have played in human development. Even Engels seems to have been unaware that the Industrial Revolution that he criticized had its roots in the machine age of the Middle Ages. Historians were "men of letters" and did not concern themselves with lowly subjects such as engineering or agriculture, and consequently the influence of technology on historical development was downplayed, if it was mentioned at all. One of the first American historians to reconsider the place of the machine was Lewis Mumford, who in 1934 wrote one of the earliest histories of technology: *Technics and Civilization.*

The premise of this work was that although industrialization had obviously begun in the second half of the eighteenth century, the transformation of society as the result of mechanization was not a recent phenomenon, but the culmination of a *series* of historical developments, beginning in the Middle Ages. Mumford identified a number of phases in the transformation of preindustrial Europe: first, the eotechnic, a kind of preparatory stage corresponding roughly to the Middle Ages, which he correctly identified as the real starting point of the Industrial Revolution. The succeeding period he called paleotechnic, which referred to what is commonly called the Industrial Revolution. He differentiated this period from our own stage of development, which he referred to as the neotechnic, which is characterized by automation, new sources of energy, and above all by the use of science.

Technics and Civilization, written by an American in the period between the wars, is an optimistic book. Unlike Engels, Mumford did not blame technology for social problems. "The machine itself makes no demands and holds out no promises," he wrote; "it is the human spirit that makes demands and keeps promises." Mumford, born in 1895, was essentially a humanist, and his book strongly maintained the pre-eminence of man over machine. While acknowledging the ill effects of the paleotechnic phase (e.g., the First World War, which he described as a "disastrous interlude"), he saw it primarily as a troubled but necessary step between the eotechnic and neotechnic economies. The attraction of Mumford's schema was that the curtain could be rung down on difficult times, only to rise again on a new setting.

Of course, Mumford's tripartite division of history is too simple. It refers only to Europe and America and does little to explain the growth of other civilizations. Its evolutionary character was due to the influence of Mumford's mentor, the biologist Patrick Geddes. The use of pseudo-scientific prefixes, such as eo-, paleo-, and neo-, reflected a conscious parallel between the evolution of technology and the evolution of man. Throughout the book there was an attempt to show that things were getting better as technology ascended the evolutionary ladder toward the neotechnic, which, according to Mumford, was barely beginning and promised a kind of superior *machina sapiens.*

Mumford's optimism about technological progress was due to his belief that neotechnic machines could be assimilated by a culture that would nevertheless remain essentially nontechnical. He felt, erroneously as it turned out, that certain technical limits had already been reached. The printing press, he wrote, is practically perfect—not imagining the photocopier, the offset printer, and the word processor. "What could improve the telephone?" he asked, not knowing the impact that satellite transmission and optical fibers would have on communications.

That Mumford conceived of modern technology as having reached a kind of plateau is evident in his discussion of the writing pen. The eotechnic phase of this device was the goose-quill pen—made by hand, related to agriculture, crude but effective. The steel-tipped dipping pen represented the paleotechnic phase—cheap, uniform, and mass-produced. The culmination of this evolution was the neotechnic fountain pen, made of high-quality materials, with its own reservoir and a tip which, for all practical purposes, never wears out. The limitation of Mumford's "theory" becomes evident if one considers that it completely fails to foresee the writing invention that only a few years later would sweep the world—the ball-point pen. The ball-point is mass-produced, but otherwise has little in common with the fountain pen. Not only is it not long lasting, its writing tip is actually *designed* to be thrown away. Its successor, the felt-tip pen, is even shorter lived. This admittedly minor example illustrates a shift in the development of technology that was to catch many, including Mumford, unawares. Things were moving further than even he had thought possible.

With the rise of the consumer society (which Mumford also failed to foresee)—typified by the ubiquitous ball-point of the 1950s, and later by the inexpensive watch of the sixties and the calculator of the seventies—came more sinister technological developments. The automobile and the exodus to suburbia began destroying the cities, massive industrialization began destroying the countryside, while militarization, in the form of the atomic bomb, threatened to destroy the world. If this was the neotechnic phase, it was not what it was cracked up to be.

Lewis Mumford's volte-face with respect to technology paralleled the disillusion that many felt in the years following the Second World War. *The Myth of the Machine,* a two-volume epic which he completed in 1970, is a massive study of culture and technology which re-examines his earlier premises and almost reaches an opposite conclusion. In it Mumford abandons his earlier view of history as an orderly progression, and instead describes a kind of metaphysical conspiracy whose aim is nothing less than the coercion and subversion of all decent human values. Pointedly, he calls this evil force, the *megamachine.*

The Myth of the Machine expands Engels's view of the "guilty machine" to include the whole course of history. It is Mumford's thesis in this work that the modern industrial state represents only the latest incarnation of the megamachine. This sinister force, like Count Dracula, seems to emerge periodically to ensnare unwary victims. Its manifestations, according to Mumford, are visible in pharaonic Egypt, feudal Europe, the absolute monarchy, princely despotism, fascism, communism, even the welfare state. Mumford argues that the megamachine has undermined virtually all of what is called civilization, with the exception of certain aboriginal and village cultures.

Is the megamachine just a metaphor? If not, it has severe limitations as an explanation of history. For example, Mumford cites Adolf Hitler as one of the chief modern agents of the megamachine, yet there is plenty of evidence that Hitler's attitude to modernization was at least as ambivalent as Mumford's own. Hitler, who loved cars and delighted in knowing the mechanical details of many military technologies such as the tank, at the same time polemicized against the "soulless machine" and promoted "folkish" culture; Albert Speer, in his Spandau diaries, went so far as to call Hitler "downright antimodern." This may have to do with the fact that Hitler and Göring forbade Speer, then minister of armaments and war production, to employ German women in his factories, arguing that this would damage their child-bearing capacity as well as the integrity of the family. There would be no Rosie the Riveter in the Third Reich.

Indeed, the much-admired Nazi wartime industry seems to

have been promoted by Speer in the face of strong Party opposition. Otto Ohlendorf, Himmler's deputy in the ministry of economics, rejected the principle of efficiency in industry on the grounds that it would endanger the German *weltanschauung*. Hitler and Himmler, who grudgingly allowed mass production to be used—although only in wartime—were afraid that postwar industrialization would have negative effects on the German people. "Industrialization," said Hitler, "has made the individual completely unfree . . . it is a workmill in which any originality or individuality is totally crushed." The postwar German economy was to be based on quality, rather than quantity, on craft production, rather than on the assembly line. In his last book, *Infiltration,* Speer, an admirer of Henry Ford, noted sardonically that the highest-quality German product of the time, the BMW aircraft engine, was actually mass produced on an assembly line manned by unskilled Russian prisoners of war. It was pure romanticism, according to Speer, to imagine a return to a preindustrial economy, but that, in effect, was what Hitler, the "agent of the megamachine," actually wanted.

Mumford's rejection of "massification" is not so different from Hitler's, although he sees it in a much larger perspective. His unconvincing prescription for a nontechnocratic future consists in individual acts of "dematerialization and etherialization," whereby the person, acting on his own, will detach himself or herself from the system.* "What if they had a war and nobody came?" was a popular slogan of the antiwar movement in America in the 1960s. Mumford's "solution" to the problem of the megamachine amounts to virtually the same thing: if everyone were to withdraw from technological society, it, and its problems, would cease to exist.

The difficulty with the idea of the megamachine is that, char-

*Mumford's proposal is close to anarchism, although as an establishment figure he never publicly identified himself with that movement. However, Murray Bookchin has indicated to me that in private conversation Mumford did acknowledge the influence of the Russian anarchist Peter Kropotkin.

acteristically, Mumford carries his metaphor—for surely that is what the megamachine is—too far. Having abandoned his earlier concept of an evolving technology, he goes to the other extreme and makes a machine out of civilization itself. The result is that *The Myth of the Machine* fundamentally fails to convince, except as a *tour de force* which ranges through history cramming various events into the constraining jacket of an exaggerated theory that never quite fits.

Mumford was by no means alone in denouncing modern society as mechanistic; some years earlier, the French sociologist Jacques Ellul had coined the term "technological society." Ellul, an ex-Marxist and now a Catholic activist writing one hundred years after Engels, takes a position that is at once less political and more moral. In his masterful analysis, *The Technological Society,* he expands the meaning of technology—*la technique*—to include not just machines, but all methods arrived at rationally and used to promote efficiency in any field. He deals not so much with the mechanics of technology, but with the values that the use of the machine implies. The urgency that is unquestionably present in his writing is due less to a fear of technology and more to an apprehension that contemporary man is unaware of the technological forces that are conditioning him.

Ellul suggests that technology, in the broadest sense, is *the* most important constraint on modern man, and that this situation represents something fundamentally new. He avoids Engels's sentimentalism by avoiding the past: "I make no reference to a past period of history in which men were allegedly free, happy, and independent," he writes, at once rejecting history and condemning it. Ellul is much more concerned with the uniqueness of modern technological civilization, a civilization that has given rise to a new set of social determinants which did not exist in the past. "The new milieu has its own specific laws which are not the laws of organic or inorganic matter."

Ellul studiously avoids value judgments in his analysis of this new "artificial" environment, although his dry, seemingly objective writing is a devastating denouncement of modern technical society. While showing the pervasive influence of *la technique* on everything from politics to religion, he rarely says whether he believes this to be good or bad, although occasionally he allows himself an opinion which reveals that he thinks that it is a very bad thing indeed. Still, most of the time he contents himself with bearing witness, thoroughly but not hopefully.* Technology must be transcended, he writes. But how? "I do not yet know."

The answer was not forthcoming, even when, twenty-five years later, Ellul wrote *The Technological System.* In this companion work his attitude hardened into the conviction that not only is technology the determining factor in the modern world, it actually constitutes a system. According to Ellul causes and effects are interrelated. The technological system is not, like the megamachine, a metaphor, it is real. His point is not that society has become a machine, but rather that it has become dominated by a group of technologies that function as a separate system.

In Ellul's view, the technological phenomena that characterize this system have a number of common characteristics. They are autonomous; that is, they depend only on themselves, and are also self-augmenting, since they tend to respond only to inner directions and limitations. Furthermore, this system is unified: various technologies interact in intimate ways with one another. Engineering affects health care, for instance, and advertising affects politics. The technological system is also universal, not only geographically but also in its impact on every possible human activity. Finally, the system, in Ellul's words,

---

*Langdon Winner has pointed out that for Ellul technology is often Satan's modern variety of temptation. A similar attitude is evident in the work of Roman Catholic moralists such as Ivan Illich and E. F. Schumacher.

tends to "totalize" society: as it affects the various aspects of human life it tends to restructure them according to its own rules. It is not so much that man is subordinated by technology, but that it tends to reconstitute his reality.

Whether or not one believes that the technological system is a good or a bad influence (a question that Ellul implies is immaterial), its existence is hard to dispute. The relationship of man to this new technological reality is shaped by a number of conditions. First, we are born into what is increasingly a technical environment, and hence we take it for granted. We no more question it than a Maya Indian questions the Yucatan jungle, or a Polynesian questions the Pacific Ocean. Through formal and informal education we are prepared to accept the technological environment in a largely positive way, much as a rural civilization is prepared to accept the natural environment. Furthermore, the technological environment tends to assimilate and reform what is nontechnological, and as a result we have fewer and fewer reference points for criticizing the technological system.

Examples of the overwhelming presence of technology are everywhere. Consider the domestic environment. The main difference between, say, the house of one hundred years ago and one of today is that the latter contains a great deal of machinery. For a long time the only machine in the American home was the wood-burning cook stove—most of the other implements in the kitchen or in the workroom were hand tools. The contemporary house, as the French architect Le Corbusier remarked, has become a "machine for living," that is, it has become an environment that is conditioned primarily by technology. Electricity powers pumps, motors, furnaces, air conditioners, toasters, and hair dryers. There are technologies for providing hot and cold water, and for getting rid of it. There are telephone systems and cable television systems; unseen waves carry radio and television signals. The house is also full of automated devices—relays and thermostats—which turn these machines on and off, regulate the heat and cold, or simply open the garage door. Remove technology from the modern house and most would consider it uninhabitable. Cut off the power that fuels the machines for long enough and the dwelling must be evacuated.

But if we are surrounded by machinery, are we really, as Ellul implies, its victims? The cinematic visions of dysfunctional futures, such as *Modern Times* or *Sleeper,* are entertaining precisely because we know they are untrue. Even as we watch the film, we are confident that the projector bulb will not burn out. Any critic of the technological system, as Ellul admits, must face the fact that, on the whole, the system does work. The telephones, automobiles, refrigerators, elevators, subways, and communications systems *do* function. Large-scale electrical blackouts are "disasters" precisely because they are so rare. Contrariwise, power failures, or poorly functioning telephone and water systems, are commonplace in most developing countries, and hence are not considered disasters, but part of everyday life. The reservation of a plane ticket, or the use of an intercontinental telephone, are unconscious acts of immense technological complexity. It is a measure of the success of the technological system that it is so completely taken for granted, even by its critics.

The earliest tools simply strengthened man's body: the club extended the arm, the shoe hardened the foot, clothing protected the peltless skin. Some tools enabled man to cut, to cook, to play music. Others facilitated labor or relieved burdens: the pulley, the wedge, and the wheel. All of these tools were, in one way or another, auxiliary members, but, as the social theorist Arnold Gehlen pointed out, technology does more than simply imitate nature. Tools such as the knife, the bow, or the wheel have no counterpart in the natural world, even though, obviously, they must follow natural laws. They constitute what Gehlen calls *artificial* nature.

According to Gehlen, the desire to create an artificial environment is more than a reaction to utilitarian demands; it demonstrates, above all, a desire for predictability. Consider, for
example, one of the earliest technical activities—agriculture.
Pretechnological agriculture consisted primarily of foraging or
harvesting whatever was at hand. But the natural environment
is extremely unpredictable. There was no guarantee that food
would be available as required. And so, with the simplest crops,
technology begins. Rain cannot yet be controlled, but irrigation
can be. Nutrients are not always present in the land, but they
can be added through fertilizers. Many crops in their "natural"
state do not optimize food production, but the technology of
plant breeding can produce stronger, and more productive,
hybrids. Looked at this way, industrialized agriculture, whatever its faults, is still well within the mainstream of agricultural
development, since it reflects the same desire to create a more
predictable environment.

Other examples abound. The open fire heats well but needs
constant care throughout the night. The fireplace and chimney
reduce the rate of burning and control the smoke. The enclosed
stove continues this process, while the oil furnace automates the
procedure on the basis of a thermostat setting.

The field of communication is another case of evolution toward predictability. During the early part of the nineteenth
century, before the invention of the telephone, communication
between people occurred either face-to-face or by letter. The
technology of the letter is not very predictable. How many
romantic novels were based on the dramatic device of a letter
lost, delivered late, or delivered to the wrong person? With the
invention of the telephone many of these drawbacks disappeared, but since direct dialing was not yet possible, all calls had
to be put through a central exchange. One result of this, as Mark
Twain observed humorously, was that husbands had to place
calls for their wives, since it was considered indecorous for them
to call an unknown operator. The human intermediary was

eliminated by the introduction of personal dialing, and the control of the person using the telephone increased proportionately. Nor is this evolution complete. With increased automation, direct long-distance dialing to virtually anywhere has become possible. Automation has even solved the problem of the (unpredictable) call that reaches the house when no one is home—with the answering machine.

Three stages of technical development are apparent in most of these devices. First, the tool stage—human energy guided by human intellect. Second, the machine stage—human energy replaced by some outside, nonhuman source, which continues to be guided by human intellect. Finally, the third stage—the automated machine, which guides itself. To a greater or lesser extent, *all* technologies follow this evolution. For example, the problem of hammering nails is first resolved by a man swinging a hammer. The hammer is then replaced by a pneumatic hammer, which the worker aims, but whose energy source is nonhuman. This leads to the automated gang-nailing machine, used in prefabricated house factories, which descends onto the required component, according to a predetermined setting, and simultaneously fires a few dozen nails or staples.

The evolution of technology toward automation is everywhere—in the domestic hot-water heater, the automobile choke, the solar water heater, the self-winding watch, or the traffic light. It is curious that automation has been so frequently portrayed as a frightening, unnatural invention, that until recently the robot in science-fiction literature has been an ominous, not a chummy, character. It is curious because automation is the most natural of phenomena (most of our body is automated), and the desire for automation—and the predictability it brings with it—is simply the human desire for a technology as stable as the human heart, or as dependable as a sunrise.

Arnold Gehlen characterized the human fascination with automation as an instinctive need for stability within the environment. It is precisely those aspects of nature that are stable—the tides, the seasons, the solar system—that have acquired symbolic importance in the religions and cultures of many civilizations. It is the idiosyncratic events—accidental death or natural disaster—that have required superstition, myth, and legend to order them. The odd and inconsistent can be explained by magic; the vagaries of personality are regulated by astrology. These supposedly irrational practices reflect man's desire for order in the environment, and, like science, depend on laws and rules to impose predictability on otherwise random events. But perhaps the reason that so many people are prepared to accept spoon-bending rather than cybernetics is that magic has become more comprehensible to the general public than science and technology have.

Increasingly, one must be an expert to understand even a single aspect of the technological environment, and few experts can master more than a small part of the whole. Yet in a democracy people are compelled to form opinions and to make decisions about technology that are far outside their intellectual and emotional acquaintance. Someone whose only contact with the so-called Third World is the airport at Cancún is supposed to form an opinion about foreign aid. People who barely remember their high school physics are required to take sides in the nuclear power debate. The fragmentation of modern society, and the reduction of the number of shared experiences, mean that the only way to form opinions on most subjects is on the basis of secondhand experience.

While secondhand experience still depends, to a certain extent, on personal contact—rumor and hearsay—the greatest single source of most people's secondhand experience is neither education nor conversation but the media: newspapers, magazines, film, radio, and television. Nowhere is the influence of these ragmen of information felt more than on the public perception of technology. It is not a question so much of manipulation of information as of the tendency of most media, especially of television, to condense and to clarify, and in the process to replace reflection and judgment with predigested "facts." The result was apparent to Gehlen even as early as 1949: "A reality that is infinitely complex, many-sided, and changeable is thus made artificially simple and graspable."

The media have a tendency to focus on bad news rather than on good, on the aberration rather than on the norm. In this they probably do no more than reflect public taste. But the result of this emphasis is that the failures of technology tend to receive considerably more of the public's attention than its successes. Thus the accusation of the consumer activist Ralph Nader that the Corvair was an unsafe automobile received much more publicity than the finding of the National Highway Traffic Safety Administration, a decade later, that the Corvair was no less safe than the average car of the day. It is the electrical power failure, the man-made disaster, and the factory recall that catch the baleful eye of the news commentator. Though this bad news does not alone create a distrust of technology— the failures are, after all, real—it does promote the stereotype of technology as a threat to society, a benevolent despot who, more often than not, runs amok. In the nineteenth century the media enthusiastically promoted the machine; in the second half of the twentieth century they are casting it in the role of a villain.*

The public accepts this negative view of technology all the more easily because it has never properly understood the new technological environment. The great Spanish philosopher José Ortega y Gasset represented modern man as a *naturmensch*, a primitive in the midst of a civilized world, who used technology without really understanding it. As he described him, "The new man wants his motor-car, and enjoys it, but he believes that it is the spontaneous fruit of an Edenic tree. In the depth of his

---

*A 1980 University of Michigan study of how fictional scientists are characterized on American television concluded that they were usually shown as somewhat unstable, often threatening, usually unpleasant, and (the kiss of death) short in stature.

soul he is unaware of the artificial, almost incredible, character of civilization, and does not extend his enthusiasm for the instruments to the principles which make them possible."

This lack of understanding of the principles of the technological environment is particularly visible in cultures that are in the process of modernizing. There is a desire for the fruits of modernization, but only a partial grasp of the changes that are required to achieve them. The result has often been a retreat to religious or political fundamentalism when modernization is found to be simply too difficult to comprehend.

The struggle of the less-developed countries to come to grips with technology is described later (see Chapter 4), but even in fully industrialized countries such as the United States the technological environment is ill-understood. One reason for the great psychological shock of the 1973 Oil Crisis, at least as important as its economic impact, was the discovery that petroleum did not come from beneath gas stations, but often originated in other countries, and actually belonged to other people. The idea that they might be dependent on others hit the independent Americans hard, so disparate were the much-vaunted politics of self-reliance and the reality of the interdependent global technological system. Another reason for the shock was that technology has generally been so successful in America that lines, such as those that occurred at gas stations in 1973, were taken to mean that the technical system was in the process of collapse. While both conservatives and conservationists made political hay out of the Oil Crisis, the public installed backyard gas tanks, bought diesel-powered automobiles, and invested in expensive solar water heaters, all strategies intended to bring a measure of predictability and control to a situation which, at least at the time, seemed characterized by unpredictability and loss of control.

As the Oil Crisis demonstrated, the aspect of technology that concerns us most is the control of technology. Whether one is an environmental lobbyist, a Third World nationalist, a businessman facing depleting resources, or a politician caught in the nuclear debate, the issue of controlling technology surfaces sooner or later. Even the individual realizes that, as a consumer, he or she can accept or reject technologies. But if control is possible—and even that is not clear—then how is it to be exercised? And what would be the result if it were attempted?

There are two positions in this debate that accept the possibility of controlling technology. The first posits the proposition that even if there really is such a thing as a technological system, it too will be controlled, in much the same way as in the past, by the development of further technologies. Thus, air pollution can be eliminated by the invention of catalytic converters for automobiles and scrubbers for smokestacks, while water pollution can be avoided with the use of better treatment plants. As long as there is enough warning given, the argument goes, there will be enough time to invent technological solutions to all technological problems.

A second stance relies on the development of a new creature —technological man. This mutant will feel quite at home in the technological system, of which he will have complete understanding and over which he will exercise complete control. It is not always clear whether technological man is a literary metaphor or an example of biological adaptation. If it is the former, then he is more an example of sleight of hand and wishful thinking than a realistic proposal. But if it is the latter, then one searches in vain for examples of the new breed. Henry Ford the industrialist and J. Robert Oppenheimer the physicist might qualify. Both were surely "technological men," at the forefront of their respective fields. But Oppenheimer, in a most dramatic way, spent a good part of his life promoting a technology—the atomic bomb—that he would later denounce. It is not recorded that Henry Ford ever had qualms about the assembly line, but although his company was an undoubted success, it was frequently propelled forward by external forces, and did not always develop in the direction that Ford had mapped out for it (see Chapter 3). Both of these prosthetic gods could appear magnificent, but both experienced trouble with technology. While it is true that man will try to adapt to the machine, the idea that he will himself become machinelike does not address the question of control.

A different assessment of the relationship of man to technology concerns what is loosely termed the "Appropriate Technology" thesis. According to this analysis, what is required is a new type of controllable technology that will replace the present-day system. This prescription relies primarily on choosing small-scale technologies, small presumably being easier to control than big ("small-is-beautiful"), but is brought up short by a problem. The movement has not developed any method for deciding what "small" is; nor has it shown how, if a small technology is chosen, it is to be kept from becoming big. Another difficulty concerns the dismantling of the existing technological system. As Ellul has shown, this system consists not of a collection of discrete machines, but is an integrated, overlapping, syncopated whole. Not only is it difficult to remove one element from this house of cards, it is sometimes even impossible to know which card to remove.*

The complicated nature of technology is illustrated by the conflict between the desire to control the machine, on the one hand, and the need to automate it, on the other. Most demands for a controllable technology reject automation in favor of direct human control. This sounds convincing, until one realizes that many of the most controllable technologies are precisely so because they are automated. The cause of most airplane accidents is what engineers refer to as "human error," as opposed to machine error, which is much rarer. Drunken drivers cause more deaths than malfunctioning automobiles, and it has been estimated that *automatic* seat belts and *self*-inflating air bags

---

*A critique of the small-is-beautiful approach to technology is fully developed by the author in *Paper Heroes: A Review of Appropriate Technology.*

could save 12,000 lives annually in the United States. Likewise, more domestic fires are caused by people who smoke in bed than by exploding furnaces or by defective wiring, and the smoke detector is so effective because it is automatic. Examples such as these indicate that technology that is directly under human control is neither more predictable nor safer.

What about the idea of controlling technology by returning to earlier, better understood, machines? This is the theme of a number of utopian novels, such as Austin Tappan Wright's charming *Islandia*. Wright chronicles the adventures of a young American college man in Islandia, a remote nation technologically in the sixteenth century, and apparently much the better for it. He describes the mores, geography, and even the history of Islandia in great detail. There is a curious prescience in much of Wright's imaginings (the book was published in 1942, after his death), and his Islandians resemble young Americans of the 1970s both in dress and behavior. Still, like all utopias, it can exist only in fiction. The novelist can freeze technological development at one ideal stage—the Islandians are philosophizing homesteaders—but the real world will not wait. In any case, the past had its own, often unresolved problems with the machine, and even if it were possible to "go back," these same problems would have to be faced all over again.

No. The problem of controlling technology must be faced. But is it really vain, as Ellul warns, to pretend that the monolithic aspects of technology can be checked or guided? By ignoring history, Ellul and others have focused attention on the modern technological system, at the same time giving the false impression that the problems it poses have never been encountered before. But the shock of having to deal with the machine is not restricted to the twentieth century; it has occurred many times in the past, and societies have reacted in many different ways to the sudden and violent effects that have accompanied technological innovation. Frequently there has been a collision between the machine and cultural values; by no means has the machine always emerged the victor.

And yet the domination of man by machine is today taken for granted. It is assumed that we must always "cringe before technology," to use George Gilder's memorable phrase. But there is plenty of evidence that, in the past, individuals, groups, and even entire nations have resisted, opposed, or otherwise attempted to modify or direct specific technologies. Though not always successful, these examples can teach us a great deal about the relationship between technology and society. They can also serve to remind us that the machine is a human creation, and that inventing and using technology is a human activity—not an inanimate force—which has the same capacity for error as other human activities.

The shock of the machine was never more strongly felt than at the beginning of the Industrial Revolution in England. From this period has emerged a figure who is by no means unique, but who has come to typify modern opposition to technology: the machine-breaker. The following chapter examines the Luddite uprising with a view to understanding why a large group of people reacted to technological innovation in such a violent way. The caricature of the Luddite—a grinning oaf smashing weaving looms—is a popular but erroneous view; the true story is at once less romantic and more tragic.

CHAPTER 2

MACHINE-BASHING

Men and women who see their livelihood taken from them or threatened by some new invention, can hardly be expected to grow enthusiastic over the public benefits of inventive genius.
—J. L. and Barbara Hammond, *The Skilled Labourer*

If machine-breaking is the most dramatic method of controlling technology, it is also the least subtle. The machine-breaker cries "No more!" and draws the line. Most would argue that a direct physical attack on technology is hardly a method at all, but simply the mindless lashing out of desperate persons, a hopeless last resort born of frustration rather than reflection. Sometimes it is, but not always.

Machine-breaking is usually described as a nineteenth-century phenomenon, probably because the most well-known example dates from that period: the Luddite uprising of the English textile workers. It would be comfortable to consign machine-breaking to the distant past, along with child labor and the almshouse, but the fact is that it has continued up to the present.

33

On February 11, 1969, two hundred students occupied the main building of Sir George Williams University, an urban campus in the center of Montreal. There was nothing particularly unique about the event in the year of student unrest—similar sit-ins were taking place in colleges and universities all over the United States and Canada. The issue in Montreal was not the war in Vietnam, but racial discrimination. Most of the protestors were from the West Indies, and they were trying to force the administration to reopen an investigation of alleged racial discrimination on the part of a professor. The occupation was in two areas of the twelve-story building—the faculty lounge and the computer center. On the morning of the eighth day the occupiers of the computer center, apparently fearing police intervention, barricaded themselves in and threatened to destroy a hostage if their demands were not met. The hostage was a Control Data 3300 computer. To show that they were serious, they began throwing out of the ninth-story windows computer cards, tapes, and files. The street below was soon awash with payroll data and student records. The final act of this bizarre incident occurred when nervous police finally pushed their way through the barricades, and the occupiers, true to their word, attacked the CD 3300 with fire axes and finally set the whole floor on fire.

The students' attack on the machinery was greeted with incredulity by the public, the politicians (who engaged in enraged debate in the Canadian Parliament), the university (whose principal resigned), and by the majority of students (who cheered, "Go, cops, go!" as police entered the building). There was the illegality, of course, not to mention the sheer destruction—two million dollars worth. But it was above all the attack on the computer that aroused public feeling. For the public, not threatened by technology, as the transplanted West Indians perhaps felt themselves to be, the act of machine-breaking appeared immoral in itself. Although there may be a vicarious thrill derived from watching expensive automobiles being destroyed and that scene is the staple of many popular films, the fact that it occurs as part of a fictional story only underlines the basic respect that most middle-class Canadians—and Americans—feel for the machine. Hence the disbelief when machines are destroyed "in cold blood."

Inevitably, twentieth-century machine-breaking, whether committed by workers or students, is described as an anachronism.* When automobile workers in Detroit recently smashed a new Toyota with sledge hammers as a symbolic protest against Japanese imports, the journalist Morley Safer bemusedly referred to the incident as "modern Ludditism." When California Rural Legal Assistance filed a lawsuit against the University of California, seeking to stop research on large-scale agricultural mechanization, an editorial in the *Los Angeles Times* compared the rural workers, on whose behalf the suit was brought, to "the pathetic Luddites," even though machine-breaking was not involved. Just the name evokes images of resistance to progress and thinly veiled threats of physical violence, and, for most people, the destruction of machinery and the Luddite uprising have become synonymous.

The Luddite uprising took place in Regency England during the years 1811 to 1816, and is usually described as an outbreak of violence directed against labor-saving machinery by disgruntled workers who felt that their employment and way of life were threatened by the Industrial Revolution. The term "Luddism" is also used generically, to describe the various kinds of machine-breaking by workers that have occurred since "King" Ludd cracked looms, and heads, in the English Midlands. Part of the popular understanding of both Luddism and later machine-breaking is reflected in the view that the worker is inevi-

---

*In a book written soon after the Montreal incident, Dorothy Eber observed that, "Among the University people I speak to there is a lot of talk of Luddites. . . . It's a temptation to speculate on the symbolism involved in an attack on computers."

tably hostile to mechanical innovation, and that he romantically, and poignantly, expresses this hostility by periodically going on antitechnological benders. This is a simplistic view.

In order to understand the Luddite uprising, it is necessary to appreciate that during the early years of industrialization (1760–1830) England was experiencing less an Industrial Revolution than a protracted civil war, to echo J. L. and Barbara Hammond's description of the period. The term "Industrial Revolution," which was popularized by the historian Arnold Toynbee, is a misleading one. Not only does it imply that the technological changes were sudden, while in fact the process lasted more than a century and had its roots in the earlier industrial revolution of the Middle Ages, but it also implies that the changes were only industrial, while as T. S. Ashton reminds us, they were also social and intellectual.

The main themes of the Hammonds' books on the period are the social changes that constitute the "civil war." They suggest that a key ingredient of this "civil war" was not so much the introduction of mechanization as the fact that the existing social system transferred the benefits of this industrialization primarily to one group—the owners of the factories. In such a system the workers—or working poor, as they were then called—had less and less control over the way they lived and worked, and virtually none over the technology they used.

Mechanization did not descend on the English countryside overnight, as it seems to do today in some of the developing countries such as Nigeria or Saudi Arabia. It was a much more gradual process. Most of the industries that became industrialized—coal mining, wool and silk weaving, knitting—had actually been so since the seventeenth century or earlier. The first form of this industrialization was the cottage industry, in which workers labored at home. The "master" rented out looms, provided raw materials, and organized the distribution of the finished goods; the cottage worker provided the labor. The only thing that was missing was mechanization.

The knitting industry had begun in London in 1589 with the invention of the stocking loom, or frame, but it was the Midlands (Nottingham, Leicester, Derby) that became the center of the English knitting trade. The journeymen knitters worked at home on frames that they rented from the hosiers. Following the 1770s, the knitters made a number of attempts to obtain higher wages, but when these proposals were rejected by the hosiers, the knitters resorted to violence, smashing more than three hundred knitting frames. This proved persuasive, and a new schedule of prices was agreed on which lasted more than twenty years. Another sore point with the knitters involved the use of "cut-ups," which were made on wide looms. These wide looms had been used in the past to produce pantaloons and fancy stockings, but when these went out of style some hosiers began to employ the looms to manufacture material that was "cut up" into gloves, socks, and stockings. They were cheaper than the same goods made on narrow looms but considered to be of lower quality since they were stitched rather than selvaged.

Since the market for knitted goods was depressed at that time, there was a tendency by the hosiers to use cut-ups to reduce prices, underselling the traditional product. The knitters, with the support of some of the more scrupulous masters who saw the entire industry threatened by this practice, attempted to get official prohibition of the wide frames. They were not successful. Perhaps remembering the frame-breaking of 1799, the Nottingham knitters, in 1811, once more took to the streets. During the next eleven months they destroyed over one thousand frames, virtually all of them of the wide variety.

The frame-breakers had sent a letter to the English Parliament explaining that, under the charter granted them by Charles II, they considered their actions to be legal. The declaration was signed "Ned Ludd, Sherwood Forest." Ludd was supposed to have been an apprentice weaver who, some thirty years before, had destroyed his master's knitting frame after being whipped for laziness. Sherwood Forest had been the home of the folk hero Robin Hood, and suggests the popular support that the Luddites hoped to receive. Subsequently, "General Ludd" or "King Ludd" was taken as an alias by numerous local leaders, partly for recognition, and partly to confuse government spies; a Lady Ludd led food riots in Leeds.

The initial outbreak of Luddism had none of the manic frenzy or wild abandon that contemporary observers, as well as some historians, attempted to ascribe to it. It was an act neither of desperation nor of anger against labor-saving machinery. Later outbreaks, however, were aimed at the machine itself. This was especially true in Yorkshire, where shearing frames and gig mills threatened to replace the wool-finishers' trade.

The work of the shear men, or croppers as they were called in Yorkshire, involved raising the nap on the newly woven cloth and then cutting, or shearing, it off. The nap was traditionally raised by hand, using implements called teazles, and was then cropped with extremely large shears. This highly specialized process required a good deal of dexterity, and the cropper was relatively highly paid and considered to be the aristocrat of the cloth-workers. As a result, the croppers were well organized; they maintained a closed shop and their craft was protected by a number of laws and statutes. One of these laws, which had been enforced since the time of Edward VI, more than two hundred and fifty years before, outlawed a device called a gig mill, a machine that simplified and speeded up the work considerably. It consisted of a large cylinder, covered with teazles, over which the cloth was pulled. But in the 1800s the outlawed gig mill began to reappear, together with a more recent invention called a shearing frame, which consisted of several pairs of shears fixed in a frame that was moved across the cloth. Both the gig mill and the shearing frame increased productivity—the gig mill was seven times faster than manual methods, the shearing frame five times so. More important, they also dispensed with the need for skilled craftsmen and threatened both the prestige and livelihood of the croppers.

The wool croppers petitioned Parliament to enforce the old laws, but without effect. Their legal actions against masters who employed the labor-saving devices were equally ineffective. Finally, in 1809, Parliament repealed all protective laws in the woolen industry, leaving the way open for the widespread use of both shearing frames and gig mills. Frustrated after ten years of fruitless opposition, the croppers followed the example of their Nottingham neighbors and began destroying the hated shearing frames and gig mills.

There is little doubt that the Luddite revolt was characterized by machine-breaking. "Man versus machine" was a convenient explanation, not least because the machine was politically easier to blame than the entire social system. Lord Byron referred to "men sacrificed to improvements in mechanism," but many historians dispute the claim that Luddism was motivated by resistance to the machine. While the Luddites are often described as a contrary mob, stoutly refusing all attempts at modernization, the historian Malcomb I. Thomis has expressed the view that the machine was attacked less because it was hated, and more because it was a conveniently exposed target. This opinion is supported by the Luddites themselves. George Beaumont, who was a convicted Luddite, produced a pamphlet entitled "The Beggar's Complaint," in which he wrote: "With regard to the conduct of the Luddites in breaking machinery, I wholly disapprove of it: it is altogether condemnable. . . . They [the poor] are oppressed exceedingly, but not by machinery."

Given the fact that mechanization was affecting virtually every trade and industry in England, it is surprising that there was not more opposition. What concerned most workers, however, was not the machine itself, but the threat that it posed to their employment and income. In industries such as mining and printing, where mechanization did not pose such threats, it was accepted without opposition. There was likewise no resistance to innovation in those rare cases where the advantages of the improvement accrued to the worker. The fly shuttle, for instance, which revolutionized hand weaving, enabled weavers to triple their incomes; no breaking of fly shuttles has been recorded. It is important to note that workers did not oppose technological innovation out of mistrust or ignorance. As Thomis says of the Luddites, "They were tactically wrong in believing that they could successfully resist mechanization in their own industries, but they were not wrong to wish to do this when their very existence might seem to be, and might in fact be, threatened."

But if machine-breaking did not do the workers much good, neither did it do them much harm, as the historian E. J. Hobsbawm observed. Trades that did not resist mechanization with violence could be just as severely affected as those that did. The case of the wool-combers is an example.

The craft of wool-combing involved preparing the sheared wool so that it could be spun. It was a medieval skill which was carried on by a group of craftsmen who, like the croppers, had a long and independent tradition. In spite of the fact that trade unions, or combinations as they were then called, were illegal, the wool-combers had established a powerful position, usually through group action. Even in the eighteenth century they functioned much as a medieval guild that the authorities were powerless to suppress.

The wool-combers prepared raw wool by repeated combing with two heated combs. The mass of wool was thus turned into slivers, which could be spun into yarn and ultimately woven or knitted. Between 1785 and 1800, an inventive clergyman named Edmund Cartwright, perfected a mechanical method for combing wool. His manually operated machine consisted of combs mounted on rollers, and with it a single comber, with the assistance of four or five children, could do the work of *thirty* manual combers.

The wool-combers felt confident that they could face down this threat, as they had done others, with political lobbying and, if need be, a collective work stoppage. But a peaceful six-month strike in 1825 proved unsuccessful; the masters were too strong, and an economic depression eroded the workers' bargaining power. Within twenty-five years the "aristocracy of the worsted workers" was reduced to penury and replaced by the machine.

Perhaps the main reason why machine-wrecking in general, and Luddism in particular, are considered to have been failures is that they ended so quickly and so conclusively. The English Parliament dispatched 12,000 soldiers to put down the riots, and, although few people were actually arrested, the more than fifty people who were either executed or deported to Australia included all the leaders of the rebellion. Their removal had a conclusive effect and the uprising came to a swift end.

What exactly was Luddism? The traditional view of the machine-breaker is a condescending one. The view of the Hammonds is more sympathetic to the plight of the workers and sees them as the casualties of history. Some have seen Luddism as the forerunner of trade unionism; Hobsbawm has called machine-breaking "collective bargaining by riot." E. P. Thompson, in his work on the English working class, goes even further and describes Luddism as a "quasi-insurrectionary movement, which continually trembled on the edge of ulterior revolutionary objectives."

Incipient trade unionists or erstwhile revolutionaries, the Luddites were certainly casualties of history. It is easy enough, with hindsight, to say that theirs was a lost cause. But even that much is not clear, as the following example illustrates.

The agricultural workers' rebellion of 1830 is one of the rare examples of successful opposition to mechanization of that period. To understand the causes of this rebellion it is necessary to appreciate the fact that rural England of the time was unique in Europe in that there was no peasant class. This had nothing to do with the Industrial Revolution but was a centuries-old fact. The majority of agricultural land in England was owned by a small number of landlords. Their farms, usually over a hundred acres in size, were rented out to tenant farmers—manag-

ers who in turn hired agricultural workers. Unlike their counterparts in France or Germany, the English rural folk were
really proletarians; they owned no land of their own but only
worked the land of others.

The Industrial Revolution had an important effect on these
people. The rapid growth of industrial towns and cities created
a growing demand for food, which resulted in an agricultural
boom. Landowners expected an increase in production from
their tenants, who were rapidly being turned into businessmen
by the new economic conditions. Whereas the rights of the
rural poor had previously been protected by various forms of
paternalistic custom, under the new conditions these traditions
went by the board, and the financial condition of the workers
worsened. As the pressures on the tenant farmers (who were
economically better off, but still squeezed by the landlords)
increased, they were passed down to the farm workers. Employment was always temporary—at best seasonal, sometimes
weekly or daily. Whereas payment in the past had usually been
in kind (food and lodgings), it was now monetary, and the
worker was no longer protected against inflation. Since the
farmer and laborer no longer lived under one roof, the social
and economic gap between them widened.

According to a recent study of the period by Hobsbawm and
Rudé, the cause of this imbalance was a built-in contradiction.
The landlords, and to a lesser extent the tenant farmers, wanted
to have the benefits of a free market economy without abandon-
ing the hierarchical stability of an eighteenth-century agricultural system. The poor, as a result, were caught in the middle,
losing the small measure of security that tradition had accorded
them, and unable to participate in the economic benefits of the
new market economy. What finally brought the agricultural
workers together, and galvanized them into brief but violent
action, was the hated threshing machine.

The threshing machine had been invented in Scotland as
early as 1785, but it had not been introduced into England until
the nineteenth century. The machine saved labor, which was

not in short supply, and it was expensive. It was only during the Napoleonic wars, when manpower was not available, that the threshing machine was taken up by English farmers. When labor became available again, farmers were loath to give up the machine. Although machine threshing was more expensive, it was faster, and grain marketed more quickly fetched higher prices.

For the rural workers this was the final straw. The threshing machine threatened to eliminate the main source of employment during the winter—the hardest season—and while it was hardly the cause of rural poverty, it was a visible symbol, and one that could be attacked.

The first threshing machines were destroyed at the end of August 1830, and although the main uprising lasted only three months, it spread to over twenty counties, virtually all of cereal-producing south England. It is estimated that in that brief period almost four hundred machines were destroyed, and, in addition, numerous other machines were broken, barns where the machines were kept were burned, and the foundries and workshops of threshing-machine manufacturers were sacked. Arson, in particular, was widespread. Raiding parties numbered from a few hundred to a few thousand, and they called themselves the followers of Swing, after Captain Swing, an imaginary Ludd-like figure.

A Swing attack was often preceded by a letter to the farmer, such as this one quoted by Hobsbawm and Rudé: "Sir, this is to acquaint you that if your thrashing [sic] machines are not destroyed by you directly we shall commence our labours. Signed on behalf of the whole Swing." It turned out that many of the small farmers were not averse to seeing the threshing machines destroyed, since their only advantage was speed of delivery to the market. It was obvious to many that the "threshing-machine gap" was closing, and that when all farmers used threshing machines, prices would drop, and they would be left with only an expensive method of threshing.

But the Swing movement was not long-lived. While it threatened the property of the richest and most powerful group in England—the landed gentry—it was neither a political movement nor a forerunner of trade unionism. It was born in isolation and essentially out of desperation, its bitter violence not a little tinged with hatred and revenge. The retribution against the rebels was much harsher than that which the Luddites met with. Roughly 2,000 were arrested, of whom some 500 were deported to Australia, 644 imprisoned, and 19 executed.

It is all the more surprising, therefore, that the Swing uprising did achieve some of its goals. In almost all the counties affected, the threshing machine did not return, and mechanization was halted for twenty years or more. This was due partly to the influence of the rioters, partly to a fear of future disturbances, and partly to the lack of enthusiasm on the part of many of the tenant farmers for the threshing machines. In any case, judged by the immediate results—and machine-breaking is above all an act of immediacy—Swing was a success, or at least a good deal more successful than Luddism was.

To read about the relationship between man and machine during the Industrial Revolution can be profoundly depressing. Apologists can protest that the side effects of modernization were only short-term, but in this case they lasted for more than a hundred years. It would be easy to conclude from the experiences of the preindustrial crafts that the predominance of technology, if not its dominance, was inevitable. If one ignores the "civil war" of the nineteenth century, one could also arrive at the conclusion that the machine, and not society, was to blame for the ill effects of industrialization.

There is some evidence, however, that the disruption of social conditions that accompanied industrialization was not inevitable. In a different time and place it might have been avoided altogether. An example of how this might have occurred is the cottage factory.

The city of Coventry, in the English Midlands, was one of the centers of a particularly nineteenth-century industry: ribbon-making. Ribbons were an important part of female fashion at that time, and no dress was complete without yards of variously colored silk ribbons. The raw silk was brought from France, Italy, Turkey, and the Far East, and dyed and woven by the manufacturers, who were located in England, Switzerland, and France.

Ribbon-making began as a cottage industry. The cottages were actually town houses, usually with two or three floors. The residence was on the lower two floors, with a large, windowed workshop above. The independent journeyman weaver in Coventry usually owned his own loom, or looms, but produced ribbon for a merchant, who handled the supply of raw material, and the distribution of the finished ribbons. Prosperous weavers set up loom shops, in which they employed a number of workers, and some of the larger merchants were likewise manufacturers who employed relatively large numbers of weavers in factories. While the whole trade in Coventry was controlled by about a dozen merchants, in the 1830s there were still slightly more independent weavers than factory employees.

Innovation in the ribbon-weaving trade had begun in the late eighteenth century when the hand loom, on which only a single ribbon could be woven at a time, had been replaced by the Dutch engine loom, which was not, in spite of its name, machine powered, but which did allow the weaver to make several ribbons at once. The Dutch engine loom was superseded by the French Jacquard loom, which had the added advantage of being able to weave (automatically) fancy decorative ribbons as well as plain ones.

The innovation that directly affected the independent weavers was steam power. The factory that first introduced steam-powered looms, in 1831, was almost immediately attacked and burned down by an enraged mob of weavers. The factory owner was paraded through the streets, sitting backward on a donkey, and was rescued finally by a remarkably reticent constabulary. Like the Swing movement, the destruction had its desired effect and nothing more was heard of the steam-powered loom for six years. Then it was reintroduced in Coventry to compete with the neighboring town of Derby, which had started to use power looms. By the 1850s, all new factories in Coventry were equipped with steam power, and the effect of powered looms was to raise immensely the output of the weaver. Typically, the economic advantage accrued to the manufacturer and the price of piecework dropped, seriously threatening the independent weavers, who used only human-powered looms.

A familiar story now took a different turn. At this point, one might have expected that the journeymen weavers would either have tried to smash the offensive power looms, or at least have gone on strike in an attempt to have the new invention proscribed. They did neither. They realized that the use of power was inevitable if they were going to compete with the other English weaving towns, which were already using power, and they were not averse to using steam power since it would increase their income as well as eliminate a laborious part of the weaving process. Of course, they could have gone to work in the factories, but this was an almost unthinkable alternative; they were too proud of their independent position and way of life (weaving was a family activity in which all took part).

Thus they established what became known as cottage factories. Since their adjoining houses were built in rows, it was relatively easy for a group of attached houses to run a continuous power shaft through the upper-level workshops, powering each individual loom. A steam engine which drove the shaft was located at one end of the row. These so-called factories could be as small as two or three houses or as large as a hundred, but in all cases, the steam plants themselves were not cooperatively owned but were leased from an operator.

The cottage factories began to make their appearance in 1847, and it is recorded that by the 1850s there were about

1,250 power looms in cottage factories, which was about the same number as there were in the masters' factories. Though less efficient in strictly economic terms, the cottage factory was certainly successful in combining technological innovation with a desired way of life.

Not all the cottage factories were built by the independent weavers. Eli Green, a well-meaning manufacturer, built a group of sixty-seven houses with a central steam plant in 1858, and two Quaker capitalists, John and Joseph Cash, planned a cottage factory of one hundred houses (of which only forty-eight were built) on four sides of a block. In the center of the court stood the power house, surrounded by vegetable gardens for the weavers.

One of the drawbacks of the Coventry cottage factories was that although they appeared to be cooperative ventures, and in the case of the Cash brothers were intended to be communal, they were never so in practice. The independent weavers remained independent. They never managed to develop any true cooperation, a flaw that proved to be their undoing.

By 1860, factory productivity was rising, owing primarily to better management and new equipment. The cottage factories were having difficulty competing, and the gap between the wages of the independent weavers and those of the factory workers began to widen. As the price for piecework fell and negotiations with the merchants broke down, the independent weavers went on strike. Unfortunately for them, the long strike coincided with the lifting of the English tariff on French ribbons. Since French wages were generally lower, French ribbons soon pushed English prices down. Fifty of the large manufacturers went bankrupt, and the independent weavers finally had to accept even lower prices. The ribbon industry in Coventry was never to recover fully.

Under the new stringent conditions of a very competitive market only the most efficient factories could continue, and almost one-quarter of the cottage factories were forced to close, including that of the Cash brothers. Although the rest of the cottage factories hung on for a number of years, they ceased to expand; their decline put an end to this unusual experiment.

Had all the independent weavers been able to follow the cooperative social aims of the Cash brothers, the outcome of this story might have been different. John and Joseph Cash were influenced in their ideals by the British reformer Robert Owen, who deserves mention here. Owen's career had spanned the Atlantic. In Scotland he owned and operated a cotton factory, which he successfully turned into a model of enlightened capitalism. He placed particular stress on improving the workers' living environment and on providing education for their children—a radical idea in an age when children began working at five or six. Owen was by no means antagonistic to new technology, only to the merciless way in which it was applied. After a career as a factory reformer in Britain, and finding little support there for his idea of small, self-contained farming communities, he went to America, bought 30,000 acres of land in Indiana, and established a community he optimistically called New Harmony. No romantic, Owen made use of advanced farming machinery in his new venture, but the experiment was not a success. His social utopian ideas proved difficult to put into practice, and Owen returned to England, where he continued to be active in organizing some of the earliest trade unions.

Meanwhile, in France, there were also attempts to "colonize the wilderness of industrial barbarism," as Mumford colorfully put it. The most influential figure there was Charles Fourier, a contemporary of Owen, who likewise believed that industrialization should not be resisted but should form the basis of a new, cooperative social order. His ideal communities were to be housed in large structures, which he called *phalanstères*, and which resembled the Louvre. Fourier, a traveling salesman and bachelor, elaborated the cooperative life he envisaged in great detail, and although he never realized any of his ideas, his writings became quite influential and led to the establishment of a number of small communes, among them Brook Farm in the United States.

The most impressive *phalanstère* ever built was realized by André Godin, a French industrialist who moved his ironworks to the small town of Guise in 1846, and, following Fourier's precepts, built a large "family palace" which finally came to house 1,200 persons and included a theater, school, laundry, and dining rooms. The provision of proper ventilation, water-flushed toilets, showers, even garbage chutes, contrasted with the typical worker housing of that period. Godin himself lived in what he called the *familistère,* and on his death the factory, already partially owned by his workers, was fully purchased by them.

The great buildings of Godin's *familistère* in Guise can still be seen today, but little else remains of this brave experiment, which was not repeated elsewhere. Subsequent attempts to found ideal communities tended to be rural and agrarian. The Owenites and Fourierists, the cottage factory and the *familistère* have become obscure footnotes to the Industrial Revolution, a forgotten anomaly instead of the beginning of a different sort of industrialization.

CHAPTER 3

WOODEN MILLERS

The human mind seems incapable of believing anything that it cannot conceive and understand. . . . I speak from experience, for when it was first asserted that merchant flour mills could be constructed to attend themselves . . . the projector was answered: You cannot make water run up hill, you cannot make wooden millers.
—Oliver Evans, *The Young Steam Engineer's Guide* (1804)

Henry Ford is popularly credited with inventing the assembly line, but in fact its origins are much older than the Michigan inventor and even predate the Luddite uprising. Oliver Evans, a Delaware engineer and a pioneer in steam-engine development, built a flour mill in 1783 that used a variety of waterwheel-powered devices to move grain from one milling process to another. Evans's mill, which was built in Philadelphia, used very few workers; grain was automatically weighed and carried vertically, by a screw conveyor, to a storage area on the top floor of the four-story building. From there it descended on a belt conveyor to one of six millstones, and after milling, the flour was raised again by bucket conveyor to another storage area. Finally, it was moved back to the lower level, where it could be loaded aboard a waiting ship.

Although Evans patented his device in 1790, he did not reap much benefit from it. Envious millers petitioned Congress in 1813 to lift the patent because they did not want to pay Evans royalties. With the aid of no less eminent a witness than Thomas Jefferson—himself an inventor—they succeeded in convincing the authorities that the automated mill consisted of nothing really new, but of devices that were well known.* Of course, in one sense they were right, but the combination of these conveying mechanisms into a functioning whole was still a staggering achievement. As the historian Siegfried Giedion wrote, "Evans' invention opens a new chapter in the history of mankind."

Evans's case was not an isolated one, although the degree of automation in his flour mill was exceptional. Most of the early assembly lines did use mechanical transportation systems, but in conjunction with hand labor; automation came later. Hardtack, or ship's biscuit, was the staple of the English navy, and in 1804 a factory was built that rationalized the production process by having five bakers work in a line, each performing one step of the operation. Such a systematic division of labor, rather than any mechanical device, was the beginning of the assembly line. Eventually, twenty-nine years later, the process was mechanized so that all operations save one were carried out by machines connected to one another by a series of rollers.

The Swiss inventor Johann Georg Bodmer is credited with a number of inventions that advanced the development of the assembly line, among them the endless belt, the traveling crane, and the traveling furnace grate, used for the continuous stoking of furnaces. Bodmer built a number of factories in England in the 1830s which incorporated the principles of

---

*Jefferson's famous house, Monticello, included an automatic device for conveying bottles from his wine cellar to his dining table.

planned production, with stationary workers linked by various kinds of conveyance systems.

Rationalization and division of labor, step-by-step assembly, even automation occurred quite early in the industrialization of the workplace. Just as the English Industrial Revolution was the result not of mechanization, but primarily of the organization of capital and workers, so the assembly line was less the result of any particular technological breakthrough than of the perception of a different way of using technology.

The immediate predecessor of the modern industrial assembly line is generally acknowledged to be the Cincinnati packing house of the 1860s. In this widely used system, the animal's carcass was conveyed by means of overhead rails from operation to operation, moving both horizontally and vertically. While Evans had managed to move a granular material, such as flour or wheat, it was quite another thing to move objects, particularly odd-shaped objects, as the hog-packing plants did. The technological stage was now set for another revolution in industrialization, or, as the Boston businessman Edward A. Filene put it, for the "Fordizing" of America.

Henry Ford built the first automobile assembly line in a factory in Highland Park, Michigan, in 1913; it was used to assemble magnetos for his Model T cars, which had been introduced five years earlier. Ford did not invent either the automobile or the assembly line, although he did make important improvements to both. Ford understood that the assembly line, with its rationalization of work, could achieve more than simply greater profits. He was critical of Frederick Winslow Taylor's idea of "scientific management," which was popular at the time, caustically describing it as a method for increasing efficiency so that a workingman could load 47 ½ tons instead of 12 ½ tons of pig iron a day. What interested Ford was a technology that would make it unnecessary for a laborer to carry 106,400 pounds of pig iron for $1.85.

Ford saw that the assembly line would facilitate real mass

production. Mass production, he reasoned (the revelation must have come in a blaze of light), was the ability to satisfy mass *consumption*. The two, he wrote later, went hand in hand: increase production and lower costs and you can raise wages; raise wages and you will raise consumption, which in turn leads to higher production, and so on. Incredibly (for such a chicken-and-egg theory) it worked. In the first seventeen years the Ford Motor Company produced one million cars; in the next twelve years this figure increased to fourteen million. The first Model T cost $850 in 1908; twenty-eight years later the price had dropped to $310. Wages rose from year to year. In 1914, when the rest of the automobile industry was paying $2.40 a day, Ford paid a minimum of $5 a day; by 1926, although there was no inflation, the minimum wage at Ford was $6 a day, while the average wage had risen to $8 a day.

Ford's principle of high production, low product cost, and high wages was coupled with a decentralized production system of manufacturing and assembly, which further reduced costs, as well as an integrated supply of raw materials. Ford acquired coal and iron mines, forests and sawmills, railways and steamships, and he ran them all according to the same principles. He started foreign branches in Europe and Russia, employing only nationals and paying the same wages as he did in America, all in order to stimulate consumption.

Henry Ford was not unaware of the shock that this new technology would have on the assembly-line worker. He acknowledged that mass production increased repetitive work and could become monotonous, although he felt that this drawback was more than offset by the reduction in needless physical hardship by mechanizing the most laborious work processes. He argued that the only way to achieve inexpensive, high-quality results, previously accomplished expensively by hand, was to replace the craftsman with the machine. In addition, he pointed out that, while common work had always been done by unskilled labor, common work in mass production required higher standards of education and intelligence than before.

It is easy to overlook the social experimentation that went on in the early days of mass production. Ford established a valve plant eighteen miles out in the country so that he could employ farmers on a part-time basis, still permitting them to carry on their agricultural activities. This and other attempts to bring industry to the countryside—and avoid the creation of more Manchesters—were successful, and the suburban subdivision became the housing prototype of the new workers' housing. On the other hand, the hope for a decentralized industry, almost a network of cottage factories, never materialized. Instead, companies such as Ford and General Motors simply grew larger and larger.

Another idea of the early days of mass production that failed to materialize was the concept of industrial democracy. Liberal businessmen such as Edward A. Filene advocated a democratization of the workplace as not only desirable but inevitable. Filene reasoned that many of the difficulties of the Industrial Revolution in England had been due to the loss of independence and freedom on the part of the craftsmen who had been replaced by the machine. In the United States, while political life had been growing more democratic, industry had continued to be organized into two distinct classes—"the boss and the bossed." Filene, hardly a socialist, saw this as a dangerous anomaly, and warned that if the situation was not changed, the bossed would resort to left-wing political ideology to fight back. In the event, few businessmen followed the example set by Filene's own department stores, and most industries continued to be organized along strictly undemocratic lines.

No one was more autocratic in the running of an industry than that benevolent dictator Henry Ford. He rejected the idea of democracy in the factory altogether, even though he paid higher wages and provided better working conditions than other factory owners. But he became the victim of his own success. The mass consumption he stimulated also resulted in new and changing mass values. Mass production improved the lot of the workingman, as Ford had intended, but it also inevitably changed him, which Ford did not expect.

In 1949, two years after Ford's death, Yale University released one of the first social studies of the automobile industry—the famous *Man on the Assembly Line*. The study made some surprising discoveries. It found that the majority of the assembly-line workers disliked the mechanical pacing, repetitive tasks, and their inability to do quality work; a good number resented the fact that their jobs had been so simplified as to require virtually no skill (the average training period for assembly-line workers at that time was two weeks); and more than 80 percent said that the *only* thing they liked about the assembly-line job was the generally high wages. Henry Ford had succeeded in reducing onerous physical labor and in raising wages, but apparently this was not enough. He did not realize that as material needs became satisfied, other, non-material aspects of the work became more important than they had been.

In the Yale study some workers expressed satisfaction with their jobs; but significantly, these tended to be repairmen and utility men, workers who performed a variety of tasks up and down the line, either filling in where needed or troubleshooting. Many of the assembly-line workers expressed a desire for these types of positions, and the principal reason for wanting a transfer or promotion was not a desire for increased wages, but a desire to get away from production-line jobs.

The drudgery of work on the assembly line was further demonstrated by the finding that the "quit rate" for automobile assembly-line workers was higher than that for other industries, and furthermore, that within the assembly plant, mass-production workers had both a higher quit rate and higher absenteeism. The study also found that 90 percent of the workers expressed dislike for the mass-production aspects of their jobs, and that they disliked their jobs to the degree that they embodied these characteristics.

The lesson of all this is not that the assembly line is a "bad" process. A similar survey of a Manchester textile mill of the 1840s would find much more physical misery. Improvements in working conditions, wages, and standard of living stimulate new expectations on the part of the worker. It appeared from the Yale study that these expectations were not being met. But in spite of its rather bleak findings, *Man on the Assembly Line* ended on a cheerfully optimistic note: "Since these problems exist, let us get all the facts we can. In time we shall be able to solve them."

It was easy to be cheerful in 1949. After all, the assembly line had played a major part in winning the war and turning the United States into a world power. While workers might complain, they did acknowledge the advantages of high pay, company health plans, and retirement pensions. In any case, a team of university professors could hardly do anything about workers' complaints. Perhaps industry should have been listening.

Man on the Assembly Line made no mention of any violent resistance to the machine. The assembly line may have been disliked, but it was never physically attacked. But reading between the lines a reader could perceive hints of suppressed violence. The high rates of absenteeism. The attitude of the workers. "The guys yell hurrah whenever the line breaks down," one worker is quoted as saying; "you can hear it all over the plant." It is hard to believe that the breakdowns were always accidental.

If American assembly-line workers seldom indulged in overt machine-breaking, they did demonstrate resistance to the machine in more subtle ways. According to the sociologist Pierre Dubois, it is possible to distinguish at least three types of active opposition to mechanization that qualify as industrial sabotage. The first includes all attempts to destroy or break machinery. This occurs sometimes as a tactic in a labor dispute, as when pressmen of the *Washington Post,* prior to a 1975 walkout, damaged the presses to prevent publication of the paper during the strike. Also, machine-breaking can simply be the less-focused result of pent-up frustration with a tedious or monotonous job, or it can even be, as has been documented in some cases, purposeless destruction—sabotage as fun.

Two other types of sabotage are less dramatic and sometimes difficult to distinguish. They consist of actions that are meant to stop production without actually destroying machinery or to reduce the actual amount of work done. Thus, under certain circumstances, a "go-slow" or working-to-rule are forms of sabotage. Similarly, activities that halt production for a time, though often impossible to differentiate from authentic accidents, are likewise sabotage whose aim may be to take a rest and get some "catch-up time," to make a point in a larger labor conflict, or just to relieve boredom. For example, during a lengthy confrontation over automation and job supervision, Canadian postal workers "lost" a fairly significant number of letters. An article by Judson Gooding in *Fortune* refers to automobiles that left the assembly line with screws left in brakedrums, tool handles welded into fender compartments, paint scratched, and upholstery cut. This kind of sabotage is often mistakenly described as "productivity problems" or "industrial accidents"—terms that give the impression that nothing is wrong. But, as a Virginia coal miner told Michael Yarrow, "If you work to rule you can really hurt them, and then you can deliberately sabotage the stuff. You can run over cable. You can just drive your buggy real slow. 'Can't you go any faster?' 'No, sir!' Nothing in the contract that says how fast you have to work."

Less violent, perhaps, but with just as much impact on production, is absenteeism. Gooding estimated that absenteeism in the automobile industry rises to 15 percent on Fridays and Mondays, and that overall absenteeism in the last ten years has doubled. In some plants there is even a black market in blank doctor's chits, which are required for medical excuses.

The final form of sabotage is for the worker simply to quit. Chrysler reported in 1970 that 50 percent of its workers do not complete the first ninety days of employment. As early as 1913, the turnover rate at Ford assembly plants was over 380 percent. This turnover in workers has important effects on productivity because of the time spent training new workers and reorganizing the line.

Dubois implies that continued outbreaks of industrial sabotage are due to an unresolved conflict that has been present in the factory since the earliest days of the Industrial Revolution and has been institutionalized by the growth of trade unions. Many writers argue that it is the technology of the assembly line itself that is responsible for industrial sabotage. But if the assembly line is to blame, it is not in quite the way that Ellul and Mumford would have us believe. The key change that has taken place in the factory, and which is due to the assembly line, is the character of the workers themselves.

A recent study by the W. E. Upjohn Institute for Employment Research points out that workers today do not always accept the type of work that may have been acceptable in the past. This was found to be particularly true of young workers, who were better educated and had higher aspirations than their parents. The young worker still places importance on pay, security, and fringe benefits, but tends to take these for granted. In addition, the young worker places more importance on interesting and challenging work. The difficulty is that most of the work available to young workers does not fit this description. The Upjohn study also found that what set young American workers apart from their predecessors was a marked antiauthoritarianism.

The same year that the Upjohn study was published, 1971, some of its findings were dramatically highlighted by events that took place at the Lordstown General Motors factory. It had taken almost fifty years for Filene's prediction to come true, but when it did the workers, instead of resorting to left-wing politics, turned to a much older technique—machine-bashing.

The automobile plant that General Motors had built in Lords-

town, Ohio, in 1970 was planned to be the most efficient in the
industry, which at that time meant in the world. It was to be the
American industry's response to the "Japanese challenge," and
would produce a new compact car—the Vega. According to
Fortune magazine, the automation of various laborious and tedious operations in the Lordstown factory would resolve the
problem of the workers' dislike of the assembly line. Lordstown
was planned on a scientific basis and incorporated the best
techniques that the largest manufacturing corporation in the
country could devise.

Shortly after the plant went into operation, worker resistance
to the new machinery became apparent, and a year later there
was an outbreak of planned and systematic sabotage. An editorial sympathetic to the workers that appeared in *The New York
Times* referred to the situation as "guerrilla warfare." Workshops were flooded with firehoses, automobile engines were
intentionally exploded, and banana peels found their way into
the innards of cars on the assembly line. At the same time, the
workers' dissatisfaction with what they felt to be a poor-quality
car resulted in the rejection of dozens of engines at the final
inspection, until the whole shop was crammed with rejects.

Since Lordstown was a brand-new factory with a newly re-
cruited workforce, it was almost a case study of how young
workers (whose average age was under twenty-five) reacted to
the assembly line. Most of their protest was against the rigid
controls imposed by the "scientific" management of General
Motors. For instance, the assembly line at Lordstown moved at
almost twice the speed of lines at other plants—a car came by
every thirty-six seconds. It was working conditions, not wages
or benefits, which were the issue. Fundamentally, the dispute
was about who should control the machine.

All the machine-breaking at Lordstown took place while the
plant was in operation. Finally, in March 1972, the eight thousand workers walked off the job. The strike lasted only twenty-
two days but was particularly bitter. Still, it was almost an

anticlimax to a more historic occurrence—General Ludd had finally crossed the Atlantic.*

The events at Lordstown—there was later talk of a "Lordstown syndrome"—focused attention on mass-production technology as the source of the problem. Suspicion of the machine has never been far below the surface of American opinion, in spite of popular heroes such as Thomas Edison and Henry Ford. In the 1970s it emerged as a widely held view. The origins of this attitude can be found in the early days of the Republic, with such men as Henry Thoreau, Nathaniel Hawthorne, and especially Ralph Waldo Emerson.

When Emerson visited England in 1847, the Luddite uprising was a faint memory and the Industrial Revolution was in full swing. While Emerson had been an ardent apologist for mechanical innovation in the United States, his contact with the new industrial environment had been minimal, since that country was then just beginning to industrialize. Emerson was shaken by the violent, and apparently negative, impact of English industrialization on virtually all aspects of everyday life. Like the young Engels, his indignation was aroused by the misery and squalor in cities such as Manchester. His enthusiasm considerably dampened, he reflected, on his return to America, that "The machinery has proved, like the balloon, unmanageable, and flies away with the aeronaut."

Emerson's view of a runaway technology was not particularly fashionable in his own day.† Nevertheless, it has become more

---

*A few years before Lordstown, in a book about technology and employment, A. J. Jaffe and Joseph Froomkin had written, "The American worker may go on strike, fight his employer through a union, or even [!] write to his Congressman. When faced with new machinery, he may refuse to operate it. But he does not wreck factories and new machinery, nor does he threaten the lives of inventors."
†Fifteen years before Emerson's visit to England, Charles Babbage, the pioneer of the computer, published *On the Economy of Machinery and Manufacturers.* This book, which lauded the new "self-acting machines," was the equivalent of

and more accepted. The idea of an autonomous, sometimes vengeful, and always pitiless technology has become an unquestioned truism. But although Emerson was right to assert that *control* was the most important issue raised by the Industrial Revolution, he misunderstood the nature of this control. What was at stake was not control of the machine but control of the workers.

At this point a slight digression is in order to discuss a red herring that is often thrown into the discussion about technology. It concerns the difference between tools and machines. It is obvious that there is a difference; while definitions vary, it is generally agreed that tools are instruments that are manually operated, while machines transmit some sort of external force. While it is sometimes useful to differentiate between the two —in describing the evolution of a technology from the tool phase to the machine phase, for instance—it is misleading to overemphasize the change that occurs as a result of this evolution. As Arnold Gehlen warns, "the difference between tool and machine is not the key qualitative difference involved in the transition from premodern to modern technique."

Unfortunately, many writers cannot resist focusing on this difference, rather than on the change in technical (and social) activity that caused handicraft production to be replaced by factory production, and only incidentally caused the tool to be replaced by the machine. Ivan Illich, in *Tools for Conviviality*, contrasts the skilled user of a hand tool with the "mere operator" of a machine. Ellul, in *The Technological Society*, ascribes regional stability, a high degree of skill development, and aesthetic value to the tool phase of civilization, and loss of these to the machine phase. Is it caviling to point out that many hand tools require absolutely no skill at all, and that their use

---

a best-seller, went to four editions, was reprinted in the United States, and translated into four languages.

involves primarily drudgery? At the same time, most machines require dexterity and a high level of hand-eye coordination. Ellul claims that tools are inherently deficient and hence rely on, and develop, the skill of the user. But is not the same true of many large machines? Had Ellul or Illich ever had the opportunity to operate a bulldozer, or a hundred-ton crane, they might be less prone to denigrate the skills required to coax these awkward monsters into useful life.

Throughout the Industrial Revolution the workers' reaction to the machine cannot be satisfactorily explained as a reaction to the shift from tools to machines. As I have pointed out, the shift sometimes occurred before, and sometimes after, industrialization. It could even occur outside the factory system, as the Coventry cottage factory shows. What the machine-breakers were opposing was not the "oppressive machine" but rather the way the machine was *used* to oppress—which is not at all the same thing.

In the "civil war" that characterized the Industrial Revolution in England, technology was frequently a weapon in the hands of the factory owners who were attracted to mechanization as a way of undermining the power of the more troublesome craftsmen. The Hammonds describe how the wool-combing machine, for instance, was adopted by the masters precisely to destroy the independence of the wool-combers who had given their employers so much trouble in the past. The attraction of steam power was not that it lessened human exertion, but that it reduced the number of skilled laborers required. Emerson himself observed that the manufacturers in England preferred the machine, "this peaceful fellow, instead of the quarrelsome fellow God has made." The replacement of men by children and women was likewise not an accident of mechanization; it was frequently a deliberate tactic on the part of the manufacturers, and an effective way to minimize the possibility of labor conflicts and keep wages low.

The use of technology as a kind of brickbat can still be found today. In the telecommunications industry, for instance, the computer may do to the skilled telecommunications worker what the gig mill did to the wool cropper—replace him. But, contrary to the popular image of automation, the computer does not always reduce employment; the total number of jobs in the Bell System is expected to increase, not decrease, as a result of automation. However, the kinds of jobs will change drastically. In effect, there will be a shift from nonmanagement to management categories, and from technicians to clerks. Electronic switching systems, like the gig mill, dispense with skilled craftsmen. They can diagnose their own faults, and repairs involve simply replacing one circuit pack by another.

The Communications Workers of America, like the croppers' institution, has largely lost control of the technology in the workplace. In one case the union protested the assignment of clerical workers to a new type of computer that runs a complex series of tests on telephone equipment, work that had previously been performed by a skilled, unionized technician. The arbitrator found that the previous human skill was now invested in the machine, and so there was no "skill parity" between the present and the previous job, and hence the company had the right to assign it to an unskilled clerical worker.

It is important to note that the real issue in confrontations such as these is not just that machines take away jobs from people (as the unions sometimes assert), but that the new machines take jobs away from one person and give them to another. Automation could just as easily allow blue-collar workers to perform management functions, though this possibility is rarely discussed.

It is not necessary to argue that industrialization is *always* introduced specifically in order to control the worker; but as machines are increasingly used, their role as controlling mechanisms is soon appreciated by management.* No one appreciated this characteristic of industrialization more than Henry Ford. His famous three principles of mass production all have to do with controlling the worker by means of the machine. The line itself regulates the pace of work; it controls the worker's mobility by organizing operations along the line so that the worker does not move around; and it controls the worker's skill by breaking down the assembly process into a large number of simple operations. Of course, Ford's assembly line was not devised to coerce an unruly work force or to undermine the power of a traditional guild—it was instituted in the name of efficiency —but the effect on the worker, as the results of the Yale study showed, was that he felt controlled by the machine.

Sometimes efforts were made to camouflage this control. In 1928, Elton Mayo, a Harvard professor of industrial research, was asked to suggest ways of making improvements to an electrical assembly plant in Chicago. His finding was that flagging production was due to the fact that supervisors were too visible, and he suggested a "freer" work environment, where supervision was less apparent. After instituting Mayo's recommendations the Chicago plant did in fact increase production. In a revealing aside, Mayo observed that "Many times over, the history sheets and other records show that in the opinion of the group all supervision has been removed. On occasion indeed they artlessly tell the observer, who is in fact of supervisory rank, very revealing tales of their experience with previous 'bosses.' Their opinion is, of course, mistaken: in a sense they are getting closer supervision than ever before, the difference is in the quality of the supervision." But whatever the quality of the supervision, the line between the bosses and the bossed remained.

*The chairman of agricultural engineering at the University of California at Davis, which has developed an automated tomato-picking machine that is now widely used, is quoted as saying, "The machine won't strike. It will work when [the growers] want it to work." (See Bernard Taper.)

All in all, democracy has been slow in coming to the work-place. A number of corporations have been experimenting with job rotation, vertical job enlargement, and redefining the division of work to give employees an increased sense of participation and authority. Many of these attempts, however, are simply "experiments in management," that is, attempts to find less visible methods of control. In the telecommunications industry, automation has played a major role in this process. Some American Telephone and Telegraph companies are now using a computer system called FADS (Force Administration Data System), which measures the flow of information traffic and plans employees' work schedules to suit. The computer regulates coffee breaks and lunch periods, and it also provides the supervisor with a record of exactly how much traffic has been handled by each operator. Robert Howard, a journalist, quotes one operator as saying, "The computer watches you for the supervisor. It is constantly alert to the atmosphere in the office." Another system called TSPS (Traffic Service Position System) is a computer program that routes long-distance telephone calls. It times each operator for half an hour, randomly, twice a week, to determine his average working time, and to record the time the operator takes to answer the call. No longer able to schedule his work pace, the operator must now conform to management norms. If the terminal is put on "busy," or if it is left unattended for·a few minutes (a common practice with the old cord switchboards), the machine knows. And the machine tells.

It will be interesting to see whether the automation of the office—the replacement of typewriters with centrally computerized word processors—will follow the same pattern. The new office worker will be connected to a Big Brain; what is typed, when it is typed, even how quickly it is typed will be recorded and, theoretically at least, could be available to management. But most workers and unions are resisting automation for the wrong reasons: the threat of unemployment will not be the only problem; they must also deal with the nature of the new jobs that automation will create.

A contemporary of Oliver Evans called his automated flour mill "a set of clap-traps," and indeed it has taken more than a hundred and fifty years to develop the wooden miller into a functioning steel-collar worker. Although automatic riveting machines were used on automobile assembly lines as early as the 1930s, full-scale automation had to await the development of the computer some thirty years later. Konrad Zuse, a Luftwaffe engineer, built the first electric computing machine in 1941, and it was soon succeeded by the electronic computer, built at the University of Pennsylvania in 1946. The first generation of computers was characterized by low memory capacity, slow operating time, large energy consumption, and rather huge space requirements. The second generation, which used transistors rather than electronic tubes, worked more rapidly and had a larger memory. The transistor was soon replaced by the integrated circuit, which spawned the so-called third-generation computers.

During the 1950s, there was talk of factories run by master computers which would control all the production processes. In fact, few such factories were ever built. They would have been too costly and, more important, too risky: a small computer failure would have brought the entire factory to a halt. It was the microprocessor—the computer on a chip—that rendered the supercomputer obsolete.

The microprocessor made it possible to build small, inexpensive computers with extensive feedback and memory storage— the minicomputers. It now became practical for a series of minicomputers, each doing a single, simple task, to be linked to one another in a hierarchical system. This arrangement became the basis for the automated factory.

In 1977, the Philip Morris tobacco company built a large plant in Richmond, Virginia, that is automated. The tobacco arrives at the warehouse, where laser optical readers and photoelectric cells identify various grades of tobacco and instruct one of five computer-controlled stacker cranes to pick up the bales and store them. The location of the bale is recorded and forwarded to another computer. This machine plans manufacturing programs based on market data; it selects various grades of tobacco which are then blended and processed by another computer. In the out-going stockroom cigarettes arrive at the breakneck speed of sixty cartons per second; a small computer coordinates stacking, palleting, and storage of the finished product. When a delivery truck pulls up at the dock and the driver (finally, a human) opens the doors, a computer-controlled drone is waiting for him with the specific cargo. In this $200 million factory, 5,000 workers annually produce 140 billion cigarettes; or, to put it another way, each prosthetic god produces goods worth $280,000.

Similar developments are taking place in the automobile industry. There are presently fewer than 5,000 robots scurrying around factory floors in the United States, although it is estimated that in less than twenty years, second-generation robots, equipped with rudimentary sensory capability and some feedback capacity, could be performing the equivalent of 2.3 million jobs. In the automobile industry, robots are currently used for welding, painting, and metal-cutting. Some of the benefits may be economic: a $60,000 welding robot costs only $6 an hour to operate, compared to the average assembly-line worker's wage and benefits of almost three times as much. The "peaceful fellows" carried out 98 percent of the 3,000 spot welds on the 1981 Chrysler K-model car. Robots can also do higher-quality work, and the American switch to robots partly reflects an effort to produce cars of a quality equal to that of the Japanese, who use robots extensively. Robots can also perform tedious or monotonous tasks; General Motors is developing machines that will be capable of such simple operations as selecting parts from a bin and examining them for defects.

The dire consequences of using robots and automatic manufacturing techniques have been foretold for a long time. It is
commonly said that the worker will be even more alienated,
unhappy, and bored. But evidence is accumulating that this is
not happening. Jon M. Shepard, a sociologist, has conducted an
extensive survey of workers in mechanized and automated environments. The purpose of his research was to discover
whether the changed relationship between persons and machines that is caused by automation affects levels of alienation
among workers. The survey examined both industry (an oil
refinery and an automobile assembly plant) and commerce (in-
surance companies and a large bank).

Alienation in the workplace results from a number of person-
machine relationships. Most obviously, alienation consists of a
feeling of powerlessness, or lack of control over work processes.
Lack of understanding of the work, or of how it relates to the
overall process, can also result in a feeling of meaningless-
ness. Another aspect of alienation consists of what Shepard calls
"normlessness"—the perceived lack of promotion through legitimate means—a common experience in industries with a
highly developed division of labor. Alienation can also be characterized by low self-esteem as regards the work—a feeling
that the job is unimportant or inferior to other activities. The
conclusion of Shepard's detailed study is that automation does
not increase alienation, as defined above: it actually seems to
decrease it. This apparent anomaly can be explained by the
nature of work in an automated environment.

There are generally considered to be two types of automation: "Detroit automation" and "continuous-process" automation. Detroit automation, which is really semiautomation,
involves an assembly-line process with automated work stations
replacing hand assembly. Continuous-process automation is
characterized by the integration of both materials handling and
processing with automatic regulation by the computer. The
speed of continuous-process technology—whether a word

processor or an oil refinery—is enormous. Whereas mechanization and the assembly line force the worker to adapt to greater speeds—with potentially disastrous consequences, as at Lordstown—the computer-controlled continuous process moves at a speed that can be measured only in microseconds. The worker cannot keep up with this machine. Instead, work in a continuous-process plant consists in periodic monitoring and occasional maintenance, done at the worker's pace. Remember that *Man on the Assembly Line* found that the most satisfied assembly-line workers were the repairmen and troubleshooters, who enjoyed a high degree of freedom and variety in their jobs. In a continuous-process plant, such as an oil refinery, maintenance craftsmen make up the majority of the labor force. A similar situation occurs in the office, where Shepard found considerably less alienation among clerks than among assembly-line workers, and less alienation among computer operators and software personnel than among clerks.

Whether automation will have a beneficial effect on the work environment will depend to a great extent on the way in which it is introduced, on how it is used, and on who makes these decisions. Since industrial democracy has been slow in coming, it is likely that labor unions will have an important say in this transitional period.

In its 1979 negotiations with the Ford Motor Company, the United Auto Workers union had a number of demands specifically related to the introduction of new automated technology. They included union access to all computer data bases, no use of computers to monitor or discipline workers, and the right to strike on technology conflicts. The union won agreement on the establishment of a National Committee on Technological Progress and programs to train workers in operating computer-controlled machinery, and it was given assurances by Ford that new technology would not be used to take jobs away from unionized employees. Similar contracts were also signed with Chrysler and General Motors.

The result of these agreements is that UAW workers are being integrated with computers and robots and not simply being displaced by them. Technicians now operate, service, and maintain computer terminals, program industrial robots, and reprogram computer chips—all jobs that had been previously done by nonunion personnel when the new technologies were first introduced. This example indicates that this latest industrial revolution need not result in worker displacement or alienation, although a lot will depend on the unions' ability to shift exclusive control of technology at least partly to their members.

Swedish industry has experimented with various methods of transferring control from management to labor. In 1972, the Saab/Scania Company opened an engine plant in Soedertaelje, a suburb of Stockholm, which introduced some new concepts of *arbetsmiljo* (working environment). Industrial robots have taken over the more monotonous and the more laborious jobs (most of the workers are women, from neighboring Finland). Final assembly of the engines is done by teams of four workers. Each of the seven teams assembles the entire engine, and the members of the team can decide whether to work individually or together. Volvo has built a plant at Kalmar, Sweden, where the assembly of entire automobiles follows similar principles. Larger teams of workers are responsible for assembling entire sections of the car; the team has control over internal job assignments and over the pace of work. Absenteeism, which is endemic in the Swedish car industry, also becomes the responsibility of the team.

Volvo also operates an engine plant at Skövde that has a unit organized on the team principle. Each team, consisting of about twenty workers, has shared responsibility for maintenance, organization, and quality control; the division of labor is drastically reduced—all members of the team have an opportunity to learn all the tasks within the unit, both informally and in organized training sessions. Workers are not paid individually but as a team, according to output.

A study of this novel system was conducted by Jan Forslin, about a year after its inception. Production quality, quantity, and costs were comparable to those of the more traditional Volvo assembly lines, but absenteeism and labor turnover were significantly lower, and, more important, the attitudes of the workers in the new unit tended to be more optimistic about technological change and further automation.

Whether or not the Swedish examples are adaptable to the much larger-scale American (or Canadian) automobile industry, they indicate that the technology of the assembly line can be directed to give greater control to workers, if that is the goal of the parties concerned.

Automated machining, originally a highly skilled traditional craft, today consists of the conjunction of machining tools with minicomputers (Computer Numerical Control, or CNC). The operator retrieves the required program from the minicomputer, although it is also possible for him to modify or reprogram on the spot. David Noble, a historian at the Massachusetts Institute of Technology, contrasts the application of automated machine tools in the United States with its application in Norway. He has purposely chosen two plants of similar size that use a similar process and make use of automated machining tools.

According to Noble, at the General Electric plant in Lynn, Massachusetts, machine operators may not alter or rewrite programs; this is a management function performed by programmers. This restriction on the initiative of the operator affects the quality of the product. The Norwegian factory, which makes aircraft parts using CNC machinery, operates in a different way. The operators have direct access to the minicomputer program, that is, they routinely modify, rewrite, and rearrange a program until they are satisfied with it according to their own criteria of efficiency, quality, and convenience. While both the American and Norwegian operators are told *what* to do, the Norwegian is considerably freer as to *how* he is going to do it. The introduction of the minicomputer to the shop floor has permitted the shift of former management functions to the machine operator and, coincidentally, has improved the quality of the product. It has also, Noble found, significantly improved the quality of the operator's job.

Computer time is now so inexpensive that very little skill and training are required to create new programs. But the way that this new capability is used in the Norwegian plant contrasts sharply with the way it is so often introduced to companies such as the Bell System, where automation was used to downgrade, rather than improve, the tasks of skilled workers. As Noble concludes, "How this technology will actually be employed in a plant *depends less upon any inherent nature of the technology* [my emphasis] than upon the particular manufacturing processes involved, the political and economic setting, and the relative power and sophistication of the parties engaged in the struggle over control of production." Or, to put it more crudely, we often get the technology that we deserve.

It is obvious that the suspicion of the machine in the workplace is not a nineteenth-century phenomenon; it continues with regard to the automation and computerization that characterize the present industrial revolution. Many of the contentious issues are similar and are concerned with control of the machine. And the issue of control is not, as some philosophers and historians would have us imagine, that of man versus machine. It is the much older conflict of man versus man.

The democratization of the factory has occurred very slowly, when it has occurred at all, and, as a result, the "civil war" that the Hammonds described, although it has abated, has not disappeared altogether; instead, it has become a permanent state of unrest—not quite strife, not quite armistice. It is hardly surprising that in such a climate technological innovation often becomes a weapon in the hands of the antagonists.

The labor unions, although rarely opposed to "progress" in theory, have often resisted automation in practice, and there are a number of understandable reasons for this. Increased automation usually has the effect of decreasing the number of so-called blue-collar workers and increasing the number of clerical jobs, thus reducing union strength. Even if clerical jobs are not classified as management, the growth of white-collar unions has been slow and they are usually separate from the industrial unions. The traditional power base of the unions has been the industrial worker who, through automation, is gradually being replaced by the skilled worker and the craft union, which is causing a shift in the relative strength of these groups.

But the biggest threat to unions is the effect that automation has on labor's chief bargaining tool: the threat of a strike. Whereas a labor-intensive industry can be halted by a worker walkout, the same is not true of automated industry, where nonunion management can easily replace workers. This applies particularly to continuous-process automation, in which monitoring and maintenance represent the chief worker activity. As early as 1961, during a seventy-five-day strike in a Texas oil refinery, supervisors were able to keep the plant operating at 65 percent capacity. More recently, during the 1981 strike of 12,000 air controllers throughout the United States, supervisors (with the help of military controllers) prevented any major disruption of air traffic. Strikes in other industries with a high degree of automation, such as communications and newspaper publishing, have proved considerably less effective than in the past.

The opposition of labor—and especially of labor unions—to automation could thus be described as Luddite, not because it is mindless or antiprogress, but because, like Luddism, it opposes the use of the machine to control. As in the past, the distinction is an important one.

The struggle for greater democracy in the factory will continue, and as long as it does, technology will be disputed in the process. But this does not mean that a Megamachine or a Technological System is imposing itself on a hapless society. The

relationships between persons and machines are not conditioned solely by technology, they are shaped above all by the
social conditions within which technology is being applied (see
Chapter 7). Whether or not the computer operator will also be
a programmer is a social decision. Whether or not word processors are used to monitor office workers' performances is likewise
a social, not a technical, choice. If automation means that blue-
collar workers are always replaced by nonunion employees, and
not the other way around, that is a choice dictated by the existing relations between labor and management and not by the
technology involved. The fact is that all too often we pretend
that decisions are technologically determined when really they
are conditioned by other factors.

It has been said that technological innovations, such as automation, create new social problems, the implication being that
perhaps we would be better off if such innovations did not
occur. It would be more accurate to say that technological
change in the workplace throws a new light on old problems.
Arresting technology will not make these problems go away. In
the end, whether or not we get the technology that we deserve,
we will get the technology we have chosen; and what is chosen
may be less important than who makes the choice.

CHAPTER 4

THE WAND AND THE BOOK

The wand and the book come to be regarded as themselves potent, and not merely the symbols of potency.
—Michael Oakeshott, *Rationalism in Politics*

I f the shock of the machine was deeply felt by the English wool-cropper, or is still being felt by the American assembly-line worker, it is not hard to imagine how much more aggravated the impact of industrialization is on persons who live in societies that are themselves, on the whole, not yet technological. Here too the issue of who chooses and, above all, who controls technology is paramount. And just as the Luddites vented their anger on specific machines—more symbols of change than its real cause—so also cultures that are assailed by rapid, overwhelming, technical change may misunderstand the source of their difficulties.

Technology, because it is physical and explicit, is often perceived as the prime cause of technical change. In fact, technology is itself the result of technical activity. Once technology is perceived, rightly or wrongly, as embodying technical change, whether one is trying to resist or promote technical activity, the temptation is to view the machine as either culprit or hero. The wand and the book, which are only the symbols of authority and knowledge, come to be seen as embodying power themselves. For example, every nation, no matter how small or poor, feels the need to maintain a national airline, as if that were somehow a sign of national technical accomplishment, even if—as in the case of Nigeria—this airline is managed by someone else (Royal Dutch Airlines).

The perception of technology as a *thing* rather than as an *activity* is common enough in our own culture. It is all the more understandable in nontechnological cultures that see only the results of technology, while the process remains hidden. This was the case with the cargo cults that occurred in New Guinea between 1910 and 1940, forms of which continue until the present day. They began as an attempt by nineteenth-century Melanesians to understand the great wealth and power of the white foreigners. Unlike the natives, the whites seemed to do no work, but possessed an advanced technology that was obviously the source of their power. The Melanesians reasoned that the goods and technology that the cargo ships, and later airplanes, brought to the islands could not be the product of such idle people, but must have come from a mystical source. Some versions of the cult claimed that the goods were the result of the spirits of the whites' ancestors who toiled in a far-off factory. One chauvinistic variation had it that the goods were actually made by the Melanesians' own ancestors, and had been hijacked by the whites on the open seas. In any event, the major theme of this early North-South conflict was that, just as the whites received the gift of technology from their ancestors, so too the time would come for the Melanesians: ships would arrive bearing not only goods and cargo but also their resurrected ancestors and dead relatives. At this point, they too would be rich and powerful.

The cargo cult proved to be a powerful belief. Buildings were prepared to receive the ghostly crews, and in one bizarre case in the 1950s, dummy runways and mock air-control towers were erected, not to decoy unaware Pan Am Clippers, but to receive the long-awaited ancestral cargo plane *(The Ghost Dance)*. A large airplane was even built out of sticks and leaves in an effort to woo its mate to the ground.

Few countries today are as isolated, and as technologically backward, as New Guinea. If there are few cargo cults, it may be because technology is now taken for granted. Like a consumer in a supermarket, the nontechnological culture, surrounded by an increasingly technological world, is faced with a *fait accompli*. The goods are, almost magically, on the shelves, and for the jaded shopper their source is immaterial. For people in technologically underdeveloped countries the world has become, in V. S. Naipaul's words, "a new universal bazaar . . . where goods [are] not associated with a particular kind of learning, effort or civilization, but [are] just goods, part of the world's natural bounty." Ortega's *naturmensch* has suddenly proliferated on a world scale. But when the shopping cart is full of strange and exotic products, the difficulty of what is to be done with them becomes paramount.

Virtually all African capitals boast at least one skyscraper—the ultimate empty symbol of modernity, particularly when the elevators don't work. Discarded machinery, unused-because-never-finished housing projects, and abandoned factories have all become characteristic features of the perilous development landscape. My point is not to ridicule the mishaps that can occur when new technology is introduced; but there is serious confusion between the symbolic and real value of technology—the investment in autoroutes when few own cars, or in expensive sewerage systems when the majority lack running water. This confusion can lead to wasteful and harmful choices. The government of Ghana, under Kwame Nkrumah, indulged in a great deal of symbolic technological development—building a dam or a new port here, twelve miles of superhighway there—but was unable to establish any real economic activity as an alternative to growing cocoa, a product that had been introduced to that country by the British. When international cocoa prices fell, the twelve miles of superhighway were of little help and the near-bankrupt government was overthrown in a military coup.

The misunderstanding of technology often results from an inability to appreciate all the implications of a particular technical choice. Almost all the countries in the world have built television transmission facilities. The People's Republic of China operates several stations, even though there are only 100,000 sets in the entire country; India, a country with many other problems, is nevertheless introducing color television. It is not surprising then that Saudi Arabia, with sufficient funds for both transmission facilities and individual television sets, should have bought a broadcasting system. A difficulty has arisen, however, in the area of programming: orthodox Islamic belief prohibits Saudi women from appearing on TV. Since this restriction does not apply to foreigners, many programs must be imported, primarily from Egypt. The predominance of Egyptian programming, as well as of American all-male wrestling (apparently a favorite), has given rise to concern about cultural dependency. Although the public demands entertainment, it resents the appearance of non-Saudi Arabs and infidels on the screen. Will a new type of programming develop according to the beliefs of a conservative, medieval religion? Or, as in so many other parts of the world, will tradition bend to the demands of modern technology?

Saudi traditions also conflict with Western urbanization. The Saudis have chosen to build their housing on the model of Bel Air and the Côte d'Azur—large villas on individual, and widely separated, lots. Since women in Saudi Arabia are not permitted to drive automobiles, or even to take taxis, families without chauffeurs are restricted to an isolated existence, unfamiliar to those accustomed to the traditional, congested Arab towns.

If the Saudis want orthodox Islamic television, or town planning, they will have to create it themselves—not an easy task, especially for a nation characterized by acquisition rather than invention. Nor is it easy to differentiate between what is threatening and what is simply new. The educated Saudi computer engineer wants to move out of the family compound; he wants to read *The New York Times* and watch international programs on television. Is this cultural dependency, or progress?

Information has always been a source of power. Dutch pilots in the seventeenth century were jealously possessive about their ruttiers, or navigation instructions, which gave them the sole key to the sea routes to the East Indies. The first marine charts were likewise considered important military secrets which the early sea captains, now independent of the pilots' personal knowledge, were expected to guard with their lives. But even more crucial was dynamic information—news—about political and economic events that might be taking place a great distance away. The daily newspaper, which in its modern popular form dates from the second half of the eighteenth century, owes its existence to the development of a number of technologies— cheap, wood-pulp paper and improved printing techniques.* As newspapers expanded, so did the demand for information, which soon led to the establishment of the news service.

The pioneer of the news service was the Frenchman Charles Havas who, in 1835, established one of the first information businesses. Two of his employees, Paul Julius Reuter and Bernard Wolff, both Germans, later established their own agencies in England and Germany and, until the Second World War, the

---

*The first American daily was the *Pennsylvania Evening Post* (1783), while the first dailies appeared in Britain in 1702 *(Daily Courant)* and in France in 1777 *(Journal de Paris)*.

Havas, Reuters, and Wolff services dominated not only Europe but the world. Reuters alone survives today; Havas, which collaborated with the Vichy regime during the war, was replaced by Agence France-Presse, while Wolff was disbanded after the fall of the Third Reich.

The news agency, unlike the newspaper, is a distinctly modern invention. The immediate predecessor of the agency was the courier service, which used horses and ships. Reuter himself started by transmitting market quotations from the Brussels stock exchange to Aachen by carrier pigeon (seven hours faster than by train). But it is unlikely that news agencies would have come into existence if it had not been for one particular invention—the telegraph.

The first successful commercial use of the telegraph was by the Great Western Railway in England in 1838, and a few years later Samuel Morse finished perfecting the dot-and-dash code system that bears his name. The spread of telegraph wires was phenomenal. In less than ten years there were 4,000 miles of telegraph wires in Britain; in a brief four-year period the telegraph linked the whole American Atlantic seaboard. Even more important to the story of the news agencies was the laying of submarine cables that linked one country to another. The first such cable, under the English Channel, was laid in 1851; a transatlantic cable was completed fifteen years later.

Britain led the world in building telegraph networks, a political and economic necessity given the far-flung empire. In 1872, the mayor of Adelaide, Australia, and the mayor of London were able to exchange messages, and the British telegraph, like the British Empire, covered the world. Meanwhile, Reuter, seeing a business opportunity, had emigrated to London in 1858, and had established a telegraph news service for newspapers, bankers, and brokers. With his European contacts and his imagination and flair, his agency soon became a success. Since he insisted that newspapers using his dispatches should carry the "Reuters" by-line, the agency became well known and syn-

onymous with British imperialism—as British as John Bull or
Queen Victoria herself. Reuters' position was strengthened by
the British government, which needed an accurate (and firmly
British) information system, and thus allowed preferential rates
for the agency on its telegraphs.

In just ten years, Reuters achieved pre-eminence in the
world, and in 1869 the British agency convinced its two smaller
European rivals—Havas and Wolff—that it would be in the
interests of all three to limit competition and to form a cartel,
dividing the world according to the political influences of their
respective nations. Thus the British Empire, North America,
and the Far East were reserved for Reuters, which dominated
the triumvirate. The Austro-Hungarian Empire, Scandinavia,
Russia, and the German states were Wolff's preserve; and the
French and Portuguese empires, Italy, Spain, and ultimately
Latin America were to be covered by Havas. These so-called
Agency Treaties held for sixty-four years.

Meanwhile, two large American agencies had been trying to
break into the territories of the Europeans, especially in those
two American "backyards," the Far East and Latin America.
The Associated Press had been established in 1848 as a cooperative of a number of newspaper owners; the United Press Association (later renamed United Press International) was more
recent, and was privately owned. Unlike the European agencies, the American agencies were not associated with their government. And, in the case of the larger Associated Press, the
agency was not intended as a profit-making venture. This last
point is important, for much of the state influence on Reuters,
for example, was due to government business, subsidy, and
preferential rates, which the private company was under considerable economic pressure to accept. The American companies, then, were a free-enterprise David that had to compete
against a state-backed Goliath.

In 1893, Reuters sold AP the exclusive rights for North
American coverage, in return for which the American agency

agreed to respect the property rights of the cartel in the rest of the world. This arrangement became strained when agreement could not be reached on who should have exclusivity in Japan, which AP felt to be within the American sphere of influence, and into which UPA, not bound by any agreement, was moving.

The monopoly of the Victorian news agency was finally broken in 1934. AP, with the support of UPA and the Canadian Press, forced Reuters to sign an agreement that permitted free access among all agencies and terminated the practice of regional exclusivity. This capitulation was due in part to the fact that stock control of Reuters, which for eighty-four years had been a family business, had just been obtained by a cooperative of British newspaper owners who were sympathetic to the idea of free information flow.

The situation today is only slightly changed from that in 1934. There are a few dozen news agencies that operate internationally. Some are national, such as Kyodo of Japan or Deutsche-Presse Agentur, the successor to Wolff, and a small number of news services are operated by some of the largest newspapers, such as *The New York Times* or *The Washington Post*. But the gathering and dissemination of international news has become completely dominated by the two American agencies (Associated Press and United Press International), the one English (Reuters), and the French (Agence France-Presse), known collectively as the Big Four.

Since few publishers can afford to support foreign correspondents, contemporary newspapers in almost all countries have come to rely on the Big Four for their international news. The agencies maintain reporters in the field, gather and edit news, and distribute it to their subscribers. This makes them very powerful indeed. The source of their power, in addition to their historic head start, is their access to large newspaper-reading markets and, equally, their access to worldwide communications systems, which now include teleprinters, direct satellite links, information banks, and computer-assisted video-editing.

The scale of the operations of the Big Four is global. All of the Big Four maintain regional offices, which collect news for exclusive regional redistribution and forward select news to the head office for international transmission. The international clientele of the large agencies is prodigious: AFP reaches 147 countries in four languages; Reuters sells its service to newspapers in 153 countries in six languages. It has been estimated that the number of readers and listeners of AP's 8,500 subscribers in America, Latin America, Africa, and Asia approaches a billion persons. The result is that most, if not all, of the foreign reporting in virtually *any* newspaper of the world is likely to carry the by-line of one of the Big Four. Argentines read about Brazilians through the eyes of a UPI (though not necessarily an American) reporter; Kenyans learn about Nigerians through Reuters; while Agence France-Press interprets Ghanaians to the Senegalese. This has begun to irritate many of the politicians in the less-developed countries.

What stands out about the Big Four—other than that they are so big, and only four—is that they are all located in the industrialized countries of the West, and that they are privately owned companies.* Natural enough, one might say, as the majority of newspaper readers and newspapers are to be found in the countries where the agencies are located; and if they are private companies, they have, after all, themselves invested in developing these vast information networks. But it is also true that the Big Four are a symbol of both the technological predominance of the West and the recent colonial past (particularly in the case of the European agencies). Their activities appear, at least from the point of view of less-developed countries, as economic and cultural domination. The resentment of the power of the Big Four, and of the influence of Western media in general, has given rise to an interesting debate about cultural oppression

*AP, the largest of the Big Four, is a nonprofit cooperative of 1,350 American newspaper publishers; UPI and Reuters are privately owned companies; AFP, though privately owned, is heavily subsidized (and most say influenced) by the French government.

and one-way information flows. But again the real issue is not so much the technology itself as who is going to control it.

The prime mover behind what is portentously referred to as a "New World Information Order" has been UNESCO—the United Nations Educational, Scientific, and Cultural Organization.* The New World Information Order is a contentious idea whose main goal seems to be to shift control over the flow of news away from the private companies and toward national governments, especially those of the less-developed countries. It is no coincidence that UNESCO, like many of the United Nations agencies, is dominated by these same less-developed countries, who have, on this issue, the support of the Communist bloc. Nor is it a coincidence that most of the countries of both groups do not tolerate a free press within their national borders. It appears that the main characteristic of the proposed New World Information Order would be an expansion of control over information from the national to the international level.

The limits to press freedom in the Communist bloc are well known. It was Lenin, after all, who asked, "Why should freedom of speech and freedom of the press be allowed? Why should a government which is doing what it believes to be right allow itself to be criticized?" Less well known are the severe limits placed on the press in the non-Communist, less-developed countries. For instance, a 1975 study by Dennis L. Wilcox found that 70 percent of the thirty-four nations of black Africa had only state-owned newspapers, and 90 percent prohibited newspapers published by opposition parties, while more than half explicitly endorsed an authoritarian press philosophy. Since

---

*The New World Information Order is a conscious partner of the "New International Economic Order" that was proposed by the so-called Group of 77, representing nonaligned, less-developed countries. The term has unfortunate connotations; the first New Order was proposed by Hitler for restructuring the economy of postwar Europe.

that time the situation has worsened, and today only Kenya, Senegal, and Nigeria have anything even approaching a free press.

India experienced twenty months of press censorship in 1975 during the Emergency. This period was marked by many New Order policies: the four private Indian news agencies were nationalized; journalists had to follow a government-legislated code of ethics, and all news was subjected to the scrutiny of the censor, to ensure that "no news is published in a manner that contributes to demoralization." The Middle East press is characterized by "semiofficial" newspapers, a more covert form of control. In the Philippines, a country that actively demands the New World Information Order, the press is an advocate of "developmental journalism" and a strong supporter of President Ferdinand Marcos's New Society politics. This is not surprising since Manila's four daily newspapers are controlled by the President's brother-in-law, his ex-military aide, his wife's official biographer, and a fraternity brother who also owns four of the country's five television networks. In Argentina, despite Juan Perón's official policy of state control over all media, an independent news agency—Noticias Argentinas—was established in 1972. Its operation has not been without difficulty: its first chairman was assassinated, and state interference is a continued hindrance. Although the official UNESCO delegates who advocate a New World Order depend on *Le Monde* or the *Times* for information, state control over the media in their countries is the natural order of things.

These bureaucrats, with the support of some European and American academics, assert that the standards of a "libertarian press" are inappropriate to the needs of the new, emerging nations, whose priorities are such that open discussion of political issues must wait for a future, more settled time. It is not clear how this argument applies to Latin America, which has had a free, though at times repressed, press for a long time, or to India, which likewise has had a long tradition of free discussion.

What about the newly independent countries of black Africa, where, as some national leaders would have it, the public is not ready for the responsibility of a free press? During the preindependence period, an indigenous press existed in virtually all of the African colonies. Although these newspapers and magazines were usually severely restricted by the white authorities, they were at least free enough to form the focus for the growing agitation for national emancipation. The first presidents of Kenya, Tanzania, and Zaire—Jomo Kenyatta, Julius Nyerere, and Joseph Mobutu—were *all* editors and journalists in the preindependence black press, as were the first leaders of Nigeria, Ghana, Senegal, and the Ivory Coast. The power of a free press could not have been lost on them. Even after independence, the press continued to be a power base for people such as Patrice Lumumba, the first premier of secessionist Congo-Kinshasa, himself an ex-editor.

The repressive press laws of the outgoing colonialists were preserved intact in most of the new African republics, and even the small amount of press freedom that the indigenous press enjoyed was curtailed. As the Ugandan writer Ali Mazrui wryly noted, "It is felt by many African leaders that the journalistic freedom which had helped to create African nationalism could not be trusted to create African nationhood."* It was as if the free press that had been used against the colonialists could no longer be continued by the new élites lest it be turned against them.

Some of the resentment that has given rise to the attack on the Big Four by the Paris-based UNESCO is directed against the Anglo-Saxon domination of the news agencies, of newsmagazines, and of television production. The director general of UNESCO who initiated the information debate was a Frenchman—René Maheu—and his successor and the main architect of the New Order is Amadou-Mahtar M'Bow, a Senega-

*Quoted by Dennis L. Wilcox.

lese educated at the Université de Paris, which is also the alma mater of Mustapha Masmoudi, Tunisia's secretary of state for information and the coordinator of the nonaligned nations' New Order activities. Likewise, many of the criticisms of Latin American "communications experts" are barely disguised anti-Americanisms. The English-language domination of the world media also rankles governments in Havana, Warsaw, and Prague, which all tend to be favorably inclined to the ideas of the New Order.

What chiefly seems to concern the advocates of the New Order about the international media is the fact that they are, for the most part, privately owned and not under direct state control. Perhaps this explains why the debate over who is to control the media has so little discussed a technology that is much more representative of twentieth-century mass communications—the radio.

One has only to think of the effective use of the radio made by such disparate politicians as Hitler and Roosevelt, or the influence of Churchill's broadcast speeches on wartime Britain, to recall that between 1935 and 1960 it was radio, and not newspapers, that dominated the mass media. While radio has ceded its primacy in the West to television, it remains as important as ever in the less-developed countries. Moreover, the ownership of radios has risen dramatically, thanks to the availability of cheap, portable, transistorized receivers. In a world that is still largely illiterate it is the radio, not the newspaper, that is the most potent communications device.

Why then is there not more objection to the one-sided use of the airwaves by the so-called superpowers? The British Broadcasting Corporation, the Voice of America, and Radio Moscow all have powerful transmitters which beam their broadcasts far beyond their national borders. While transmissions are occasionally jammed, as was the case in Poland during the recent period of martial law, they are generally tolerated. It appears that because these radio services are under direct state control their "propaganda" is acceptable, while that of the private media is not.

There is something very crude about the calls for an international supervision of the media, which is to be achieved by the state licensing of journalists, international codes of conduct, and state responsibility for national media. Perhaps because print media and news agencies, despite the satellites and computers, are nineteenth-century inventions, their link with the colonial past invites retribution, at least in the eyes of the less-developed countries. Control over the print media is easily achieved. Indeed, much of this control is already practiced in the Third World, where many countries regularly censor newsmagazines such as *Time* and *Newsweek* by removing the pages containing offensive material. Furthermore, in most of these countries, the Big Four sell their news not to individual papers but to national news agencies, usually state controlled, which are able to censor or delete reports before they are passed on to local papers. All this tends to call into question the urgency of the need for additional restrictions.

Control over the international media exists already and sometimes produces unexpected results. A comparison of the 1973 coup that overthrew Salvador Allende in Chile with a similar military takeover in Argentina three years later is instructive. The Chilean military introduced censorship, restricted news coverage, and for two weeks refused entry to all foreign media, so that journalists had to rely on rumor and hearsay as well as on reports from refugees. As news of murders and assassinations trickled out of the country, it was quickly picked up by the waiting, and by now suspicious, foreign reporters. The result was that the Chilean junta was portrayed, not unfairly, as repressive and cruel, and junta pronouncements were treated with skepticism. The Chilean generals acquired an international reputation which would tarnish them for many years to come.

On the other hand, when the Argentine military decided to

overthrow Isabel Perón in 1976, they learned from the Chilean experience and exercised control of the international media in a much more subtle way. According to Mort Rosenblum, an American reporter, journalists were informed of the planned coup even before it occurred. Local papers were strictly controlled, but foreign newsmen were not censored, although their access to news stories was restricted. The result was that the Argentine coup, which was just as vicious, bloody, and repressive as the Chilean, was presented as considerably less so in the international press.

The military junta that took control of the Polish government in 1981 exercised a similar form of indirect censorship. While international reporters were allowed to enter the country, their movement within it was mainly restricted to the largest city, Warsaw. Thus, while Polish émigrés were warning of imminent starvation, television broadcasts from the capital showed prosperous-looking Warsaw crowds. News of disturbances in provincial towns would have received considerably more attention had not the press been limited in its access to them.

The People's Republic of China has not, until now, played a major role in the demand for a New Order. This may be because the "Middle Kingdom," while politically supporting the so-called Third World, has never felt itself to be a part of it. It may also be because China does not feel threatened by the Western media; indeed, it has shown a masterful ability to manipulate foreign journalists to its own ends, especially during the period of the Cultural Revolution. It was so difficult to visit the country at that time that any reporter who was finally granted a visa tended to bend over backward not to insult his hosts—and forfeit a second invitation. The result was that a cruel, anarchic, and destructive episode in China's history was often described as a successful social experiment. This was evidence of how successful Chinese control of the international media really was. Visitors were shown only selected sites, met only briefed officials and interpreters, heard only prepared speeches. The same model factories, even the same workers, formed the basis for what could be described as an elaborate theater piece. Understanding the media's need for "human interest," the Chinese authorities provided taciturn peasants and contented workers. The foreign journalists, usually lacking the language and having to rely completely on their guides, dutifully wrote as they were told. If they did not, they were not invited back.* It was not until after the death of Mao Zedong that the truth about the Cultural Revolution began to be told, and then only because it suited the new regime.

Very few countries have achieved the sophisticated control of foreign media that is evident in China and more cruelly in Argentina. Occasionally, despots such as Idi Amin of Uganda or the late Shah of Iran are able to project an image of bonhomie or withdrawn majesty which diverts attention from their policies, but most governments prefer a more direct control. Mort Rosenblum, in a *Foreign Affairs* article, quotes an African UNESCO delegate as saying, "We don't want Western journalists in our countries. They should take their news from us."

One aspect of information that the New World Information Order barely addresses is the technology involved in news gathering. The experts hired by UNESCO (who are almost never professional journalists) constantly reiterate the need for less-developed countries to have their own information systems. But the technology of news collection and dissemination is expensive. It has been estimated that the cost of maintaining one newsman abroad, including the cost of communication, is about $100,000 a year. UPI's computer storage and retrieval system in New York cost $12 million, and the operating budgets of the Big Four are as much as $100 million a year each. The UNESCO

---

*One of the earliest critics of the Cultural Revolution was Pierre Ryckmans, a Belgian Sinologist, who wrote under the name Simon Leys. This subterfuge allowed him to revisit China, even after publishing his critical books. He was subsequently exposed by European Maoists and denied further entry.

theorists tend to ignore the fact that the cost of maintaining the international news-gathering apparatus is almost completely underwritten by the American and European operations of the Big Four, not by their clients in the less-developed countries. How are poor and technologically backward countries to support these kinds of activities? Although UNESCO ominously refers to information as "the oil of the 1980s," there can be no OPEC of news, and the analogy is inappropriate. The Big Four may superficially resemble the Seven Sisters, but information is hardly a national resource like oil, and an embargo on news would hurt only the less-developed nations. At the same time, it is unlikely, as Jean-François Revel, the editor of the French newsmagazine *L'Express,* pointed out in an editorial, that the capitalist countries will be prepared to finance a policy which, at least in the field of information, aims to eliminate them. The less-developed countries cannot expect to get Western approbation, recognition, and financial support for an information policy that goes against Western interests.

The attempt to found a New Order seems unlikely to become successful. Any restriction on the flow of news out of the less-developed countries through the licensing of journalists or constraints on travel will be a Pyrrhic victory for those countries. They will either find themselves accused of censorship and authoritarianism and held up to international ridicule and scorn or, worse, they will be ignored, and the controls, instead of increasing coverage of the less-developed countries, will have the opposite effect.*

Except for Reuters, whose subscribers are largely international, the Big Four do not depend on subscribers outside their own countries for the majority of their income. The annual turnover of the "news imperialists" is small ($300 million for the

---

*In 1982, Uganda withdrew accreditation from the last Western correspondent. Countries such as Angola and Mozambique impose severe constraints on foreign journalists, who may travel outside the capitals only with a state-appointed interpreter and guide

combined Big Four in 1977); and three-quarters of it comes
from Europe and the United States. The closing of news bureaus in the less-developed countries would not affect the large
agencies at all financially, and would only reduce the already
narrow coverage of these countries.

And the coverage is narrow. Just as Indian papers contain
very little international news, and Nigerian papers focus primarily on local politics, so also the American and European
papers, and the agencies that serve them, tend to give most
space to information that is of primary interest to their readers.
It is also true that news of the less-developed countries tends to
be about political upheavals and famines, and gives a distorted
image of these countries.

There is no simple solution to this problem of distortion. One
suggestion has been the formation of a so-called Third World
news pool, an alternative to the Western-dominated agencies.
Such a pool was established in 1976 by the fifty-eight nonaligned nations with the moral and financial support of
UNESCO. The technology for the pool was provided by Tanjug,
the national Yugoslav news agency, which serves as a clearing-
house for the forty countries that contribute to the pool. In
practice, the pool is dominated by a small group of fish—the
national news agencies of Yugoslavia, Cuba, Iraq, and India.
The pool transmits dispatches from its members unaltered and
unedited—the constitution of the pool requires "mutual respect" for news selection—so that they often consist of lengthy
political speeches or dull descriptions of government policy.
Since many are little more than government press releases,
they can be considerably more biased than the reporting of the
Big Four and are of limited news value. The pool seems to be
viewed by its members more as a public relations office than as
a news agency. Its aim, in the words of British author and
journalist Rosemary Righter, seems to be to increase the flow of
views, rather than of news.

What about the idea of making the news agencies responsible

to their national governments, of nationalizing them in practice, if not in fact? It is very likely that national control would affect the credibility of the large agencies. Rather than hobbling them, as UNESCO hopes, it would probably cripple them altogether. The fact that AFP is so heavily supported by the French government already makes its coverage of certain types of political news suspect in the eyes of many. The Soviet news agency Tass (Telegrafnoye Agentstvo Sovietskovo Soyuza), which was founded by the Tsar before the First World War and later renamed by the Bolsheviks, has always been under complete state control. Tass is only slightly smaller than any of the Big Four: while UPI serves 92 countries, Tass serves 80; AP has 62 foreign bureaus, Tass has 40; AFP has 12,000 subscribers, Tass has 13,000. But these figures are deceptive, for while Tass is large and technologically sophisticated, it has not been the object of UNESCO attacks. This is partly because it is a state-controlled organization which makes no pretense at objectivity; Tass is not criticized—it is usually ignored. Its huge clientele is largely in the Soviet Union and in the vassal states of the Eastern bloc, and in spite of the fact that it distributes news to foreign media free-of-charge, it has only 325 foreign subscribers. UPI, which charges for its services, has 2,282 clients outside the United States. Tass is a clear example of how state-controlled media quickly lose credibility, influence, and, above all, readers. A New Order based on sanitized government bulletins and predigested handouts would inevitably produce an alternative underground press—a kind of global samizdat—which would attempt to circumvent official channels. Perhaps Reuters would be forced to revert to carrier pigeons once again.

It is ironic that the debate over a New Information Order should center on the lack of government control over the news agencies. When Associated Press started its struggle to break away from the domination of Reuters and the other "national" agencies, one of its objections to the cartel was that its members were in practice extensions of their respective governments. During the First World War, for instance, Havas refused to carry German dispatches, while both Havas and Reuters tended to play down the American contribution to the war effort. The cartel of Reuters-Havas-Wolff was supported by Britain, France, and Germany because it furthered their political and economic aims. The New Order would have the effect of returning to this earlier period.

The ultimate contradiction of the New Order is that it does not recognize the main reason for the existence of the Big Four, which is not to exploit the less-developed colonies, but to service the enormous newspaper-reading public in the industrialized countries of America and Western Europe. There are more than 180 million newspapers read daily in Europe and North America, compared to 23 million in Latin America, 6 million in Africa, and only 3 million in the Arab countries (*UNESCO Statistical Yearbook*, 1976). These numbers reflect not cultural domination but cultural habits and literacy. Book publishing further supports this thesis: each year 264,000 new titles appear in Europe, 29,000 in Latin America, 11,000 in Africa, and 5,000 in the Arab countries. The preponderance of publishing in the West is also a reflection of the large population of this part of the world. Professor Julian L. Simon has demonstrated the causal connection between large populations and various types of cultural, technical, and economic achievements. His point is that large populations not only permit economies of scale, but also facilitate creative innovation and technical invention. Thus the imbalance between UPI and the Arab Revolution News Agency of Libya or the national agency of Tanzania is above all the imbalance between a very large country and two very small ones; between an agency that serves hundreds of millions and, in the case of Libya, one that serves, at most, three million. Even when readership rises in the less-developed countries, as it must do with the growth of literacy and political awareness, one would expect only the largest countries to field powerful news agencies. It is very possible that Samachar (India) and Hsin Hua (People's Republic of China) will eventually be referred to as Number Six and Number Seven.

The supporters of the New Order describe access to information technology as the right of all nations, big or small, and have chosen to ignore the relationship between the size of nations and technological development. Yet the relationship is obvious. India is one of the poorest, and one of the most populous, nations; but because it is populous it is also powerful: it has been able to launch a communications satellite, support a large number of active daily newspapers, and maintain a number of internationally active news agencies. One looks in vain for Reuters or AP by-lines in Indian papers—the majority of foreign stories come from Indian agencies. It is India's size that has made this possible; Malawi or Afghanistan, equally poor but so much smaller, could never hope to emulate India's example. Industrial productivity (and news-gathering is at least partly industry) increases with size; that is, large industries can be expected to be more productive than small ones. Simon describes the phenomenon as "learning by doing": the more units produced, the more people develop better and more efficient methods of production. Although the New Order calls for a "new equilibrium and greater reciprocity in the flow of information," it ignores this vital characteristic of technical development.

The latest communication technology is not only so expensive and so complex as to be out of reach of most of the less-developed countries, but it may also, paradoxically, permit the Big Four to respond to at least some of the grievances voiced by UNESCO. The telegraph and teleprinter were both technologies that tended to centralize the operation of the agencies; news was forwarded to London, New York, or Paris by a foreign correspondent, but editing and dissemination was done in the head office. Both time and money precluded all but the most cursory verification of the final copy with the original reporter.

With satellite connections and video-editing, it is possible for the reporter to edit a piece instantaneously from a distant computer terminal. The new technology thus allows significant decentralization, and hence regionalization, of the agencies' operations.* This will tend to introduce a much higher degree of autonomy to the regional bureaus and reduce the head-office bias of which the agencies are often accused.

But new technology can be a two-edged sword. During the 1960s, UNESCO promoted the use of television as an educational tool for the less-developed countries. Twenty years later, there are more television sets in Hong Kong than in all of black Africa. Furthermore, those countries that invested heavily in television's infrastructure have found that the public demands not educational programs but entertainment. Instead of promoting national culture, television becomes, as in Saudi Arabia, one more open door to foreign influence. The cost of producing television programs is so high that it is cheaper simply to buy from abroad. This self-inflicted cultural dependency, typified by Hong Kong kung-fu adventures or Indian melodrama, is deplored by UNESCO, all the more because it seems to be enjoyed by the public.

Television broadcasting is under direct state control in most less-developed countries (Latin America is an exception), so that programs from abroad can be rejected or edited before being aired. But with the advent of direct satellite transmission, this situation is changing. It is already possible for individuals to purchase relatively cheap dish antennas and receive programs directly from the orbiting satellites, bypassing any state control. As ownership of television sets increases in the less-developed countries, and as the technology of personal satellite antennas becomes cheaper, it will be as easy to receive international television programs as it is now to receive shortwave radio

---

*Decentralization is not automatic, however. AFP is highly centralized even though it has been computerized since 1976.

transmissions. Since so few countries have the resources to launch satellites or to rent satellite time—or to jam transmissions—direct transmission will tend to short-circuit any attempt to control the flow of information.

Another television technology that has made state control of media obsolete is the video-recording machine, which enables the owner of a television set to bypass the propaganda that passes for national programming in many countries, and purchase, legally or illegally, any television material that is available. The fact that video tapes can be so easily copied makes state control of this technology extremely difficult. It is possible that in wealthier underdeveloped countries such as Saudi Arabia and Nigeria more people are watching video films than broadcast television.

While critics of television insist on describing it as a one-way information flow—from the West to the rest of the world—this is not always the case. Various resistance groups, such as tribesmen in Afghanistan or *Solidarność* members in Poland, have become quite adept at reversing this tide. The Viet Cong, during the recent war with the United States, permitted various reporters and public personalities to visit North Vietnam precisely because they were aware of the effect that television coverage of these visits would have on American audiences. The Palestine Liberation Organization has been equally adept at using television to make its point to an international audience. The Iranian students who occupied the United States embassy in Teheran in 1980 were very conscious of media coverage and staged a number of events specifically for the visiting journalists; the most memorable tableau was probably the picture of two Iranians using the American flag as a garbage bag. The slogans daubed on the embassy wall were as often in English as in Iranian, and American television cameramen were never prevented from entering Iran (and felt safe doing so) because the Islamic fundamentalists correctly perceived the press as a crucial ingredient for a successful blackmailing of the United States. It was undoubtedly the Ayatollah Khomeini who inspired this curious combination of Islam and McLuhanism; he had, after all, smuggled tape recordings of his speeches to initiate the revolution in Iran while he was exiled in Paris.

The relationship between the governments of the less-developed countries and the Western-dominated media is ambivalent. It is reflected in the statement of one of the members of Willy Brandt's North-South Commission, who was quoted by Anthony Sampson as saying: "If there's one thing worse than being exploited by a multinational, it's *not* being exploited." The freedom of the media is appreciated when they report—and hence tacitly support—the views of the underdog, the oppressed, the victim; the same coverage is criticized when it embarrasses or accuses. Lack of coverage of so-called development issues is deplored, with some reason; but the baleful eye of the foreign correspondent sees different things from the blind eye of the local lackey. The free-wheeling global news agencies are an unpleasant reminder of colonial dependence, but dependence on their news-gathering capability is real nevertheless.

To the governments of the less-developed countries the news media appear to be Excalibur—a prize held in the stony grip of the big agencies; it would suffice to pull the sword from the stone to become information king. On one level the New Order debate is really that simple: Who is going to write the news, "us" or "them"? Just as automation is often a weapon in the power struggle between management and labor in the factory, so also the UNESCO-inspired attempt to give greater control over the news media to the less-developed countries is part of a global ideological struggle. But while the news agencies are symbols of technical achievement, unlike Excalibur, they do not automatically bestow power on their owner. Just as Reuters reflected the real power of the British Empire in its heyday, so too do the Big Four reflect the real domination of world culture by the United States and northern Europe. It is a domination the New World Information Order is unlikely to affect.

The benefits of technology come as the result of indulging in technical activity; but this technical activity has its own demands. The problem, to paraphrase the British political scientist Michael Oakeshott, is that technology stems from a particular tradition of technical behavior, reflects social manners and arrangements, and is not simply a piece of machinery to be transported around the world indiscriminately. It is relatively easy to import a foreign machine. But it is much more difficult to undertake the technical activity that makes the machine useful, especially if the required social manners and arrangements are not indigenous.

It is impossible to discuss the impact of the international media, or of any technology, on the less-developed countries without encountering the issue of indigenous culture and, more specifically, its preservation. Cultural dependency and cultural aggression are thorny issues that give rise to much UNESCO rhetoric; but underlying them is the concern that traditional ways of life in the less-developed countries are in a very real way threatened by technical change. It is not much help to point out that it is above all the small countries that suffer most from this threat; or to give examples, such as Japan, which have successfully undergone rapid development without necessarily losing their cultural identity. These arguments do little to soften the impact of jeans, video games, and mopeds on the consuming countries of Africa and Asia.

The search for cultural authenticity preoccupies the less-developed countries and forms the cornerstone of almost all United Nations pronouncements on North-South relations. It is likewise present in the New Order programs. Cultures, according to a UNESCO book on the New World Information Order, are like individual persons and have a "right to privacy." According to this analogy, just as journalists should not be permitted to intrude on the private lives of individuals or "to expose harmless personal eccentricities to public ridicule," the international media should observe limits when dealing with issues that might affect the "self-respect of a national culture." The idea of national culture as personality is intriguing in that it implies that society is both fragile and inviolable. Change is regarded as an intrusion, outside influence as a violation. It also implies that if societies were left alone they could lead long and happy lives.

The concept of hermit-states asserting their cultural independence and right to privacy raises an interesting question as far as technology is concerned. While cultural purity is being restored, technology will also be affected. Since foreign technology is a part of foreign domination, it too will have to be relinquished; a self-sufficient hermit cannot be expected to continue shopping at the local grocery store. If a country has adopted television but finds itself unable to produce indigenous programs, and if it wishes to spare its citizens the influence of imported shows, what option is there except to dismantle the television system? If modern medicine leads to dependency on the outside world, better to return to traditional folk cures. If literacy has lead to the dominance of foreign media, perhaps it is better not to read. After all, if technology can be invented, surely it can be uninvented.

Or can it?

CHAPTER 5

GHOST DANCING

Nothing can be uninvented.
—Daniel J. Boorstin, *The Republic of Technology*

The historian Daniel J. Boorstin has suggested that technology is irreversible; that is, while cultural and political concepts can seemingly be turned 360 degrees—from democracy to dictatorship and back to democracy—technology can be added to but not subtracted from. We cannot go back and forth between the kerosene lamp and the electric bulb, he argues. Furthermore, "There is no technological counterpart for the political restoration or the counter-revolution." On the face of it this is an eminently sensible observation; the failed attempts of the Luddites to halt mechanization seem to be proof that you cannot turn back the clock. But it is not that simple. The Luddites were largely unsuccessful in their aims, but Luddism occurred at the end of a very successful proscription of a number of mechanical devices. The croppers, for instance, had the gig mill declared illegal for two and a half *centuries;* agricultural workers retarded the introduction of the threshing machine—which had been waiting on the sidelines forty-five years—and kept it from being used for another twenty-five. Much of the violence of that period was due to the fact that postponed inventions were finally being put to use. In many of those cases, the technological clock had been turned back, or at least stopped.

But what about a technological restoration? Has there never been a Napoleon who wished to turn back the march of modernism? Has there never been a culture that wanted to discard what was then considered progressive in order to return to earlier techniques? Is it true that whatever can be invented will be invented and, once invented, must be used? Is it impossible to uninvent the past?

These questions are particularly important if we are considering how technology can be controlled, or what the effects would be if a turnaround were attempted. Some critics of contemporary technology, such as Mohandas Gandhi and, more recently, Ivan Illich, have suggested that not only *can* the clock be turned back, it *should* be turned back. Most opponents of nuclear technology do not want it improved or changed—they want it stopped—and implicit in their argument is the acceptance of a return to earlier energy technologies, if necessary. Another popular view is that modern society will undergo a vast transformation in which contemporary technology will be uninvented (or abandoned) and replaced by as yet unspecified but superior substitutes. But whether the New Age is solar or entropic or ecotopic, it will require a considerable technological counter-revolution.

Such counter-revolutions have been attempted, Boorstin's claim notwithstanding. This chapter examines a number of incidents in which entire societies rejected contemporary technology in order to return to more traditional techniques, or in order to replace it with some substitute. Of course, none of these examples is limited to a rejection of the machine alone; the technological counter-revolution must inevitably be part of a much larger rejection—of culture, religion, or simply foreign influence. Then, as now, feelings about technology have really been feelings about values.

The conflict between the person and the machine is frequently portrayed as the struggle of an individual, or at most of a group of individuals, against the onslaught of an industrializing society. Thus the machine-breaker, whether bludgeoning computers in Montreal or burning threshing machines in Devon, is always the underdog. He is doomed to failure by force of numbers alone.

But there also exists what could be called state Luddism— technology control imposed by *society* against the individual— and such control is not uncommon. The first documented example of machine-breaking in the weaving industry, for instance, concerned an early version of the mechanical ribbon loom, which was invented in Danzig in 1661. But it was the Polish authorities, not the weavers, who, fearing the effect that this device would have on employment, destroyed the machine and drowned its hapless inventor.

German National Socialist students, encouraged by Dr. Goebbels, ceremoniously burned "decadent" books outside the University of Berlin in 1933; similar bonfires occurred during the Chinese Cultural Revolution in the 1960s. The Philippine government is currently waging a war against video games. At various times governments have proscribed, and destroyed, slot machines, whiskey stills, marijuana plantations, and poppy fields. Even the destruction of shantytowns and slums, which is carried out with depressing regularity by the authorities in most less-developed countries, could be described as an attempt to control low-cost-construction technology by means of state Luddism. However, there are few modern examples as dramatic as Democratic Kampuchea—an example of state technology control directed not against a group or against an economic class, but against an entire nation.

Democratic Kampuchea was formed in April 1975, when the

Khmer Republic (previously known as Cambodia) was defeated by Communist revolutionaries, the Khmer Rouge. Their short-lived forty-four-month Kampuchean Republic is best remembered for a Guinness Book of Records–like achievement—the overnight deportation of the population of an entire city of two and a half million people. While it was characterized by the world press as a cruel and bloodthirsty regime, Kampuchea was not just a mindless exercise in self-destruction: it also represented a large-scale and extreme rejection of modern technology and of modern institutions. It was an attempt to "turn back the clock." For Democratic Kampuchea, 1975 was to have been, as one observer put it, Year Zero.

Kampuchea was that rare example of history following theory —rather than the other way around—for the leaders of the new state were above all theorists. What was remarkable about the new leadership (whom the Vietnamese called the Gang of Six) was not just that five of them were related to one another by birth or marriage, but that all had been teachers of one sort or another. Many had been educated in France, but if this was a revolution carried out by the book, it was according to Mao Zedong's Little Red Book, which they had had the opportunity to study in the People's Republic. There they had also observed the Cultural Revolution in full swing, and had decided to undertake the same technological and social revision in their own country. But whereas Mao had waited seventeen years after coming to power before launching his cultural reforms, the Kampucheans were in a greater hurry. Barely five hours after the capital city of Phnom Penh fell to the Khmer Rouge, its entire population was ordered to leave. The dismantling of Cambodia had begun.

What impressed the rest of the world was not only the rapidity of the Kampuchean de-urbanization—it was accomplished in a matter of days—but the disregard for human suffering that this extreme action entailed. As events progressed it became apparent that the forcible evacuation of Phnom Penh was part of a master plan to restructure Cambodian society; but whether this was to be a socialist utopia or a barbaric authoritarian state was unclear. There was a good deal of self-righteous indignation on the part of most Americans, tired and embittered by the Vietnamese war. Henry Kissinger, who as secretary of state had secretly planned the bombing of Cambodia six years before, called the evacuation "an atrocity"; his colleague President Richard Nixon referred to the government as "one of the most ruthless, cruel, vicious communist dictatorships in the world." The correspondent William Shawcross, a strong critic of both Kissinger and Nixon, nonetheless agreed with them that Kampuchea "seemed a vast and somber work camp where toil was unending, where respite and rewards were nonexistent, where families were abolished and where murder was used as a tool of social discipline."

Shawcross's description of the country as a work camp was based on rare and unreliable accounts that had begun to trickle out of the country. Between 1975 and 1979, no foreign journalists were allowed in Democratic Kampuchea. During its three-and-a-half-year existence, the country cut itself off from the rest of the world and imposed a Lhasan shroud of mystery over itself. So complete was this isolation that for the first few years not even the real names of the Kampuchean leaders were known. While a small number of (mainly Communist) diplomatic delegations were permitted to stay, these were not allowed outside the empty city of Phnom Penh. Finally, the only persons who were able to relay information about conditions in the country were the refugees, and there were many of those. It is estimated that in the twelve months following Year Zero, 200,000 Vietnamese nationals returned home, while 50,000 Cambodians fled to Vietnam, and 35,000 to Thailand, considerable numbers for a country whose total population numbered less than eight million persons.

The refugee accounts were luridly exploited by both the Americans and later by the Vietnamese, who were preparing to invade Cambodia and re-establish an old fiefdom (in the nineteenth century, Cambodia had been a Vietnamese province). One of the accounts which seems to be at once better informed and more disinterested is that of François Ponchaud, a French Jesuit missionary who had been living in Cambodia for ten years and had been one of the last to leave the country, one month after the establishment of the new regime. Ponchaud, who spoke Khmer, interviewed dozens of Cambodian refugees, both in Thailand and in France, and was able to paint at least a partial picture of life in the new society.

Ponchaud disputes the view that events in Kampuchea were brought on simply by wartime conditions. Some observers, such as George C. Hildebrand, have suggested that the relocation of city dwellers was simply a "monumental reorganizational task" necessitated by the large destruction suffered by Cambodia's agricultural base during the American aerial bombing.* This was also the official position of the Kampuchean government, but, as Ponchaud points out, wartime conditions do not explain either the haste or the totality of the move. Nor do they explain why similar "evacuations" were found to be necessary for virtually all Cambodian towns, and even many villages, when these were not swollen by refugees as the capital had been. The fact was that the Khmer revolutionaries had been forcibly emptying villages and towns in their occupied zones since the beginning of the war. The destruction of the *métropole* was more than a practical necessity—it was part of an ideological strategy.

The depopulation of Cambodian cities and towns was only the beginning of an attempt to "uninvent" technology on a national scale. For the Khmer Rouge, technology was synonymous with foreign (that is, French) domination. For almost a hundred years, until 1954, Cambodia had been a French protectorate, and while this probably saved the country from Viet-

---

*The American bombing was unprecedented in intensity. In four years over half a million tons of explosive was dropped—seven tons per square mile.

namese domination, it tied it firmly to the French colonial empire. What little technology there was—and there was not
much—was French, and most of it was in the hands of Chinese
and Vietnamese entrepreneurs who, like the Asians in East
Africa, tended to dominate commerce. Since the French had
done little to industrialize the countryside—except to establish
rubber plantations—foreign technology tended to be concentrated in the city. In Kampuchea, wiping the slate clean meant
getting rid of the cities—permanently.

State Luddism became the official policy of the ruling party,
which called itself the *Angka.** Machine-breaking was common. Ponchaud describes books being burned in front of librar-
ies, and a refugee recounted to him how he was employed in
transporting televisions, refrigerators, and other consumer
goods to a huge bonfire on the outskirts of Phnom Penh. This
destruction seems not to have been motivated by envy or
greed, nor was it only a symbolic act. The city and its technology
—like Sodom and Gomorrah—had to be destroyed so that history could begin anew. "There are no models whatsoever of
the society which we are creating," said Ieng Sary, a self-
proclaimed admirer of Stalin and one of the chief theoreticians
of the technological and cultural turnaround.

The Kampuchean regime put into practice many of the technological transformations that lecture-circuit revolutionaries in
America and Europe had only dared to speculate about. De-
schooling, small-scale technology, back-to-the-land—all had a
place in the new order. Having liberated the Cambodian people from affluence by returning them to the countryside, they
then undertook to free them from dependence on the tyranny
of modern medicine by promoting only traditional herbal medicines and cures. The colonialists' hospitals were emptied and
destroyed, and the doctors and nurses put into the fields to plant

---

*Angka literally means "the Organization," and in fact the party did combine
the benevolent paternalism and familial despotism that characterize the Mafia.

rice. Rural clinics were established which a refugee nurse described to Ponchaud as follows: "In the hospital where I worked there were about three hundred patients. It was a hospital in name only, because sick people were brought there so that their families wouldn't waste time looking after them instead of working. The only medicines came from the traditional pharmacopoeia. Large numbers of patients died every day."*

Death and suffering became the hallmarks of the Kampuchean experiment. The *Angka*, in an effort to still the music, had broken up the piano, and for good measure had also shot the piano player. It is estimated that during the first year of the *Angka* between 800,000 and 1.4 million Cambodians died; estimates of the final death count go as high as 3 million. Undoubtedly many died of starvation as a result of the damages inflicted by the war, yet there is plenty of evidence that the *Angka* systematically eliminated many thousands during the reorganization. After interviewing many refugees, Ponchaud reached the conclusion that "So many accounts contain similar statements that it can safely be affirmed that the revolutionaries had simply decided to kill off the bulk of the former civilian and military establishment in the hours following the capture of Phnom Penh." Ben Kiernan, an Australian historian who spent some time in Cambodia in 1980, after the fall of the Khmer Rouge, told *Wall Street Journal* correspondent Barry Wain that it would take ten to fifteen years for the country's economy to return to the pre-1970 levels of production, primarily because "the technical cadre of the country has been wiped out."

Having eliminated much of the population that might have offered obstacles to the new society, the Khmer Rouge began restructuring their country—that is, "uninventing" the past. "Rely on nothing but your strength" and "Capitalism is bad"

---

*Indigenous medicine was apparently reserved for the people; the military had separate hospitals staffed by trained personnel and stocked with European medicines.

were the slogans; money was eliminated in favor of barter. Radio Phnom Penh exhorted, "There is no need to import machines built in foreign countries—the only worthwhile ones are those invented by the peasants." Buddhism—not a peasant invention—was discouraged and the bonzes were persecuted. The French *lycées* were abolished because "It is the people alone who confer true diplomas." The postal service was closed.*

Many of these policies were copied directly from the Chinese Cultural Revolution. The emphasis on the peasants, the promotion of traditional medicine and of self-sufficiency were all based on Chinese precedents. As in China, the substitution of "our" technology for "their" technology was a key ingredient in the process, along with the "uninvention" of modern technology, which led to the use of bicycle-powered machines, organic insecticides, herbal cures, and small blast furnaces. And, as in China, very little of it worked.

By 1976, the course in self-reliance was wearing thin and Kampuchea began to re-establish contact with a number of foreign countries: not only with its "sponsor," China, but also with North Korea, Malaysia, Singapore, and Japan. Most of the commercial activity was really in the form of aid rather than trade, since production of Kampuchea's two main exports—rice and rubber—had been drastically affected by the war. With Chinese credits and a Hong Kong intermediary, industrial goods from France, England, and the United States began to be imported, among them antimalarial medicines and DDT, for traditional cures and pesticides had proved ineffective and malaria was reaching epidemic proportions. Chinese technicians arrived to man the few factories that had not been destroyed, and Chinese aid also included rice, machinery, agricultural

*After 1979, when the Khmer Rouge were once again in the jungle and no longer in power, the postal system was restored in the areas under their control. It seemed that it—and foreign journalists—were now necessary to promote foreign support.

equipment, and medical drugs. Foreign trade was not large by international standards, but it did indicate the problems associated with trying to be self-sufficient for a country as poor, underdeveloped, and war-ravaged as Kampuchea. The theories formulated in Parisian classrooms simply did not stand up to reality.

The Kampuchean experiment was not allowed to run its course. In some ways that is a pity, for perhaps had it done so it would have silenced once and for all those who demand that the less-developed countries be allowed to develop "on their own," without recourse to foreign and "alien" technologies. But "uninventing" the past turned out to be a hazardous task. Estranged from its ally China (largely because of its harsh treatment of Chinese Cambodians, 150,000 of whom had recently fled the country) and hardly popular at home, the *Angka* was not to last long. In November 1978, after a series of border disputes, the Vietnamese launched a full-scale invasion of Kampuchea and overran the country in a matter of days. The Khmer Rouge offered little resistance, and most Cambodians stood by, believing the invader could not be worse than the previous rulers. The experiment was over.

The tragedy of Kampuchea demonstrates the perils of uninventing the past. The brave statements of Year Zero, the rejection of foreign science and technology, and their replacement by traditional, indigenous techniques soon proved, at enormous human cost, to be inadequate. The increased reliance on foreign aid during the last year of the regime would probably have led to a reopening of Kampuchea in much the same way that the People's Republic of China, after the upheavals of the Cultural Revolution, returned to a more conventional pattern of economic and technological development.

A number of other societies are currently engaged in destroying parts of their technological past, notably Islamic countries such as Iran, Pakistan, and Indonesia. One of the characteristics of what has been called an Islamic revival is a rejection of what is perceived of as Western civilization. The rejection is hardly absolute, as V. S. Naipaul has observed. Even as the West is criticized, European and American goods are sought. As Naipaul writes in his book *Among the Believers*, "All the rejection of the West is contained within the assumption that there will always exist out there a living, creative civilization, oddly neutral, open to all to appeal to."

The example of Kampuchea seems to indicate that Boorstin is right—nothing can be uninvented. Technology can be rejected, but it remains as a kind of safety net, something to fall back on if the New Way proves a failure. When herbal cures prove ineffectual, pharmaceutical medicine is still there; rural clinics can be replaced by hospitals. If the universities have been closed and the professors shot, trained personnel can always be imported from another country; and, if the malarial mosquitoes survive the homemade pesticides, DDT can be counted on to do the job.

Fundamentalism, whether it is Maoist as in Kampuchea, or Islamic as in Iran, inevitably leads, in Naipaul's words, to parasitism. This parasitism is not intentional, but it is inevitable all the same. Tanzania, for example, has proclaimed a new African socialism *(ujamma)* based on rural communes and peasant technology. But the fact that President Julius Nyerere symbolically chooses to reside (part-time) in a "development village" is not enough. Tanzania, which had been a food exporter in the past, is now forced to borrow money from the World Bank in order to import food. Two-thirds of Tanzania's budget is externally funded through foreign aid, which fact underlines its parasitic relationship to the outside world.

Another example of fundamentalism that stresses self-reliance and a fusion of traditional values with socialism is taking place in Burma. This relatively small country—about the size of Texas and located in Southeast Asia between India and Thailand—has a long history. Unlike most of the less-developed countries, Burma "emerged" almost a thousand years ago. While Saxons and Normans were hacking at each other at Hastings, Burmese kings built an advanced civilization whose greatest architectural achievement was the great city of Pagan—sixteen square miles of pagodas, temples, and monasteries. During the European colonial expansion into Asia, the Burmese fought three wars against the British invaders until finally, in 1886, they were incorporated into the Indian raj.

Burma became independent in 1948, and the main aim of its new government, under U Nu, was to unify the various ethnic groups, a historical problem in this heterogeneous country where almost a third of the population belonged to small tribal minorities. Like many ex-colonies, Burma tried to follow socialist ideals; unlike most, it has tried to combine socialism with another, older ideology—Buddhism.

U Nu was never able to resolve the basic contradictions of a unified Buddhist, socialist state. One of the difficulties was that Burma is made up of many different peoples—some of whom are neither Buddhists nor Burmans. There are tribal minorities —Karens, Mons, and Arkanese—some of whom are animists and others Christians. While Burma had been a part of India, a fairly large number of Hindu and Moslem Bengalis had immigrated and formed a distinct merchant class of small businessmen and shopkeepers. Finally, as in all of Asia, there is a small but powerful Chinese community. U Nu's Buddhist policies tended to alienate the minorities, while his pluralist statements, on the other hand, were opposed by Burmese nationalists, particularly the armed forces, and his nationalist legislation antagonized the Indians and Chinese. Like any politician caught in the middle, U Nu was unable to please anybody. In 1958, his government was replaced by one led by General U Ne Win, who four years later consolidated his power by a military coup.

The new government dealt harshly with ethnic minorities. All foreign businesses were nationalized; indigenous businesses, particularly those run by people of Chinese and Indian descent, were likewise expropriated; and thousands of their owners emigrated. Discrimination against ethnic minorities, even when these people had been settled in the country for some time, was not unique to Burma. There are many other examples, including not only the expulsion of Vietnamese and Chinese by the Kampuchean government, but also state discrimination against Asians (Uganda), Ibos (Nigeria), Indians (Sri Lanka), and Chinese in a number of Southeast Asian countries. As P. T. Bauer, the British economist, has underlined, quite apart from the immorality of such discrimination, it has almost always had the effect of damaging the local economy. In all the examples cited above, including that of Burma, the persecution of ethnic minorities has had an economic background—all of these were groups that showed particular success in their economic activities. Though clothed in national rhetoric, the discrimination was not so different from European anti-Semitism; it was founded on envy and resentment.

Burmese persecution of its ethnic minorities resulted in the emigration of a large number of Indian Moslems: by 1978, there were over 150,000 such refugees in neighboring Bangladesh. Some of the tribal minorities began armed resistance, swelling the already large number of insurgents, who included Communists, Christians, and hill tribesmen. Such are the results of "indigenous development," for, if foreign influences are to be avoided, then, not illogically, this must apply not only to white-skinned imperialists but also to yellow-skinned merchants. This policy was formalized by the Burmese government in 1980: two classes of citizens were created—indigenous Burmese and naturalized citizens. The second category, which included all Indians and Chinese (about 10 percent of the population), was barred from military service and elected positions, and from belonging to political parties or holding executive positions in any economic organization. The accent of Ne Win's "Burmese Way of Socialism" was to be firmly on the first vocable.

Burma became a closed society, not only to foreigners within, but also to the outside world. It is only recently that the twenty-four-hour visa has been replaced by a seven-day visitor's permit, and even that is nonrenewable. Foreign relations are based a policy of strict nonalignment politically, and an almost unique, among less-developed countries, reluctance to accept not only bilateral aid but even multilateral assistance. For example, when earthquakes damaged the ancient pagodas of Pagan in 1975, all offers of help, including those of the United Nations, were refused. Instead, the required funds were raised from public donations within Burma. This hermit among nations was determined to go it alone.

But cracks began to appear in the international façade, first becoming apparent in regard to Burma's chief export—rice. Thanks to the construction of the Suez Canal, Burma had become the main rice supplier to Europe, and from 1852 to 1922, rice acreage increased fifteenfold and prosperity was brought to the country. Since the military takeover, what had once been the largest rice producer in the entire world became instead the twelfth-poorest country. Rice production fell year by year, the foreign deficit grew, and the goals of a series of economic plans were regularly left unmet. Not surprisingly, the Burmese peasant, seeing local food prices rise even as production lagged, has remained skeptical of the Way of Socialism. The inability to keep up agricultural production and to gain the confidence of the farmers is further compounded by other internal difficulties which are a direct result of the self-reliance policies.

A black market has grown up alongside the formal economy and provides those imported products that the government is unwilling, or unable, to produce. Most of this illegal exchange is with Thailand, and peasants hold back part of their production to exchange privately for consumer goods. This, of course, only further reduces the country's export potential. Burma's small stock of cattle is also becoming severely depleted because meat is in great demand in Thailand, and cattle is smuggled across the border by Burmese farmers. Indeed, as a result of self-reliance policies, smuggling has become a major factor in the Burmese economy. Since automobile parts cannot be imported, Burmese who own cars drive to Thailand to have repairs done. Private dentists, who are busy despite the fact that medicine is supposedly socialized, bring their equipment illegally from India. The sum of all this activity is such that, according to *The International Herald Tribune,* the daily turnover of the black market is significantly larger than that of the legitimate economy.

Even the government has been forced to bend the rules it set itself. In the early 1960s, after ending its joint venture with the British Burma Oil Company, which was one of the oldest petroleum companies in the world and had built the first refinery in Rangoon as early as 1871, Burma tried to develop its oil resources (with Rumanian technical assistance). These attempts were not successful. Sorely in need of foreign exchange owing to falling rice exports, Burma finally turned to the multinationals and invited several American companies to take offshore drilling leases. But such events were little publicized, and the myth of self-reliance continued to be promoted, at least for the benefit of the Burmese public. In private, the generals were more pragmatic. In 1970, a United States Congressional hearing revealed that nearly $80 million in military assistance had been provided to "nonaligned" Burma during the previous twelve years. Some of this aid had been solicited ostensibly to control poppy growing in the infamous opium zone of the Golden Triangle, but much of it was later shown to have been used to quell local insurgents.

The failure of self-reliance and of the Burmese Way of Socialism was publicly acknowledged when the Burmese government approached the World Bank for financial assistance in 1976. Since that time, a consortium of nations that includes the United States, Canada, Australia, Japan, and a number of Western European countries has provided aid and loans; the amount requested by Burma in 1979 was $400 million. At the same time, experts from the World Bank and from the International Monetary Fund are attempting to restructure the devastated economy.* Apart from resolving internal contradictions of the Way, this will have the effect of ending self-imposed isolation: foreign investment in joint ventures is to be allowed, tourism is beginning, and a small but revealing incident occurred—a government representative has been sent to the United States to study . . . television.

It would, of course, be possible to credit the failure of Buddhist economics in Burma to what *The New York Times* called "a corrupt, repressive and inefficient regime." On the other hand, Mya Maung, an expatriate Burmese economist, has suggested that the failure of his country's economic policies is specifically linked to its attempt to combine Buddhism with socialism. Maung's argument hinges on the contradictions implicit in the idea of Buddhist economics (though he does not use that phrase). The Buddhist view is that the pursuit of worldly goods is a cause of suffering in the world and an impediment to spiritual fulfillment. Since the aim of economic activity is precisely material improvement, it is easy to see the difficulty. The fatalism that is part of the belief in Karma also conflicts with economic planning and managerial responsibility. The parsimony and enterprise needed for entrepreneurship were not a part of the Buddhist ethic—the Indian and Chinese minorities were referred to as "stingy savers" and "ruthless money-mongers"—and when the ethnic merchants were expelled or dispossessed, there was no one to take their place. Finally, as in Kampuchea, the obsession with the integrity of traditional culture led to a closed, rather than an open, society. In Maung's words, Burma was "unwilling to pay the cultural price" and

---

*A European diplomat has been quoted as saying, "It's really quite a feat to have failed so miserably for so long with a nation so rich in resources and talent" (*The New York Times*, June 14, 1979).

hence was unable to integrate successfully foreign ideas (like socialism) or foreign technology. The preservation of national culture and traditions is the aim of many countries—of Canada no less than Burma—but, paradoxically, it cannot be achieved by an inward-looking policy that attempts to revive an outdated heritage.

The possibility of instituting Buddhist economics in Burma was finally accepted as a delusion. "The basic tendencies of Buddhism in Burma," wrote Maung, "to desocialize the individual, to develop a fatalistic attitude toward life and one's station and to encourage spending rather than saving, all seem to be incompatible with the materialism and divinity of work embodied in the philosophy of . . . socialism." Buddhism in Burma, like religion in a number of the less-developed countries, acted, in Gunnar Myrdal's words, as a tremendous force for social inertia.* Like Islamic economics in Pakistan, Buddhist economics was a political expedient that did not constitute any real basis for action.

It cannot be a coincidence that both Burma and Cambodia were once European colonies. It could be argued that the technological reformation and isolation that took place in these countries were nothing more than the rejection of a hated colonial past, and only incidentally of technology. But this argument ignores the fact that anticolonialism, if indeed that is what it was, was transformed into such an extreme form of self-sufficiency that *all* foreign influences were eschewed. It also fails to explain why the reformation took so long to surface. In Burma, fifteen years elapsed after that country became inde-

---

*It is important to distinguish Theravada Buddhism—the traditional version practiced in India, Sri Lanka, Thailand, and Burma—with Mahayana Buddhism, an offshoot that developed in China. The Chinese version reached Japan via Korea, and, under the influence of Shintoism and Confucianism, developed very differently. One Japanese sect, Zen Buddhism, became the philosophy of the military class and developed a martial aggressive ethic, Kendo (the Way of the Sword). According to Victor Harris, translator of a classic Japanese guide to strategy, Kendo still motivates many successful Japanese businessmen today.

pendent and before the announcement of the Way of Socialism. In Cambodia, twenty years passed before the independent country came under the rule of the Khmer Rouge. While the years after independence were similar in both countries, and followed a pattern repeated in other ex-colonies—that of political unrest, regional insurgency, and military coups—the period was not marked by opposition to the technological system.

An example of another country that has reacted violently to the shock of the machine is contemporary Iran. Though never part of a colonial empire, Iran has been experiencing modernization since 1925. This process was accelerated in the last decade as larger and larger amounts of oil money were spent on industrial, commercial, and agricultural projects. The violent and apparently largely popular movement that led to the overthrow of Shah Reza Pahlavi was not just a reaction to the way in which modernization was imposed, but was also due to the cultural and social stresses that were a result of this modernization process. Unlike most revolutions in recent years (those in Russia, Mexico, and Cuba), the Iranian revolution (like the Kampuchean) was directed not only at the owners of modern technology, but also at technology itself.

The Kampuchean experiment was cut short; what are the chances of the Iranian attempt at restoration, or of similar events taking place in Pakistan and Indonesia? The future of these experiments is uncertain, but it is interesting to glance at an event that took place over a hundred and fifty years ago and bears a striking resemblance to what is happening in Iran today. It concerned a country likewise under foreign influence, and likewise not a colony. There was, like the Shah, an enthusiastic, modernizing despot who was succeeded by a Khomeini-like figure—cruel, religious, fundamentalist, staunchly traditional. Instead of the Central Intelligence Agency there was the London Missionary Society; instead of F-16 fighter planes there were flintlock muskets. The export commodity was not oil, but slaves. The technology involved was much simpler, even primitive; the story, however, was distressingly similar.

The island of Madagascar is one of the largest in the world and lies off the east coast of Africa. Though mentioned by Marco Polo and "discovered" by the Portuguese in 1500, it was well known to Arab traders, whose dhows handled its main export —slaves. Attempts by the Portuguese to settle Madagascar failed, as did later efforts by the Dutch, French, and English, so that at the beginning of the 1800s, Madagascar remained uncolonized and technologically relatively backward. Our story begins here.

In 1817, Radama, the leader of one of the most powerful of the eighteen tribes on the island, made a treaty with the British governor of nearby Mauritius: in return for agreeing to abandon the slave trade, Radama would receive financial compensation, arms, and military training for his men. With the aid of superior technology, Radama quickly consolidated his power over the other tribes and was recognized as King of Madagascar by Britain. The British, in turn, got a trading foothold on the island, while the ban on the slave trade put a severe dent in the operations of the French plantations of Réunion.*

The transfer of technology from England to Madagascar proved successful, and not just in the military sphere. Under British influence, Radama reformed the primitive tribal laws, introduced mass education, built roads, and established industries. Such elementary techniques as clay-brick manufacturing, soap-making, and the tanning of hides were taught to the Malagasy natives. Other "high" technologies exported to Madagascar included the magnetic compass, the clock, the cross-cut saw, and the horse.

Although the living conditions in Madagascar in the early

---

*Slavery was not actually illegal in the British colonies until 1833; thus the ban could be said to have been instituted as much for political as for humanitarian reasons.

nineteenth century were not so different from those still found in the rural areas of India today, the level of contemporary European technology was such that it was adapted to the conditions of Madagascar with relative ease. The impact of gunpowder, or of the alphabet, was certainly great, but these technologies were integrated into local life much more easily than wire-guided missiles or computerized information-retrieval systems can be integrated into "primitive" societies today. Nineteenth-century applied science was neither as expensive nor as technologically demanding.

There were, however, difficulties. Radama was an impulsive enthusiast and a despotic ruler who is often compared to Peter the Great—the modernizer of Russia—but more closely resembles the Shah of Iran. Radama wanted to modernize Madagascar, and he wanted to do it quickly. He admired Napoleon and Frederick the Great and promoted European fashion in his court—he himself owned 155 dress uniforms. Like most modernizing tyrants, Radama was as concerned with the trappings of modernity as with its substance. He decreed that all the male nobility should have their long hair cut in the current English style. This was a direct attack on a long-held tradition and there was much resistance to his orders; when a large deputation of women remonstrated with him, he simply had five of them executed. While he was personally uninterested in Christianity, he allowed the British to send missionaries, probably because it was they who introduced many of the practical crafts and manufacturing techniques. The missionaries established a network of schools throughout the island and developed, with Radama's participation, a written Malagasy alphabet and grammar. Of course, the London Missionary Society had not come to Madagascar to promote literacy or to tan hides—it had come to baptize converts—and many thousands of Malagasy duly underwent the conversion. In a few short years, the feudal despotism of Malagasy culture—this was no Islandia—began to be undermined by the spread of technology, British values, and Christian beliefs.

Radama died at the age of thirty-six by his own hand, accidentally, in a drunken fit. He was childless, and was succeeded by his wife, Ranavalona. The succession was uncontested because the Queen had ordered the murder of the designated heir, Radama's nephew, as well as that of a number of other close relatives, acts that firmly established not only her rule but her reputation for cruelty: she became known as Ranavalona the Terrible. She did not share her husband's passion for modernization—quite the opposite. She had gathered around her a circle of conservative Malagasy nobles who felt that modernization was threatening and dangerous to their position and (secondarily) to their culture, and that it should be halted and, if possible, reversed. Like the Khmer Rouge, they wasted no time in setting the restoration in motion.

The treaty with the British was abrogated almost immediately, and the slave trade with the French recommenced. In this Ranavalona had the support of the noble families to whom she gave trade monopolies, both in slaves and in other products. She did not move against the missionaries immediately, though she did warn them that they might have to depart as soon as they had taught local craftsmen European skills, among them soap-making, which the Queen seems to have particularly prized. However, she forbade the baptism of any local people, then closed the schools, and shortly thereafter, prohibiting Christianity altogether, she expelled the missionaries.

These drastic measures, which completely ruptured relations with England, were intended not only to protect an ancient religion but also to maintain the Malagasy social order. As the writer Arthur Stratton put it, "The queen was shrewd, although illiterate. She saw that these foreigners were educating her people—teaching them to read, to write, and what was worse, to think, and to protest." But, as in Kampuchea, a double standard persisted, so that although schools were closed to the common people, the children of the leading families continued to receive an English education from private, mission-taught tutors.

During most of her reign Ranavalona succeeded in isolating her country from virtually all outside influence, and in excluding all foreigners, not just the British. When gold was discovered she prohibited mining, fearing an influx of the *vazaha* (white man). She reintroduced the traditional trial by ordeal, the *tanghena,* a process that consisted of forcing the accused to swallow a poisonous fruit. If the person vomited in the approved fashion, he was innocent, if not, he was guilty. If, as happened often, he died, he was guilty by default. The *tanghena* was used as a kind of universal polygraph (on slaves above all, for as in the American South, slaves were often considered to be liars by nature); it has been estimated that in a single year more than a tenth of the entire population underwent the test. Probably half were found guilty.

But although the Queen did not want European religion or civilization, she soon found that she required European technology. Following the rupture of the treaty with the English and the expulsion of the missionary artisans, the nascent industrial sector came to a halt. The Queen could live without Malagasy Bibles, but local insurgency could only be put down with muskets and cannon. Where would these come from now that foreign contact was forbidden? The answer arrived in the form of a remarkable Gascon adventurer, Jean Laborde.

Laborde had gone to India to make his fortune, and on the way had been shipwrecked in Madagascar. An inventive and enterprising man, Laborde, the son of a blacksmith, convinced the Queen to give him a contract for the manufacture of gunpowder and muskets. Since the British had removed their military advisers, it was Laborde who led the Malagasy army and put down a regional revolt. Soldier, engineer, businessman, architect, and inventor, Laborde seemed capable of doing anything, and excelling at everything. He introduced animal husbandry and agronomy and imported a wide variety of fruit trees, vegetables, and plants from Europe. He established a

quarry and trained masons (dressed-stone construction was unknown in Madagascar), with whom he built a great palace for
the Queen and tombs for the nobility.

Laborde's most dramatic accomplishment was the construction of an entire industrial town for 10,000 workers, which
included a cannon foundry, a sugar refinery, a paper mill, a
cement factory, a silk industry, and housing for the workers.
The whole was laid out in orderly French fashion, factories on
one side and housing on the other. Superficially it resembled
one of Charles Fourier's *phalanstères* (Fourier's *Le Nouveau
Monde Industriel* had been published just a few years before),
but there was one major difference. Laborde's model city was
not inhabited by cooperating *citoyens;* like Albert Speer, who
also had a talent for organization, Laborde did it all with slave
labor. The enlightened technology that he introduced to
Madagascar was based on the distinctly unenlightened use of
slaves. It was hardly a solid foundation for indigenous development.*

Laborde's impressive, but shaky, technical achievement exemplified the final dependence of the slave state on external
civilization. For even as the spirits of the ancestors guided royal
policy, and the ordeal of the *tanghena* determined guilt or
innocence, it was European technology that delivered fresh
water to the capital and provided glass window panes for the
palace. The Queen's fetish might be invoked during a thunder
storm, but the lightning rods that Laborde had introduced to
Madagascar were probably more effective. The parasitism of
what today would be called a "client state" was evident
throughout the so-called period of isolation.

The price that the Malagasys paid for their self-imposed self-
sufficiency was monstrous. War, religious persecution, slavery,

---

*Laborde left Madagascar under a cloud, twenty-five years later, expelled for
political meddling. Immediately after his departure his workers rioted, destroyed the machines, and razed the town. Its ruins can still be seen today.

neglected agriculture, and traditional justice all took their toll. It is not known how many died or were exported as slaves, but some estimate that Madagascar, which then had a population of about two million, was depopulated by as much as one million persons during the thirty-three-year rule of Ranavalona the Terrible. Even if the total is smaller, it is still genocide on an unprecedented scale. It is sometimes argued that we cannot abandon modern technology, even if we wish to, because the human cost would be too high. In Kampuchea and Madagascar, at least, this seems to have been so.

The technological restoration of Madagascar failed, as it had to. Ranavalona knew what she did not want, but had no successful substitute; she wanted the technology of Europe without the awkward encumbrance of an educated population or a more just legal system. The past to which she wanted to return could offer superstition but not lightning rods; it resurrected benevolent ancestors, but could not make soap.

Madagascar's modernization had been associated with Britain, just as Burma's would be many years later and Cambodia's depended on France. Burma's prosperity depended on trade links with Britain, and Cambodia's and Madagascar's modernization was based on imported ideas such as mass education, scientific health care, and the rationalization of agriculture. But because modernization was so closely associated with foreign domination, the rejection of one seemed to require the rejection of the other. This is the final tragedy of antimodernism: it confuses technology with nationalism, and in an attempt to promote the latter, it strives to destroy the former. As Naipaul wrote, in *Among the Believers,* of another fundamentalist revival in another time: "Step by step, out of its Islamic striving, Pakistan had undone the rule of law it had inherited from the British, and replaced it with nothing."

There is a curious footnote to the Madagascar incident, which throws additional light on technological counter-revolution.

When Ranavalona's son came to power after her death, he surprisingly overturned his mother's policies. A confirmed modernist, he lifted all restrictions on foreign trade, invited back the missionaries, and abolished many traditional practices, such as trial by ordeal. After more than thirty years, the modernization process begun by Radama was resumed, contact with the outside world was re-established, and Madagascar's isolation came to an end.

But much of the population reacted negatively to the innovations. While they did not prefer the rule of the cruel mother, neither were they prepared to accept the radical changes being introduced by the son. The traditionalist opposition to modernization manifested itself in a widespread epidemic of what has been called dancing-mania. Men and women began dancing hysterically in the streets for hours on end, until, exhausted, they fell to the ground in a kind of trance. This phenomenon was called *imanenjana*—the dance of death—and it quickly spread throughout the island. The dancers were said to have been instructed by the old Queen's ghost, who, displeased with her son's reforms, had returned from the dead.

A young English missionary, James Sibree, witnessed the dance and assumed it was some sort of disease. It is much more likely that, like a similar phenomenon that occurred in Germany in the fourteenth century—St. Vitus' dance—it was an example of what is sometimes referred to as a crisis cult.

The crisis cult, according to Weston La Barre, is an extreme form of culture fantasy which societies seem to develop as a protection against an otherwise clear knowledge of their predicament. St. Vitus' dance occurred during the third outbreak of the Black Death, the bubonic plague that decimated all of Europe. The *imanenjana* took place during a similar period of culture shock. In both cases, the pressure on traditional beliefs had become insupportable and the crisis cult emerged.

The most poignant crisis cult of recent times, and the most overtly antitechnological, was the last catastrophic attempt by

the American Plains Indians to resist the shock of modernization. Nobody has felt the shock of the machine more deeply
than the American Indian during the nineteenth century. A
number of technological devices—the railroad, the buffalo rifle,
the barbed-wire fence, and the plow—quite literally destroyed
the Indian way of life. Buffalo were slaughtered to feed the
workers building the railroad, fertile land was settled for agriculture, and plains were fenced in for cattle. By the 1880s, the
Indians had been pushed farther and farther west, isolated on
reservations, tricked, and betrayed, until they became dependent on the white man even for food. Their traditional way of
life still a living memory, their situation filled them with frustration and despair.

The crisis cult that arose in reaction to these circumstances
was the result of an Indian messiah—Wokova—who preached
a kind of apocalypse. According to this belief, the earth would
be reborn in a pristine state, with the traditional life of the
tribes restored and without railroads or barbed wire. The purpose of the dance he introduced was similar to that of the
imanenjana: to invoke the return of the ghosts of the dead
ancestors who would help to re-establish the old way of life. The
Ghost Dance also induced a trancelike state in the participants.

There were many versions of the Ghost Dance. Some were
pacifist and taught a strict moral code not uninfluenced by
Christianity; not all versions were inimical to the white man,
although all rejected his technology. The practitioners of the
dance discarded, as much as possible, all non-Indian tools and
implements, frequently including the metal decorations and
ornaments previously so highly prized, and replaced them with
traditional Indian buckskin. Sometimes non-Indian machinery
was destroyed. In one violent episode, large amounts of agricultural equipment, much of it belonging to the Indians
themselves, was broken up. As in all technological counter-
revolutions, there were inconsistencies: such European imports
as the steel knife or the horse were never proscribed, nor,
generally, was the gun.

The Ghost Dance proposed the ultimate technological face-lift. During the apocalypse, which was often described as a kind of landslide, all the alien artifacts that had so damaged the Indians were to be destroyed and replaced by buffalo, elk, deer, and all that was necessary for the tribes to resume their aboriginal way of life. According to some versions, the white man would be pushed eastwards, out of the plains; while according to more aggressive tribes, such as the Sioux, he too would be destroyed.

In 1890, the great Sioux medicine man, Sitting Bull, led a rebellion of Ghost Dancers against the white man. He and his followers wore "ghost shirts," buckskin shirts that were supposed to make the wearer invincible to bullets. The result was predictable: Sitting Bull himself was shot (by Indian police) and two hundred of his followers, most wearing ghost shirts and including women and children, were massacred by the United States Army at Wounded Knee. The Ghost Dance proved no more effective for other tribes than the ghost shirts had proved for the Sioux. The ghosts did not return, the white man did not disappear, and the Indians were never to regain their lands, their game, or their way of life.

It would be stretching the point to claim that all attempts at technological restoration are the result of crisis cults. Certainly, the fundamentalism of the Iranian ayatollahs and the hysteria of the Cultural Revolution in China are complex religious and cultural phenomena. Seen in a larger, historical context, however, the frenzied and short-lived attack on Western technology that took place in China in the 1960s does resemble the Ghost Dance. There was certainly a messiah—Mao; there was a dance of sorts—the waving of his little red book; and there were even dancers—the Red Guards. Likewise, the outcome of the Cultural Revolution was as futile for the Chinese as the Ghost Dance had been for the Plains Indians.

While some countries have managed to make the difficult transition from a traditional to a technological society—Japan,

South Korea, Yugoslavia, and Greece—most traditional societies experience difficulties as the result of rapid cultural and technological change. Some of the poorest countries—small and technologically backward—feel threatened by modernization. Development may bring wealth, but it also brings economic, and cultural, dependence. They are required to abandon at least a part of their past, while advancing into an unknown future.

Occasionally, the stresses of cultural change, what I have called the "shock of the machine," become too great. The traditionalists see their last chance to stop the technological system. It is at this point that technology may be kept at bay, as in Burma, or violently expunged, as in Madagascar, Kampuchea, and elsewhere.* But the ghost dance of technological counter-revolution can never succeed. At worst it is a charade that deals with the problems of development by ignoring them, and it ends by falling back on the very technology that was initially rejected. At best it buys a little time for cultures that are unwilling, or unable, to accept the technological system—it is a postponement.

---

*The Boxer Rebellion in China in 1900 and the Mau Mau uprising in Kenya in the 1950s were more than simply movements for national independence. They were both fiercely anti-Western and rejected all forms of foreign influence. Both the Boxers and the Mau Mau, like the Ghost Dancers, practiced rituals that were supposed to give immunity from enemy bullets.

PART II

THE ENVIRONMENT OF TECHNOLOGY

CHAPTER 6

FROM CABIN TO COCKPIT

It had been like seeing the inside of someone's house, and, by studying it, knowing them better.

—Paul Theroux, *The Mosquito Coast*

The machine is either loved or hated. How we try to control technology has a great deal to do with how we feel about it, for we choose to use or not to use a particular machine for reasons that may be more emotional than historians would have us believe. The fact that Henry Ford liked machinery, while Pol Pot probably did not, hardly explains either the assembly line or the evacuation of Phnom Penh. On the other hand, it is impossible to understand the Ghost Dance without understanding the deep antipathy of the Sioux for all things mechanical. The Ghost Dance was not intended to secure for the Indians the technology of the white man, it was meant to make it, and him, disappear. Conversely, it is easy to misinterpret the call for a New World Information Order if we fail to appreciate the fundamental admiration of the less-developed countries (though probably not of UNESCO) for Western technology. The New Order does not seek to destroy or eliminate the international media, only to control them.

Because the shock of the machine is emotional, and not merely a cultural or economic reaction, it is not restricted to countries that are undergoing rapid modernization. There are not a few Ranavalonas in Europe and America today, of the political right *and* left, who feel threatened and dislocated by science and technology and who, like her, fundamentally dislike the machine. The technological misanthrope emerged in America and Europe almost simultaneously with industrialization, and his or her warnings, sometimes heeded and sometimes ridiculed, have been a constant feature of technological society ever since.

Emotions are never far beneath the surface in any discussion of technology. Almost as soon as it appears, the machine is the object of both dismay and admiration. When the English writer John Ruskin saw a locomotive for the first time in 1865 he felt a "crushing humility" not only in the face of this "anatomy of active steel" but also—and this was perceptive on Ruskin's part —in the reflection of the men that built it, whom he referred to as "iron-dominant Genii," already, in some way, superhuman. The small steam engine, with its tall, decorated smokestack and open driving platform, which seems quaint and picturesque today, frightened Ruskin. It, and its creators, symbolized the industrial age he lived in, but came to detest.

But only nine years after Ruskin's death, an Italian poet, Filippo Marinetti, published a manifesto of what he called Futurism, in which the power of the machine was extolled. Instead of humility, he felt exhilaration for the "deep-chested locomotives that paw the ground with their wheels, like stallions harnessed with steel tubing." While Ruskin felt that any attempt to beautify trains, or train stations, was pointless, since such a miserable activity as train travel made the appreciation of beauty inconceivable, Marinetti wrote poems about high-speed cars and planes. He considered Ruskin a "maniac for antique simplicity" and made fun of his nostalgia for primitive pastoralism. The Futurist could not understand why anyone would wish to look back when mechanical destiny beckoned.

Marinetti would have been surprised to discover that the future, which he anticipated with relish, would consider him, and not Ruskin, to have been a maniac of sorts. Today the Futurists' optimism seems naïve, and their faith in technology unfounded, or at least compromised. While accepting the accomplishments of the machine, many would sympathize with Ruskin's skepticism and uneasiness. The positions that these two men typified have not altered much in the intervening years. Although the specific issues have changed, the battle lines of this trench war have persisted, with little movement, for more than a hundred years. If Ruskin were alive today, and assuming he could come to terms with the automobile, his car would probably sport a "Split Wood Not Atoms" bumper sticker. Marinetti, who always liked to shock, would undoubtedly adorn his Ferrari (he was a car enthusiast and a nationalist, finally a Fascist) with "Nuke the Whales."

The emotional postures present in this debate about technology were formed during a relatively short time: the second half of the nineteenth century and the beginning of the twentieth century. It is worth taking a closer look at this era if we are to understand our own attitudes and inherited preconceptions about the machine. I have chosen to examine this period by scrutinizing the attitudes of four individuals—by no means the most important, but representative nonetheless—and by looking at their lives not so much in the light of their writings or famous creations, but as reflected in the four quite different domestic environments they made for themselves.

Less than a hundred years separate Henry David Thoreau's cabin at Walden Pond from an altogether different minimal shelter, Wally Byam's Airstream trailer; less than a hundred years from ax-formed white pine to paper-thin aluminum. In 1859, William Morris, who was to become the leading figure in the British Arts-and-Crafts movement, built Red House, a neo-Gothic, hand-decorated manor. Sixty-six years later, another sort of crafts movement produced another sort of house: in Dessau, Germany, Walter Gropius, the founder of the Bauhaus, built a pristine, cubist collage for himself and his teacher colleagues.

Each of these men was born in the nineteenth century. They represent the evolution of an attitude toward the machine which is exemplified in the houses they built and in the way they chose to live. At the same time, they also represent different emotional attitudes to the machine that have persisted, in one form or another. An antimechanical pastoralism and a desire for independence have survived Thoreau, just as the lure of simpler and happier times survived William Morris. Gropius's Bauhaus became synonymous with a Machine Style that still continues, while Byam, the least known of the four, typifies a comfortable acceptance of technology that many Americans still take for granted.

We start, as we will end, in the United States. It is a paradox that a strong and long-lived distrust of the machine exists in the country that has been, for the rest of the world, a prototype of the technological society. The American affair with the mechanical bride has not been a tranquil one, and the American embrace of the mechanical environment has never been as total or as equanimous as jealous outsiders have believed. Whereas in Europe the machine confronted tradition and history and the lines tended to be drawn between technology and humanism, on the open continent of the New World, where history was short, technology confronted not man-made traditions but the natural environment. According to the historian Leo Marx, the main conflict of American culture ever since the introduction of technology has been the resolution of the problems posed by the introduction of the "machine into the garden."

It is not necessary to read the novels of Herman Melville or Mark Twain to find examples of the "push and pull" between the natural and the artificial in American life. During the last decade this country, with the largest automobile ownership in the world, has embraced running and bicycling on a previously unimagined scale, confounding earlier prophets who had foretold a metaphorically legless citizen, chained to his car. On the other hand, in the midst of physical culture, the fascination with technology continues. Every year brings new improvements to the bicycle and the running-shoe; hiking and cross-country skiing were relatively static, technologically speaking, until they were taken up by Americans. Now these apparently uncomplicated activities are characterized by continual technological change as equipment is made lighter, stronger, warmer, safer, more versatile, and more durable. It is no coincidence that the hang glider, the dune buggy, the surfboard and the sailboard were all invented in the United States, not because they are a rich man's hobby (quite the opposite, they are inexpensive) but because they characteristically combine enjoyment of nature with enjoyment of technique. The American is never as happy as when he can bring the machine right into the garden and marry both parts of the American myth: American know-how and America-the-beautiful.

No one illustrates the American pastoral ideal better than Henry David Thoreau (1817–1862). He is best remembered as a naturalist and as the author of *Walden,* which describes his two-year experiment in rural self-sufficiency. The outlines of that story are simple. The young townsman, Thoreau, fed up with urban life, decides to "get away from it all." With his own hands he builds a cabin in which he lives a contemplative life, growing his own food, independent of external society, his few basic needs satisfied either by nature or by his own labor. Through these activities, and through observation of his natural surroundings, he finds inner peace. It is a quintessentially American story; every summer cottager and weekend farmer owes something to *Walden.*

Thoreau moved to Walden Pond on Independence Day 1845, and the purpose of his experiment, as he later called it, was to demonstrate that the individual could, to a great extent, be self-reliant. His ideas at that time were influenced by the English writer Thomas Carlyle, who was a violent critic of what he called the "Age of Machinery." In *Past and Present,* published two years before Thoreau's move to Walden, Carlyle attacked industrial capitalism—the present—and contrasted it unfavorably with life in a twelfth-century monastery—the past. Although Carlyle's feudal socialism had little meaning in the context of the United States, his questioning of the material goals of the Industrial Revolution found a ready audience in Thoreau, his mentor, Ralph Waldo Emerson, and the literary circle to which they both belonged. They reacted sympathetically to the denunciation of the machine, which, Carlyle wrote, made humanity "mechanical in head and heart." Even in the small town of Concord, Massachusetts, where Thoreau and Emerson lived, the effects of industrialization were already beginning to be felt as mechanization, in the form of the factory, changed old methods of work. It was to escape this environment, and in the process to discover himself, that Thoreau moved to a piece of land that belonged to Emerson, about two miles outside Concord.

The construction of the one-room, ten-by-fifteen-foot house was simple. After digging a root cellar, Thoreau fashioned a frame from pine logs and covered it with boards. The roof and walls were shingled and the interior plastered; at the end opposite the door was a brick fireplace. It took the young writer— he was twenty-eight—three months to build and cost only $28.12 ½.

The design of the Walden cabin was probably influenced by the ideas of Andrew Jackson Downing, a landscape architect who had published *Cottage Residences* a few years before. Downing described houses whose aesthetic qualities would arise from a simple expression of purpose and from domestic features such as chimneys, doors, and windows. The symmetrical location of all three in the Walden cabin is neither haphazard nor utilitarian, nor is the total absence of ornament. Thoreau's choice of a mortice-and-tenon wood frame may also have been influenced by reading Downing, who felt that the so-called balloon frame then coming into popular use was "dishonest" because the structure was hidden. This may explain why Thoreau chose not to use the lightweight balloon frame which, since he was building alone, would have been much easier for him to erect. As it was, he raised the frame with the help of friends.

One might have expected Thoreau to build a less conventional house. He greatly admired American Indian architecture, such as the tepee and the bark longhouse, and he also mentions the underground houses that the early Dutch settlers in New England had built. Why then did he not live in a tent or a rustic lean-to? If he was really conducting an experiment in self-sufficiency, why did he not at least build himself a log cabin?

Part of the attraction of Thoreau is his common sense. He would have preferred "not to live in this restless, nervous, bustling, trivial Nineteenth Century," but his Yankee practicality precluded a retreat into authentic primitiveness, which was as inconvenient then as it is now. Like a magpie, he scavenged the detritus of the very society of which he was so critical. For the boards of his house he bought an old railway worker's shanty, gave the owner less than twelve hours to vacate the premises, and then took it apart and transported the lumber to the pond. His windows were likewise secondhand. The shingles he bought were factory rejects which he had to straighten with a plane; the bricks for his fireplace came from a fifty-year-old demolished chimney. While he did try to manufacture his own lime plaster—by burning clam shells—he made only a small quantity, "for the sake of the experiment," and used store-bought plaster instead. Most of his furniture was donated by friends.

The ambivalence of his position was evident, not least to himself. Factory-produced nails—a recent invention—held the shingles and the boards together; factory-made glass filled the windows. The homemade fireplace turned out to consume a lot of wood, and during the second winter Thoreau substituted a cast-iron stove in spite of the fact that this meant that he could no longer enjoy the sight of an open fire.* Here, as in so many other things, the pragmatic side of his nature won out over the poetic.

Unlike most of his literary friends, Thoreau had a fair firsthand knowledge of technology and things mechanical. The family business was manufacturing pencils, and while he was not enthusiastic about devoting himself to this activity, the young Henry periodically worked in the pencil factory, and after his father's death managed the business for a number of years. He showed skill both as an entrepreneur and as a chemist, developing superior leads and producing pencils of varying hardnesses, then an innovation.

Although his reputation is that of a naturalist, and although he did not hide his antipathy to the machine in *Walden*, during his short life, out of all his activities—including writing, tutoring, lecturing, and teaching—he was a recognized success at only two: pencil-making and land-surveying. Thoreau epitomized a paradox of the new technological society: what he said and what he did were often in conflict. While searching for a natural environment, he could not resist the impulse of the tinkerer to improve it. His famous frugality was less that of a hermit and more that of an entrepreneur. His meticulous ac-

---

*Although the cast-iron stove was invented by Benjamin Franklin as early as 1763, it did not come into popular use until the 1830s, and Thoreau's use of it was, to a certain extent, adventurous.

counts of every expense were a curious forerunner of cost-benefit analysis—he only wanted to get the maximum return on his investment. Far from rejecting the machine, he was trying to limit its intrusion into his life, with incomplete success.

At a practical level the pastoral ideal of *Walden* proved to be unattainable, but as far as Thoreau was concerned, the experiment was far from being a failure. If he did not become financially independent as a result of his gardening, as he had hoped, then at least he did get "to know beans." If his scavenged house was in reality a product of industrial processes, it could at least serve as a literary symbol of the sylvan arbor. It is a measure of his success as a writer that he transcends the inconsistencies of his "life in the woods," and leaves the reader with the pastoral ideal intact.

Thoreau left his cabin at Walden Pond after two years, two months, and two days. He never returned and never again undertook to experiment with self-sufficiency. Of Walden he later wrote in his journal, "Perhaps if I lived there much longer, I might live there forever. One would think twice before he accepted heaven on such terms." Americans have been thinking twice about it ever since.

Henry Thoreau died in 1862, and by then many of the gloomier speculations of the Concord literati seemed to have been justified, as some of the more horrible aspects of the world's first mechanized conflict became apparent. The American Civil War made use of a number of new inventions, including steamships, steel warships, boat-borne torpedoes, armor-plate, and, above all, the mass production of small arms. The railroad too played a major role in the new mechanical war by facilitating the rapid deployment of large numbers of soldiers. The train Thoreau had observed fondly from the shore of Walden Pond had become an instrument of death.

But that same year—1862—in England, a train traveler would have had little thought of violence. True, the train traveled at an unprecedented fifty miles an hour, but the first-class carriage was as comfortable as a good coach, which in fact it resembled. During the 1840s, private railroad companies had mushroomed across England, connecting not only the major cities, but virtually every small town in between. The North Kent Line, for instance, ten miles outside London, passed through the small village of Abbey Wood. If one were visiting William Morris that year, it would have been the place to get off.

Mechanization stopped at the station platform. The gasoline-powered engine and of course the automobile were as yet undiscovered, and even the bicycle, recently coming into use in France, was unknown in England. Apart from trains, the common form of land transport was the horse-drawn carriage, a technology that was not really much changed since the twelfth and thirteenth centuries, when most of the basic improvements to harness and carriage design had been effected. But at Abbey Wood, the cart awaiting the visitor would have been medieval in appearance as well as in technique. It was an odd-looking wagonette, gaily painted and protected with a cloth roof. The inside was covered in colorful chintz and the side curtains were made of leather. The back of this carriage was emblazoned with a coat of arms, further emphasizing its medieval character.

The drive to Morris's home was not a long one, a few miles across Bexley Heath until the final destination was reached—a large brick structure built in the center of an apple orchard. The picturesque setting seemed appropriate for this rambling, irregular building, so unlike the classical Georgian villas that were then fashionable. The doors and windows had pointed arches which, together with the steeply pitched, red-tiled roofs and the stained-glass windows, gave the house a Gothic appearance. The tile roofs and the unadorned brick walls gave the dwelling its name—Red House.

The arcadian setting, so removed from steam whistles and rattling railroad cars, might have been from another time, and this feeling would have been heightened on entering the house.

The interior, though far from monastic, resembled a manor house of the thirteenth century. The walls and ceilings were either painted with murals or covered with embroidered wall hangings. The theme of the decorations—armored knights and willowy maidens—was medieval.

A large cupboard stood in the entry hall, its panels painted with scenes from the Teutonic sagas. The furniture, like the cupboard, was oaken and massive. Speckled light fell through the stained-glass windows onto the red-tiled floor. The tall brick fireplaces, like the door lintels and the window frames, were deliberately plain and undecorated, almost rustic. Frequently epigraphs appeared in illuminated Gothic script: *Ars Longa Vita Brevis* over a mantel, *Si Je Peux* (Morris's motto) on a tapestry.

The house may have looked Gothic, but it was actually less than three years old. The owner with the brave motto was no aristocrat, but the son of a wealthy businessman; together with his friends he had designed and built the house and all its furnishings. Like Thoreau, he wanted to get away from the industrial nineteenth century; but if the Concord naturalist wanted to go back to nature, William Morris (1834–1896) intended to go back to history.

While Thoreau tried to simplify the physical demands on his life, Morris was more interested in re-creating a particular atmosphere, and on quite a grand scale. Like Thoreau, Morris was influenced by the writing of Thomas Carlyle, but unlike the American, he could actually visit and admire the churches and hamlets of the Middle Ages, and Red House was an attempt to re-create Carlyle's idealized medieval monastic community where life and work were integrated. Morris often referred to his house as a "palace of art," and it was his intention to make it the headquarters of his newly founded design firm, where he and his friends could live together and, using medieval techniques, manufacture furniture, illuminated books, dyed textiles, and hand-blocked wallpapers.

Red House resembled a fairly typical middle-class country

house in its arrangements.* There was nothing monastic about the space provided—the Walden Pond cottage would have fit quite comfortably inside the entry hall—although Red House did accommodate not only the Morris family, but also half a dozen servants and frequent visitors. It was conventionally divided into a drawing room, dining room, study, bedrooms, and a service area that included a kitchen, pantry, scullery, and stables. Technologically, it did not differ much from houses built three hundred years before. Red House stood at the threshold of a revolution in domestic environmental technologies, but was as yet untouched by it. The house had no running water— the picturesque well in the garden court was not a decoration but a functional necessity—and since there was no plumbing there were no bathrooms and no water closets. Hot water for bathing, in a portable tub in the bedroom, was heated on the coal-fired kitchen stove. Of course there was no electricity; had Red House been located in the city it would probably have had gas lighting, but as it was it was lit by candles or oil lamps. Housework was performed manually by servants.

There is one environmental technology that is absent from Red House that might have been included—central heating. The British historian Reyner Banham has observed that, "By the 1860s central heating by steam or hot water could be looked for in most buildings, public or domestic, of any pretensions" *(The Architecture of the Well-Tempered Environment)*. By contrast, Morris's house had a fireplace in virtually every room, including the entry hall. The thirteen fireplaces may have been "bold and independent in design," as the art historian Nikolaus Pevsner wrote, but they were insufficient to heat the uninsulated brick construction, particularly as the upper rooms had no ceilings but were left open to the great sloping roof, a medieval "feature" that added to their discomfort. Since almost all

---

*Though it has been described as "remarkable and revolutionary," the house did not attract much attention until Morris became famous.

of the principal rooms faced north, the house was cold and drafty; its environmental failure was one of the reasons that Morris, who had contracted rheumatic fever, was eventually forced to move back to London.

But if Red House was technologically unsophisticated, it was also considerably more conventional than it may have at first appeared. It looked like a medieval manor because it was *designed* to give that impression by an architect—Philip Webb—who was one of Morris's close friends and would become a member of Morris and Company later on. Red House was Webb's first commission, but he would go on to have a long and successful career, like many "country house architects" of the time, designing residences for the wealthy. Nor was the way in which Morris's house was constructed different from the way any other building would have been built at the time. It was not constructed by a guild of craftsmen but by a local contractor, using ordinary laborers and materials.

It is not recorded whether Philip Webb rejected central heating as being unauthentic for a medieval residence, or whether, as an inexperienced architect, he was simply ignorant of the advances that had been made in heating and ventilation.* James Watt, the inventor of the steam engine, had steam-heated his own office as early as 1784, and by the middle of the nineteenth century considerable progress had occurred in America in heating technology, not only with the popularization of the cast-iron stove, but even with the use of furnaces that heated air and circulated it throughout the house. The American architectural historian James Marston Fitch refers to at least two publications on central heating with hot air that appeared in 1844. Catharine Beecher published her remarkable *American Woman's Home* not long after Red House was built, and in

---

*The reason was certainly not financial. Morris had an independent income of five hundred pounds a year, a not insignificant sum; the average Victorian working family could live comfortably on less than a hundred pounds a year.

it she already took for granted, among other domestic improvements, a furnace located in the basement and distributing hot
air to the various rooms through metal ducts.

But that was in America. An examination of Red House underlines the very limited impact that technology had on everyday life in England in the 1860s. The Luddite uprising was a
living memory and the Industrial Revolution was almost one
hundred years old, but the main impact of industrialization had
been felt only in the workplace, not in the home. It was easy for
Morris to imagine a revival of the Middle Ages since his own life
was little touched by industrialization except for the occasional
train or steamship. When he inveighed against "modern civilization," he was primarily attacking the sweatshop and the coal
mine.

It was not surprising, then, that the positive impact of industrialization and its potential as a force for improving living
conditions would have eluded Morris. A true follower of John
Ruskin, his goal was to revive hand-crafted production of interior furnishings, an effort in which the machine was his
archenemy. Apologists for Morris's political beliefs (he later
became a socialist) have attempted to play down his opposition
to technology, but as late as two years before his death he could
still say, "Apart from the desire to produce beautiful things, the
leading passion of my life has been and is a hatred of modern
civilization." But Morris's later opposition to the machine was
neither prophetic nor reactionary; it was simply stubborn.

During Morris's lifetime, though some years after Red House
was built, a number of inventions radically altered the domestic
environment, among these the use of cast iron and, later, steel
in construction; the discovery of portland cement followed by
the invention of reinforced concrete; and the development of
the elevator, which allowed the construction of tall buildings.
Electricity, the telephone, the internal combustion engine, the
automobile, and photography all came into use before the turn
of the century. Technology was also beginning to solve some of

the problems that urban industrialization had created. Underground sewers were begun in London in 1855; the first municipal garbage incinerator was built in Nottingham twenty years later. The availability of pressurized water in the city, together with a new awareness of the relationship between personal and environmental hygiene and health, promoted significant improvements in heating and ventilating buildings and the widespread use of baths and showers. By the end of the nineteenth century, technology was becoming the most important force shaping the environment. William Morris, and the Arts-and-Crafts movement he inspired, failed to grasp this.

The Arts-and-Crafts movement was based on a rejection of the machine in favor of what had previously been crafted by hand. At best, machines might be acceptable to perform some particularly menial or repetitive task, thus freeing the craftsman to pursue his or her traditional handwork. Inspired by the writing of Ruskin and the living example of Morris, architects, painters, and craftsmen vainly strove to resurrect the traditional crafts. Vainly, because it was becoming increasingly clear that the Industrial Revolution had been only a preamble, and that what was coming was really a Machine Age. By the early 1900s, Morris's successors, feeling beleaguered by the expanding technological environment, retreated even farther into medievalism. They sought out rural craftsmen in remote villages who still practiced the traditional crafts; founded crafts schools to revive forgotten techniques; and many began to give up all modern technology, even when common sense dictated otherwise. The use of the rotary saw, for instance, was considered by some purists to be immoral—they required workmen to shape timber by hand in a saw-pit. As wages rose, this began to cost a great deal of money, and the patrons of the Arts-and-Crafts movement were limited to the upper-middle class, for whom this romantic revival of medievalism in buildings and interiors was only a fashion; the morality of opposing the machine did not much concern them. When fashion changed after the First

World War, the movement lost its only constituency. It is unlikely that the workmen in the saw-pits were unhappy to see it go.

Nevertheless, the Arts-and-Crafts movement exercised a powerful influence on public taste for many years. The art critic Philip Morton Shand wrote in 1930 that, "Rooted in the Englishman's mind is the essentially nineteenth-century idea, fostered by Morris and Ruskin, that machine-made articles must inevitably be inferior to, because a substitute for, hand-made ones." Even today, Morris's ideas have not lost their attraction, and if a serious revival of arts and crafts is unlikely, a resurrection of its bankrupt ideology is quite probable, given the continued confusion about the real character of technology.

Only twenty-seven years separate the death of William Morris and the lingering quietus of the Arts-and-Crafts movement from the house that Walter Gropius (1883–1969) built for himself in the wooded outskirts of Dessau, a small provincial capital in eastern Germany. Much had happened in the interval, not least the First World War, which so accelerated many of the technological developments that were already becoming apparent by the turn of the century, but a chain of events links the young Gropius with William Morris.

Morris's ideas had been introduced to Germany by Hermann Muthesius, an architect who had spent seven years in England studying housing and construction. Muthesius subsequently published a series of books in which he singled out the British Arts-and-Crafts movement as a model for a building style which, according to him, was both practical and honest, in contrast to the eccentric styles of the day, such as the French *Art Nouveau* or the Viennese *Sezession*. An Anglophile, the Prussian Muthesius exaggeratedly described Red House as "revolutionary . . . unique . . . the very first example in the history of the modern house." He also admired the British guilds and societies which had been established to promote higher standards of craftsmanship and, in 1907, founded a similar organization in Germany which he called the *Deutscher Werkbund*. It included craftsmen, designers, and architects, and in a few years had more than seven hundred members and sister organizations in Austria, Switzerland, and Sweden. Unlike the British guilds, however, the *Werkbund* also included industrialists, for somehow the antipathy of the Arts-and-Crafts movement to mechanization was lost in the translation, and Muthesius insisted on collaboration between art and industry and between craftsman and manufacturer as a means of producing a new industrial aesthetic.

When the opportunity came to establish a new teaching institution to promote the goals of the *Werkbund*, it was natural that the post of director should be offered to one of its members, a young but already prominent architect—Walter Gropius. In 1919, he took over what had previously been two separate institutions—a state-supported arts academy and an arts-and-crafts school—located in the city of Weimar and renamed them the Staatliche Bauhaus. The choice of name was revealing, for it recalled the *bauhütten*, or medieval guilds, within which artists, craftsmen, and builders had collaborated in the construction of the Gothic cathedrals. Like the Futurists, the Bauhaus had a manifesto, written by Gropius and influenced by William Morris. The manifesto called for a new unity of artists and craftsmen, for a return to the quality of handmade crafts, and for a new guild within which all craftsmen, architects, and artists would cooperate. There was absolutely no mention of the Machine Age, of industrialization, or of machine production. The message was clear even from the cover of the manifesto— a woodcut of a distinctly medieval-looking glass cathedral.

In spite of Gropius's later disclaimers, the Weimar Bauhaus was obviously oriented to the arts, with a secondary emphasis on crafts, and there was no recognition of industrialization whatsoever. All the professors were actually painters (including Paul Klee and Wassily Kandinsky) who, while they were assisted by journeymen craftsmen, were clearly in control. The courses themselves were almost completely preindustrial, that is, they included stone sculpture, pottery, stained glass, weaving, and carpentry, but no technical or scientific subjects. How such students would be able to adapt themselves to a "world of machines, radios and fast motorcars" (Gropius) was not clear.

The Weimar Bauhaus soon developed into a Morrisonian palace of art, though "palace" is too strong a word for the strained economic and social environment of postwar Germany. There was, though, a palace revolution. A Zoroastrian cult was established, and some of the students and staff shaved their heads, wore oriental robes, and practiced vegetarianism, breath control, and a drastic regimen of purgation. Their approach to design became more and more mystical until they finally challenged Gropius's modest but increasing emphasis on practicality. At the same time, public support for the school waned. A group of professors of the former art academy seceded and started their own school in an adjoining wing of the building; local conservative politicians complained about Bolshevist tendencies—neighbors complained about noisy parties—and finally, in 1925, the Weimar Bauhaus was closed. But in the meantime, the enterprising Gropius had found another patron —the mayor of Dessau—and staff and students moved to a new location.

One of the attractions of Dessau was that the city had agreed not only to support the school, but also to provide new accommodations. Besides a building for the classrooms and workshops, there would be seven houses for the teaching staff. These buildings would be among the first to exhibit what would become known as the International Style—the style of the early Machine Age. For Gropius, who designed all the Dessau buildings, it was as if in leaving Weimar a new leaf had been turned. There would be no more compromising with the past, no more shaved heads and mysticism. The curriculum of the Bauhaus was reorganized: stone sculpture, pottery, and stained glass were discontinued, photography and printing were added, and the metal workshop turned to industrial design. Gropius himself returned to the original aim of the *Werkbund* and established links with German industries, and a Bauhaus Corporation was formed to market Bauhaus designs.

These changes, which were above all inspired by Gropius's new confidence, were also apparent in the buildings that started to take shape in the Dessau suburb. According to Bauhaus doctrine, the modern home, like modern clothes, should be different from historical buildings and should be "equipped with all the modern devices of daily use." It was typical of the Bauhaus that clothing was used as an analogy, for it was above all the external appearance of the Dessau buildings that had the biggest impact on contemporary observers. Gropius's house, like all the other buildings, was built of reinforced concrete; the exterior was unadorned, painted white, and punctured by frameless windows that seemed to be cut out of the wall. Extensive use was made of plate glass. The roofs were flat and often accessible as terraces. There was a complete absence of "traditional" materials such as stone or brick, and all hand-crafted components and historic decorations had been exorcised.

The interiors, on the whole, resembled the exterior. The impression is sometimes given that Bauhaus buildings were white, inside and out. This is inaccurate. Colors were used extensively throughout the interior, although of course they did not appear in the black-and-white photographs of the period. Gropius's office, for instance, had brightly painted walls and a bright yellow armchair. One of the staff houses had rooms with gold and silver walls and a bizarre, all-black dining room. The furniture and cupboards were designed and built by the Bauhaus workshops. They used metal tubing, plywood (a recent invention), and no ornamentation at all. In spite of Gropius's avowed interest in unifying art and architecture, his house, like the other buildings, was devoid of pictorial art, except for a few paintings, whereas the Weimar Bauhaus, like Red House, had incorporated a number of frescoes and murals.

What distinguishes Walter Gropius's house from that of William Morris is the great number of "modern devices" that by then had come into everyday use: coal-fired central heating, hot-and-cold running water, flush toilets, and separate bathrooms. Also taken for granted were the telephone, the radio, and, most important, electricity. Electrification had spread extremely quickly since Thomas Edison built the first power station in 1882, and the manufacture of electrical appliances followed at a remarkable rate. Isaac Singer, inventor of the sewing machine, produced an electrically powered model in 1889, and a few years later, an American company exhibited electric saucepans and coffee makers at the London World Exhibition. Electric lighting became common by the turn of the century when the inexpensive incandescent lamp was perfected, and during the first decade of the 1900s, such household devices as vacuum cleaners and electric cooking stoves were also available. It is not recorded if Gropius's house contained an electric refrigerator, but it might have, since this replacement to the icebox was available in the early 1920s, as was the electric washing machine.

Many of the electric appliances available in Germany were manufactured by the massive AEG (Allgemeine Elektrizitäts-Gesellschaft) Corporation, the German equivalent of the General Electric Company. In 1907, AEG had hired a *Werkbund* architect, Peter Behrens, to design their entire line of products, from turbine factories to electric tea kettles, to give a corporate, unified, and progressive appearance to its products—the "AEG look." He was not asked to invent new devices or even improve their performance (he was an art-school graduate, not an engineer), and his function was essentially that of a stylist.* Walter Gropius was one of Behrens's young assistants and later when,

---

*As a stylist, Behrens was flexible. While he gave AEG, a "modern" company, what it wanted, when he later designed the German embassy in St. Petersburg, he reverted to a traditional neoclassic style.

as Bauhaus director, he called on the students to "invent and create forms *symbolizing* [my emphasis] the machine world," it was the visual impact of these forms that concerned him the most.

The Bauhaus buildings were certainly treated primarily as visual, not technical, structures. Flat roofs were used throughout, not because they were technically superior (in fact they leaked and needed constant repair), but because they responded to a visual vocabulary of rectangular forms that had been judged to be aesthetically appropriate to the Machine Age. If one compares a piece of furniture or a graphic design produced at the Bauhaus with Gropius's own house, the resemblance is striking: the Bauhaus Look transcends both scale and function. The difficulty was that frequently, whether in a chair or in a building, the purpose of the device was secondary, if it was considered at all.

This obsession with the visual and symbolic function of practical devices is obvious throughout Gropius's Dessau house. The hard, flat surfaces of floors, walls, and ceilings made it acoustically uncomfortable. Windows were located for the purpose of external composition and not for either lighting or ventilation, so that none of the bedrooms had cross ventilation; the staircase was lit with an enormous north-facing studio light; and the dining room became overheated in the summer because of a large, west-facing, plate-glass window. The effect of this and other large windows was mitigated in winter by radiators located beneath them, a primitive solution and one that hardly improved a technology that had been well known since before the turn of the century. The lighting, as some critics have pointed out, was crude and hardly adequate for most functions, since the lamps were invariably designed as sculptural objects attached to walls or ceilings rather than as sources of illumination; a favorite Gropius light fixture consisted of a tubular incandescent lamp which resembled a bare fluorescent tube, and was just as insufficient. Concealed or indirect lighting was com-

petely absent, even though the American architect Frank
Lloyd Wright had used it successfully in Chicago fifteen years
earlier.

Part of the reason the Dessau buildings showed a limited
grasp of the functional possibilities inherent in the new domestic technologies was that neither Gropius nor the other members of the Bauhaus were particularly knowledgeable on the
subject. In spite of the rhetoric about machines and machinery
and in spite of the decided shift to functionalism since the
Weimar days, the Bauhaus still approached technology as a
formal aesthetic problem, that is, a problem of developing a
style suited to the machine, rather than of developing products
suitable to machine production.* As Reyner Banham wrote in
Theory and Design in the First Machine Age, "they were for
allowing technology to run its course, and believed that they
understood where it was going, even without having bothered
to acquaint themselves with it very closely."

Although William Morris disliked machinery, Red House was
more pretechnological than antitechnological. Gropius's house,
on the other hand, admitted technology (there was not much
choice), but it hardly displayed more understanding of the machine than its arts-and-crafts predecessor. Like Morris, Gropius
was not comfortable with the requirements of industrialization.
Above all, he did not grasp the impact the machine was already
having on the human environment. While he was trying to
create a Machine Age style, the machine was reshaping that age
in a way that made the whole question of style secondary.

When Marinetti published his Futurist Manifesto in 1909, one
of the mechanical technologies that excited him most was the
automobile—the first mobile machines over which the nonspe-

---

*Though justly famous, the furniture produced at the Bauhaus and designed
mainly by Marcel Breuer was never appropriate to mass-production techniques, and remains to this day a handmade luxury product.

cialist had direct control. Unlike the train, the airship, or the steamship—in which most people were simply passengers—the driver of a car was an *active* participant, a perambulating prosthetic god. Marinetti was an enthusiastic, if erratic, chauffeur, and even when he ended up in a ditch, he never lost his love for this and other new machines. Not only was he prepared to challenge the ideas of Ruskin and Morris, he would stand them on their heads. "A roaring racing car, rattling along like a machine gun," he wrote, "is more beautiful than the winged victory of Samothrace."

That was much further than Walter Gropius was prepared to go, and nothing typified his grudging acceptance of the machine better than a design that he prepared for the Adler car company. Adler was looking for a designer for one of their new automobiles, and just as AEG had turned to Peter Behrens, they gave the job to Walter Gropius. The Adler 3.9 liter, which began to be manufactured in 1931, was available in a number of models, including a convertible and a four-door limousine, all with bodies designed by Gropius (who by then had left the Bauhaus). The car, which has been referred to as the *Werkbundwagen,* was characterized by a high level of craftsmanship. Following the Bauhaus Look, the rectangularity of the silhouette and the doors was broken only where absolutely necessary by the circular wheel wells. The Adler 3.9, like other luxury cars of that period, was not mass produced but individually assembled. It was popular in Britain, and in fact resembled the large English touring cars of a decade earlier. Although it incorporated some mechanical innovations, such as four-wheel hydraulic brakes and reclining seats, on the whole it continued the conventional configuration of the period—a coachlike silhouette, separate hemispherical coach lamps, large detached fenders and running boards, and an external toolbox and trunk. It was an attractive sculptural object, but one that barely acknowledged that it could move and "rattle along like a machine gun." *Werkbund* principles were simply inadequate to deal with something as new as an automobile; *Bauhauslers* were more at home designing such familiar objects as chairs, lamps, and book jackets.

The traditional orientation of the Bauhaus is understandable, but not altogether excusable. Less than half a mile from the Bauhaus buildings in Dessau stood the enormous airplane factory of Hugo Junkers, one of the world's pioneers in aircraft construction. Junkers had built the first all-metal cantilever monoplane immediately after the First World War, and by 1932 had produced a classic small airliner, the Junkers Ju-52—"Iron Annie"—the German equivalent of the DC-3. As aerodynamics and metal construction began to be better understood, his designers almost immediately abandoned the squarish, box-kite shapes that had been favored by the builders of the first wood and fabric airplanes and began to produce planes with sleek, streamlined forms. But these historic developments seemed to have had no effect on the neighboring center of Machine Age design.

The same cannot be said of American industrial designers, who, unhampered by artistic considerations, were quicker to follow the lead of their counterparts in the aircraft industry. One of the first to experiment with the effect of shape on automobile performance was the famous aviator Glenn Curtiss. By the crude and simple expedient of rebuilding a car back-to-front on the same chassis, he observed that the sloped trunk facing forward—instead of the stubby hood—improved the speed of the car, and as he further altered the shape to reduce air turbulence, performance increased proportionately. When Norman Bel Geddes, an industrial designer, was asked by the Graham Paige Company to redesign its cars, he took Curtiss's findings into account and produced a remarkably modern-looking convertible which, in addition to a rounded, streamlined (as it came to be called) shape, incorporated such innovations as a convertible top that retracted into the car body, an integrated trunk, and swiveling front headlights. Although Bel Geddes's design was not manufactured, owing partly to the advent of the Great Depression, it served to point out the difference that existed between America and Europe in the attitude of designers to the machine—Bel Geddes produced his design three years *before* Gropius's Adler.

A car that *was* manufactured, and that managed to break away from the horseless-carriage approach of conservative designers, was the Chrysler Airflow, on which work was begun in 1927, and which began to be mass produced in 1934. The design of the Airflow was distinguished by a number of devices that are now commonplace: integral headlights and fenders, and a concealed trunk. The overall shape, as the name suggested, was the result of aerodynamic considerations as well as of welded unitary construction. In any event, the Airflow was not well received by the public—it sold for about three times the price of a Ford Model A—and it was discontinued after only three years, although many of its design features were to reappear later in such famous cars as the Volkswagen and the Volvo.

Automobile design indicated that while the Machine Age may have originated in Europe, it took root more firmly in America. Even more telling than car design was car ownership. By 1930, Germany, the home of the motor car, had slightly over half a million registered private automobiles. England, with a smaller population but with a technologically more advanced economy, had about one million. These low figures were due to the fact that in Europe the automobile was expensive and considered a luxury; in general, mass-produced, inexpensive cars were not available until after the Second World War. The German *Kraft durch Freude* (Strength Through Joy) car, better known as the Volkswagen, was designed in 1938, but production was interrupted by the war, and only resumed for civilian consumption in 1949. The 1936 Italian Fiat 500—the Topolino, or "Little Mouse"—was a rare example of a real "People's car." The French version of the People's Car—the Citroën 2CV—was designed in 1939 but produced ten years later; the British Morris Minor began to be built in 1948.

In America, thanks to Ford's visionary Model T (1908) and the more mechanically advanced Model A (1929), there were *twenty-three million* private cars by 1930; one out of every five Americans owned an automobile! Almost three-quarters of all the passenger cars in the entire world were being driven between Maine and California. No wonder that the Americans, not the Europeans, would be the first to learn how to deal with the new machine environment.

What was becoming apparent in America was that mass production stimulated—indeed relied on—mass consumption. Thus the focus shifted from the methods of production—and the objects produced—to the users of these objects, or, as they were beginning to be called, the consumers. Whereas traditional production had been aimed at small, selected markets with narrow (and hence predictable) tastes, mass consumption implied mass markets; large numbers of individuals with as yet unknown demands and preferences that had to be taken into account by the producer.

Bel Geddes pioneered the use of consumer surveys to find out why people bought certain products and how they used them, information he would then incorporate into the particular object he was designing, whether it was a car or a kitchen stove. Whereas the *Werkbund* was interested in philosophically identifying industrial prototypes—and fixing them once and for all —the American view of technology was much more dynamic because it recognized that the taste of the public was itself the major, and changeable, factor. When Bel Geddes designed the streamlined car for Graham Paige, he was specifically asked to envision what a car might be like in five years, and then to work backward, to prepare designs for the intervening years, each slightly less innovatory than the last. In this way, it was hoped, technological innovations could be gradually introduced without alienating the public—an important consideration, as the ill-fated Chrysler showed.

Mass production had the effect of shifting at least some of the control over technology from the producer to the consumer. While the Graham Paige example seems on the surface to be a case of manipulating public taste, it was also an attempt to anticipate it. Although advertising would later be used to shape consumer preferences, the early days of industrialization were more responsive to public demand. How else to explain the extremely rapid adoption of such new and unlikely devices as the zipper (1896), the electric dishwasher (1932), or the mechanical kitchen-sink garbage disposal (1955)?

Of course, the public's taste could be fickle. While the Airflow failed, a few years later streamlining became so popular that it was applied even to stationary objects such as refrigerators and radios. Some new products, such as the Kodak Brownie—the first inexpensive camera—proved extremely long-lived; others were simply fads. In any event, the desires of consumers frequently were more influential than the aims of the producers. While it may seem today that the compact car was invented in Japan, an American, Powel Crosley, had marketed a small, four-cylinder car as early as 1946. The Crosley weighed less than half as much as the then-popular Chevrolet Stylemaster, was inexpensive, and consumed very little gas (thirty-five to fifty miles per gallon). Despite these obvious advantages, it was not what the public wanted, and the company did not do well, never producing more than 29,000 cars a year. In America, "good design," in the words of the famous industrial designer Raymond Loewy, meant, above all, good business.

One particularly good business in America in the 1930s was the manufacturing of automobile trailers or "trailer coaches." This industry, which was among the fastest growing at the time, produced a characteristically American creation that could not have appeared elsewhere. Because of the widespread ownership of automobiles and an already extensive highway system, demand for trailer coaches grew rapidly. By 1938, people were speaking of the Trailer Fad—that year alone over sixty stories on the subject appeared in *The New York Times*—as the trailer caught the imagination of the public. There were traveling trailer shops, trailer post offices, and trailering dentists. The New York police had a mobile detectives' office in a trailer, wheeling from crime to crime; the bishop of Cincinnati received diocesan approval to use a trailer as a temporary cathedral. But not all the trailer users were Tin-Can Tourists, as one association was named. Following the Great Depression, many workers, forced to migrate to find work, used trailers as inexpensive, and movable, housing. By 1937, over half the trailers sold were actually used as full-time homes, a trend that continued after the Second World War as defense workers, veterans, and retired couples became used to the idea of living in a home on wheels. Originally conceived for vacation use, the trailer coach was turning into the trailer home.

The early trailer coaches were not intended for permanent occupancy and lacked bathrooms and kitchens—they were little more than holiday caravans—but there were exceptions: large, custom-built trailers for the wealthy, not inappropriately called "land yachts." Glenn Curtiss, for instance, had a company that built a large touring trailer for a Palm Beach client that included a kitchen, shower-bath, "commodious" wardrobe, and even separate quarters for the chauffeur-butler. Curtiss's use of lightweight aircraft construction in his trailers demonstrated the possibility of applying mass-production and prefabrication techniques used in the automobile industry to the trailer home.

Which brings us, finally, to Wallace Merle Byam (1896–1962), who never achieved the fame or notoriety of his contemporaries Norman Bel Geddes or Raymond Loewy. While it may seem blasphemous to place him in the same company as William Morris and Walter Gropius—Byam certainly had no artistic pretensions—in his own way Byam was as idealistic as Morris, and a good deal more successful than Gropius in understanding and using technology. His famous house on wheels—the Airstream trailer—is still in production and in a form that, while improved, is not very different from what he built in 1937.

Wally Byam's background hardly prepared him for a career in manufacturing. He was trained as a lawyer and, after a checkered career in advertising and publishing, in 1930 he started a small business building travel trailers in California. Although many others were also trying to cash in on the trailer fad, Byam built trailers that were quite different. He was impressed by the Chrysler Airflow and streamlined his trailers to reduce wind resistance. Like Curtiss's experimental car, the first Airstream had a long, sloping back, although this was later rounded to allow more interior space, and, also like Curtiss, Byam followed the lead of the aircraft industry and built his trailers out of aluminum rather than wood. The semimonocoque construction resulted in a trailer that was light (it could be pulled by a man on a bicycle), extremely strong, and maneuverable.

Most startling of all was the appearance of what Byam called the Airstream: a sleek, rounded projectile with lozenge-shaped windows that were really portholes, it came in only one color —bare aluminum. Initially, the interior accommodations were relatively spartan, but they soon came to include a shower, bath, refrigerator, running water, and air-conditioning. Pulled by the large, black, rectangular automobiles of the 1930s, it didn't look like something from a future age, but like something from another planet.

But more was involved than technical progress. Although only ten years separated Byam's trailer house from Gropius's house in Dessau, a great deal had changed in the relationship between shelter and technology. While the Dessau house was referred to by the German press as a "machine for living" (a phrase coined by Le Corbusier), it had the same concern for stability and permanence as Morris's Red House. William Morris's medieval manor and Walter Gropius's constructivist lodge were built of heavy and permanent materials, and both were meant to last.* Each was a symbol of its owner's aesthetic prejudices, and neither had anything to do with industrialization, mass production, or the consumer society.

A very different concern was evident in Byam's Airstream. While the unadorned exterior certainly reflected an aesthetic prejudice, it was not related to any artistic movement but mimicked the engineering forms of the airship and the aircraft fuselage. Although its concern for permanence was no less real than that of its predecessors—aluminum is virtually indestructible—this permanence was in no way *expressed*. And the Airstream cost only a fraction of the larger European houses—$795 in 1937.

Byam was certainly not unique in trying to link industrialization and housing. In 1908, Thomas Edison had patented a formwork system for casting concrete houses, and there had been many subsequent attempts, using many different materials, to mass produce homes. The Sears Roebuck catalog, for instance, listed a wide variety of house models that could be ordered and would arrive on the building site in a package, each piece of lumber precut and numbered. Between 1900 and 1940, Sears sold more than 110,000 such mail-order houses. Less successful efforts were made by R. Buckminster Fuller, who in 1927 proposed an industrialized house (the so-called Dymaxion) which also used aircraft technology, but who in eighteen years managed to build only two of them. In France, Le Corbusier designed a prefabricated house that used metal panels in 1929, but none were ever built. In Germany, Walter Gropius was hired by the Hirsch Copper and Brass Works to design a metal prefabricated house in 1931, but, as Gilbert Herbert notes, his designs did not find much approval with the public and were soon discontinued.

---

*Red House still stands today. Gropius's house was completely destroyed by aerial bombing during the Second World War but has recently been reconstructed.

Byam's success may have been due to his very different attitude to technology. While Gropius wanted his houses to reflect their factory origins, Byam exhibited a totally different approach. True, the exterior resembled a space vehicle, but there was not a square inch of exposed aluminum visible inside the Airstream. Instead there was wood paneling, pretty curtains, and overstuffed furniture. If the exterior was Buck Rogers, the interior was strictly middle America. As Byam wrote, "A trailer is a home: you will eat in it, sleep in it, loaf in it, have friends in for dinner, watch TV, bathe, read, cook—in short, engage in the same range of activities that you normally engage in at home."

Here was technology harnessed to the needs of a consumer society. Byam saw no contradiction between the silver bullet-shaped exterior and the desire of his customers for a cosy and comfortable home, nor between the possibilities of mass production and industrialization and a product that contained a high degree of craftsmanship and durability.

Morris would have derided the idea of mass-produced houses; Gropius, while he advocated standardized, factory-built homes, was never able to come to grips with the public's desire for traditional values. Strangely enough, Henry Thoreau probably would have been more sympathetic to the idea of a small, portable home. In *Walden*, he made the novel suggestion that the large tool bins he had seen on his walks along the railroad tracks could, in a pinch, serve as a home. The only modification required, he sagely warned, was some holes for ventilation. "Many a man is harassed to death to pay the rent of a larger and more luxurious box who would not have frozen to death in such a box as this," he wrote, and added, "I am far from jesting."

We have come full circle to Henry Thoreau in more ways than one: it would not be hard to imagine the Concord naturalist, who enjoyed traveling, living in a trailer (in fact, the aluminum house on wheels was slightly smaller than his rustic cabin). Of course, Thoreau's cabin was hardly the precursor of the industrialized house, but in his ambivalent attitude to the machine there was the beginning of a recognition that to achieve the natural might require some compromise with the artificial. Thoreau may have claimed to prefer not to have lived in the nineteenth century, but he accepted its devices, even as he built a house out of its rejected materials.

The story of the Airstream would be incomplete without mentioning an associated phenomenon—the Wally Byam Caravan. Beginning in 1951, he led groups of trailers on extended trips, which came to be known as caravans, first to Mexico and later to Canada, Europe, and finally, two years before his death, on a six-month tour from Capetown to Cairo. It must have been quite a sight, up to two hundred aluminum capsules, wending their way through Mexican pueblos or trekking through the Kenyan bush. At night, the Airstreams would be formed into a huge circle, like their Conestoga forebears, and the traveling Futurists would emerge to sit around a campfire singing songs, square dancing, or indulging in other forms of traditional self-entertainment.

Marinetti would have been appalled. Where was the mechanical future? A bunch of retired folks tooling around in aluminum blimps and pretending to be pioneers? But perhaps Byam understood something his European contemporaries did not: while technology could be used to fashion a new way of life, it could also be used to redefine an old one. This was a very different way of using the machine.

CHAPTER 7

THE OPEN
DOOR

A new device merely opens a door; it does not compel one to enter.
—Lynn White, Jr., *Medieval Technology and Social Change*

No book about technology can avoid dealing with the tools of war. While it would be an exaggeration to say that all technology is linked in some way to the pointless act of killing, it is true that many useful devices have had their origin in some military purpose. The wheel as well as the horse appeared in ancient Egypt in the form of the war chariot; the first recorded horseman was a raider from the Asian steppes; the purpose of the first saddle was to steady the sword-thrusting rider; the eminently practical horseshoe was originated by the Roman cavalry. All of these devices had an enormous effect on agriculture, communications, and commerce, but all owe their existence to humankind's interest in war.

That this is so is an indication of the violence in human relations, but it is also a reflection of the power and influence of the

warlike state, in which were concentrated the resources necessary for the promotion of new inventions. The military state was
the first major client that promoted the establishment of mines,
smelters, and forges—whose first products were invariably
weapons. The earliest bronze artifacts were daggers; the first
iron and steel implements were most often spears and swords.
The first extensions of man were his "arms," and it is likely that
the first prosthetic god was really a prosthetic killer.

The effect of this gruesome interest was not always negative.
The process of mining ore for use in the production of swords
simultaneously helped to develop knowledge of hydraulics and
mechanics; gunnery advanced mathematics; naval warfare promoted navigation. More important was the effect that the military had on production techniques. Armies tended to require
large numbers of standardized products—whether shields or
sandals—and this need stimulated innovation in manufacturing
methods. As early as the twelfth century, the iron-making center of southwest England—the Forest of Dean—was so highly
organized that it could produce a single order of fifty thousand
horseshoes for Richard the Lion-Hearted's crusading force. The
first example of large-scale mass production organized according to modern methods occurred in Portsmouth in 1808, where
Henry Maudsley built a series of specialized, preset machines
that enabled ten workmen to turn out 130,000 wooden pulley
blocks a year for the British navy. In the nineteenth century,
this navy was the sponsor of a number of important innovations,
including the first assembly-line factories—turning out ship's
biscuits—and, a few years later, the first factory to produce
canned food. In the United States, Eli Whitney was unable to
find investors who would finance his cotton gin until he turned
to the army, which gave him a contract to mass produce muskets. This enabled Whitney to perfect another of his ideas, the
use of standardized, interchangeable parts in manufacturing,
which would become the basis for all subsequent successful
industrialization.

The fact that the development of technology is frequently associated with the development of weapons, or is at least stimulated by their production, is certainly not a justification for war. It is likely that the stirrup or the horseshoe would have been adopted without their military usefulness, and throughout the history of technology one finds wartime devices that subsequently shed their offensive purpose to become peaceable tools —radar and high-altitude rockets are two recent examples. Still, much of the modern antipathy to technology in general arises from a fear of modern weaponry, and the conclusion is often made that any technology that has the potential of being a weapon, no matter how otherwise useful, ought to be curtailed. At least a part of the popular opposition to peaceful nuclear power rests on the fear of its destructive use in war, and the difficulty of guaranteeing that one use is not transformed into the other. Indeed, nuclear war is a frequent example of how technology can grow out of human control, and for critics such as Lewis Mumford or Jacques Ellul the atomic bomb is a self-evident symbol of the domination of modern man by his machines. In *The Technological Society*, Ellul quotes a French politician, Jacques Soustelle, who made a famous remark about the atomic bomb to the effect that "since it was possible, it was necessary," to which Ellul adds, "Really a master phrase for all technical evolution." According to this proposition, which has many adherents, *all* technology is necessarily used as soon as it is available, without distinction of good or evil. If "anything that can be done, will be done," then any attempt at controlling technology is hopeless.

It should be obvious by now that this book is an attempt to refute such a view. This cannot be done convincingly by looking into the future, and, since the present is still unresolved, it has been necessary to examine the past. The historical record does not support the dour theory of technological inevitability. All technological activity seems to reflect a human desire to gain a greater control over the immediate environment, and every tool, according to Arnold Gehlen, is only an attempt to make life more predictable. As I have already described, the evolution of the design of machines from the tool stage to powered devices and finally to automation is a process that progressively, and specifically, increases human control.

But there is a second way in which the machine is under human control: the *choice* is made whether or not to use it. Technology is not automatically used simply because it is there. Lynn White, Jr., has cautioned: "As our understanding of the history of technology increases it becomes clear that a new device merely opens a door; it does not compel one to enter. The acceptance or rejection of an invention, or the extent to which its implications are realized if it is accepted, depends quite as much upon the condition of a society, and upon the imagination of its leaders, as upon the nature of the technological item itself." If there is a technological plot we are far from being its passive victims and are more like co-conspirators.

If all technological devices open doors, weapons do so in a particularly dramatic way. There is an urgency to war that accelerates the making of decisions; the effect of choosing to use, or not to use, a particular weapon is usually obvious and swift. War often makes the film of technical change look as if it were being run at double speed.

The development of weapons has been described as cyclical —a movement between three major axes: mobility, hitting power, and protection. At one time or another one of these three tends to predominate until a new weapon, or a new tactic, shifts the advantage to one of the other two. Protection, or armor, usually evolves to defend the soldier against projectiles or small arms, that is, against hitting power. Armor tends to be made as heavy as possible until finally, if it is too heavy, the mobility of the wearer can become so impaired that he can be overcome by a foe who is lightly armed, but more speedy or agile. At other times protection, whether in the form of armor or fortifications, can be canceled out by a new form of hitting power such as artillery. Artillery can be rendered ineffective by mobile weapons such as tanks, which in turn can be neutralized by a foot soldier equipped with the hitting power of a bazooka. And so on.

The cyclical nature of warfare and of the development of weapons-use means that making the correct technological choice—that is, recognizing the implications of a new device—can often make the difference between being the loser or the winner. Why a particular decision is made by one side, and not by the other, underlines the various nontechnological forces that come to bear on technological choice.

Whether, or when, a weapon is taken up depends a great deal on the conditions found in the society at the time. The success of the ancient Greeks in their numerous wars against the numerically superior Persians illustrates this point. The strength of the Greeks lay in their use of the hoplites, heavily armored infantry who were capable of resisting, and finally defeating, the Persian army. The Persians, on the other hand, relied primarily on light cavalry, and provided armor only to their officers because their conscript army was so enormous. The Greeks could afford to form entire regiments composed of heavily armored foot soldiers not because of any new technology but because of the nature of Greek society. The Greek army, unlike the Persian, was composed of free citizens, each of whom provided his own armor—breast and back plates, helmet, shin guards, shield, sword, and spear. But the hoplites were not just a well-armed mob; they moved in precise drill according to their officers' orders. This too was a function of Greek society, where men practiced gymnastics and dancing and came from a democratic, and homogeneous culture. The Persian army, composed of subject peoples from a wide empire, could only be roughly, and rudely, ordered into loose formations which proved to be incapable of resisting the relentless, crushing hoplites.

The hoplites depended on protection for their success, and to achieve it they had to sacrifice mobility. They were finally overcome by the Roman legions, which incorporated both disciplined movement and greater mobility and hitting power. While the hoplites used extremely long thrusting spears, the Romans had short throwing spears with which they could attack the Greek phalanx at a distance. Then, when there was hand-to-hand fighting, the more mobile Romans, trained to fight in smaller units, had a decided advantage.

The importance of the stirrup in armed combat has already been mentioned. It came to Europe from Central Asia, and by the eighth century seems to have been fairly well established. It had its greatest influence on the Franks, who, under Charles Martel—the "imaginative leader"—more than anyone else exploited the full possibilities of armored, mounted combat. Not only did the Franks develop new equestrian weapons such as the longsword and body armor, they also created a social structure which was made possible by, and centered on, the mounted knight. As Lynn White points out, while the stirrup was used by many groups in Europe, it was only the Franks who realized its full military potential. The Anglo-Saxons, for instance, used stirrups for riding and hunting, but continued to fight on foot, as tradition demanded. By the time the Norman Franks invaded England in 1066, the outcome of the Battle of Hastings was a foregone conclusion. The Anglo-Saxon farmers, fighting on foot with scant armor, were no match for the professional soldiers from Normandy, who were heavily armored and, above all, mounted.

Some technological improvements are simply a direct response to functional requirements and as such are more or less predictable: armor gets heavier, swords get sharper, cannons get bigger. But sometimes innovations seem to come out of nowhere. The longbow is a good example of a "dormant" invention, one that is known about and seemingly forgotten, only to re-emerge at a later date. Saracen archers were the first to discover that, if a bow was made long enough, it was possible to draw the bowstring all the way back to the cheek, enabling the archer to sight down the length of the arrow and shoot with great accuracy. However, when the bow became a cavalry weapon, it was shortened to enable the horseman to handle it conveniently, and sighting became impossible. When heavily armored knights began to dominate the field of battle, both sighting and the weapon itself fell into disuse. While the bow was still maintained for hunting and sport, it had become obsolete as a weapon. There was one remote region where, for some reason, the sighting technique and the longbow survived (or were rediscovered, it is not clear which). The Welsh longbow was over six feet, and this hunting tool was capable of accurately projecting an arrow that could penetrate even the heaviest armor. Once the English "discovered" the Welsh longbow, they soon incorporated large numbers of bowmen in their armies, and the days of the knight were numbered. At the Battle of Crécy, over fifteen hundred French aristocrats fell in charge after futile charge against the English archers. This marked not only the end of the armored knight, but the beginning of the end of feudalism itself.

Medieval feudalism was vanquished by two weapons, both wielded by common folk. If the longbow was rediscovered after years of neglect, the second weapon—the halberd—was hardly discovered at all. It was improvised by Swiss farmers who were struggling for independence from the barons of the German Empire and having very little success against the heavily armored horsemen. The Swiss combined a long spear with two common agricultural implements: the cleaver and the billhook. The halberd enabled a man on foot to hold a mounted attacker at bay with the spear, and either to chop him down with a forceful swing of what was, in effect, a very long-handled ax, or, better still, to haul him off his horse using the hook. It was a crude device, but it proved to be fairly effective.

Two additional factors contributed to the success of the halberd in overcoming the mounted knight. First, the halberd was an inexpensive weapon which a peasant farmer could acquire and quickly learn to use. Just as the elaborate armor and trained horse of the knight were élitist (because so expensive, and requiring so much training), the halberd was one of the first weapons of democracy. But it differed from the longbow in one important respect: while the halberd did not require great skill, it demanded considerable personal bravery. It did not take much courage to perforate an attacking French knight who was one hundred fifty feet away, but the halberd involved close combat, and until the halberdier, who wore no armor, was able to unseat or incapacitate the charging enemy, he was at great risk. Like the hoplite, who also fought hand-to-hand, the Swiss farmer was part of a citizen's militia, a free man fighting for home and family—neither a serf nor a slave—a necessary prerequisite for the bravery required to use this kind of weapon.*

More than eight hundred years after Hastings and the defeat of the Anglo-Saxons by Frankish armor, history repeated itself. The invasion of France in 1940 succeeded largely because the Germans understood the implications of another armored weapon—the tank—and how to use it in a new kind of warfare —the *blitzkrieg.* But if armored warfare caught the British and the French by surprise, it was not because the Germans had a secret weapon. The French had the most powerful tanks, and more of them, while the British had actually invented the weapon and had been the first to use it.

The door to tank warfare was opened at Cambrai in 1917, when 476 British tanks overran the Hindenburg Line in four hours. It was the first independent tank attack of that war, and although the tank emerged victorious, its immediate impact on

---

*The halberd re-emerged in seventeenth-century Japan. Women learned to use it to defend their families against mounted bandits when their menfolk were absent.

military tactics was unexpectedly minor—the final year of the war was characterized by the same sort of trench warfare as before.

One reason for this was the tank itself. When the tank was first developed in 1916, its main purpose was to cross trenches and shell-pocked terrain in support of infantry. These first vehicles—a combination of two recent innovations, the internal combustion engine and the agricultural crawler tractor—were extremely slow and mechanically unreliable. The heat inside the steel boxes was intense, and the crews had to disembark frequently, vomiting and delirious from the gas fumes. The top speed of these early tanks was less than ten miles an hour, and although they were sometimes described as armored cavalry, they could not keep up with horsemen in rapid deployment; at the same time, in frontal attacks, tanks experienced heavy losses at the hands of enemy artillery. The relative failure of tank attacks after Cambrai convinced the German general staff that this was a very inferior weapon, and although the British and the French continued to employ tanks, primarily as infantry support, the Germans made almost no use of them.

After the First World War, in spite of a number of tank enthusiasts such as General J. F. C. Fuller, the British army more or less abandoned the tank as an offensive weapon. This was not due to its mechanical shortcomings, which had by then been largely overcome, but to an inability on the part of the British officer class to accept the idea of mechanized warfare. Their attitude was summed up by Field Marshal Douglas Haig, who said in 1925, "I am all for using aeroplanes and tanks, but they are only accessories to the man and the horse" (quoted by Orgill). While Haig's view was not necessarily unrealistic (European armies would use horses for transport until 1945), his relegation of the tank and the plane to supporting roles was shortsighted.

Meanwhile, the losers were rethinking their strategy, as losers often do, and reaching very different conclusions. In 1935, when the British cavalry establishment grudgingly permitted the formation of a single tank brigade, Germany already had a *Panzertruppe* consisting of three divisions. These divisions did not yet have many tanks, but they had something much more important: General Heinz Guderian. Although Guderian had not actually driven a tank until 1929, he soon became its chief promoter in the German army. Guderian was an avid reader of Fuller's books and was successful in convincing his superiors that tanks would play a major role in any future war.

Guderian deserves the credit for pushing the German army through the door to tank warfare that had been opened by the British. He also understood the importance of the wireless radio in coordinating rapid, mobile attacks, and the changed role of the commander in mobile warfare. Traditionally, command had been from the rear, via telegraph; henceforth, said Guderian in a famous dictum, he would lead from the front—by wireless. In 1940, although German tanks were neither larger nor faster than those of the Allies, they were unrivaled in the area of radio communications.

But more than any technological advantage, other historical factors allowed the Germans to grasp the possibilities inherent in the tank. There is evidence that the concept of indirect, mobile attack actually predated the tank, for according to both Len Deighton and Kenneth Macksey, *Stoss* (assault) divisions were used by the Germans to bypass strong points and to attack artillery positions behind Russian lines as early as 1917. And even more important was the fact that a discredited military establishment was less effective than its British and French counterparts in blocking the development of new weapons such as tanks and planes. Finally, and not least, Hitler himself was a supporter of the tank. While Macksey suggests that he understood the idea of armored warfare only *after* the invasion of Poland, the fact remains that he did not oppose the *Panzertruppe*.

Like his Frankish ancestors, Guderian achieved *Stosskraft*—

dynamic punch—with heavy armor. But the advantages of the tank were soon compromised by an infantryman's weapon which, like the halberd, was light, inexpensive, and easy to use. Work on a rocket-propelled grenade was begun by the Americans soon after 1940, and within two years the bazooka was in regular use on the battlefield. As a result, the tank never again assumed the dominance it had in 1939 and 1940.

If the tank remained dormant between 1917 and 1940, at least as far as the British were concerned, another weapon employed during the First World War was so relegated to obscurity that it was not used at all during the Second World War. That weapon was poison gas. Chemical weapons had been considered, though not used, since the nineteenth century: an English chemist, J. Scoffern, published a popular book on modern weapons in 1845, and a few years later added a final chapter on "The application of chemical resources to the charging of shells." In it he argued that, inhuman as chemicals might be, it was a mistake to imagine that any "convenient mode of destruction" would not be used by one or other of the warring parties. But while a scientist might contemplate this possibility with equanimity, the military, it turned out, was much more reluctant.

As early as the Crimean War, it was suggested to the British that sulfur fumes be employed against the enemy, but this was not actually done. During the American Civil War, the Union forces considered but desisted from using artillery shells containing chlorine gas. Still, by the end of the century there was enough concern about the use of poisonous weapons that the Hague Convention specifically proscribed poison gas as a weapon. Thus it was that the British and French were completely unprepared for the chlorine gas that drifted toward them over the fields of Ypres in April 1915. It took them six months to retaliate in kind (they had no chemical stockpiles), but retaliate they did. Two years later the Germans attacked with mustard gas, a much more persistent and noxious chemical, and this time it took the Allies more than a year to catch up. The First World War was marked by an escalating use of over thirty different toxic agents, including sneeze gas, blistering gas, tear gas, and lung irritants. Although very few of the war casualties were actually due to these gases—since each escalation brought with it corresponding defensive measures—by the end of the war, at least in the minds of the public, the use of poison gas had come to typify the unholy alliance of science and war.

Even though the Geneva Convention forbade all chemical weapons, research into the subject continued among all the major powers. The American Chemical Warfare Service, which had been established in the last year of the war, was made permanent in 1920, and both Germany and Britain made extensive preparations for civil defense against the gas bombing of civilians. In 1936, the I. G. Farben Company invented nerve gas. Unlike most of the earlier gases, which irritated or temporarily incapacitated their victims, nerve gas killed outright.

In the event, neither nerve gas nor any other kind of gas was used during the Second World War (with the exception of Japan, which briefly used gas against the Chinese). While it was all very well for President Roosevelt to denounce chemical weapons as "contrary to what modern civilization should stand for," the fact was that what with concentration camps, the firebombing of cities, and the final atrocity of the atomic bombs, modern civilization took quite a beating. Yet the door to chemical weapons remained closed.

According to the historian Frederic J. Brown, there were a number of restraints that acted to prevent chemical weapons from being used in that particular war. These did not include legal restraints, which had been ineffective in the First World War, and which had not stopped the development of further poisons in the interwar period, nor was public opinion an effective restraint. The example of the earlier war had showed that the public usually called for reprisals and tended to accept the use of chemicals once they had been used by the enemy.

Rather, two different factors seem to have curtailed the use of chemical weapons. The first was the fear of retaliation by the enemy. With the advent of long-range bombers, the threat of retaliation could be carried to the civilian population. The second factor was a fear of the kind of escalation in weapon technology that had occurred in the previous war, although both sides did have plans to use chemicals as a "last resort." Hitler actually ordered the use of sarin—a nerve gas—in the last year of the war, but by then the German chemical industry was incapable of delivering any. The most effective restraint, according to Brown, was, surprisingly, the military itself. Chemical weapons were never "assimilated by the military profession" on either side. According to Albert Speer, for instance, the German army refused Hitler's orders to manufacture N-material, a kind of napalm. Some of the reluctance to use chemical weapons was based on practical considerations, since gas was difficult to control and the use of gas masks and protective clothing on the battlefield imposed awkward conditions for the attacker as well as the defender. It was not a weapon that offered the chance of victory, but, quite the opposite, it tended to prolong the conflict without providing any clear advantage to either side. The use of chemical weapons by both belligerents, as the First World War had shown, simply created a very difficult environment in which war had to continue with conventional weapons. So the door to chemical weapons remained closed because, in Brown's words, "Poison gas . . . was an unacceptable anachronism, born too early out of a unique marriage of science and war."*

Legal restraints and nonproliferation treaties did not curtail the continued development of chemical weapons, although the fact that the weapons existed by no means ensured that they would

*In the few cases where chemical weapons have been used since 1945—by the Egyptians against Yemeni tribesmen, by the Americans against the Viet Cong, or by the Soviet Union in Afghanistan—they were used against an enemy completely incapable of retaliation.

be used. In some cases, military treaties even have the opposite
of their intended effect, as was the case after the First World
War. It could be said, without much exaggeration, that the
Treaty of Versailles not only promoted a new military technology, but also had a more surprising, unplanned consequence.

The Treaty of Versailles placed severe restrictions on the
manufacture of armaments by Germany, and long-range artillery of the kind that had shelled Paris from a distance of
seventy-five miles was forbidden altogether. But there was a
technology that the Treaty neglected to mention: the rocket.
Walter Dornberger, who was in charge of the Rocket Research
Institute at Peenemünde, states in his autobiography that the
decision to begin work on rockets in 1929 was a direct result of
the limitations that had been placed on conventional artillery
research.

The foundation of the German rocket program was a group
of enthusiasts who called themselves the *Verein für Raum-
schiffahrt*—the Society for Space Travel—and who tested small
rockets in a Berlin suburb on weekends. As the name suggests,
the goal of this group was interplanetary travel, not flying
bombs, but the German Army Weapons Department was looking at possible applications of rocket technology that could be
developed without contravening the Treaty. When a rocket
research program was established, in 1931, it soon attracted a
number of key scientists from the Society for Space Travel who
saw the Department as a source of funds for their own experiments. After eleven years of work they produced the world's
first long-range ballistic missile, the V-2.

The development of the V-2 did not receive strong support
from the German military (Hitler called it a "dream toy"), and
when it was used in the final year of the war it was too late to
have a major effect on its outcome. Nevertheless, it was German
rocket technology that formed the basis for the American missile program: more than one hundred German scientists, including Wernher von Braun and other ex-Space Travelers, as

well as a number of V-2 rockets were shipped to the United States.* Under von Braun's technical leadership the American program built and successfully launched larger and larger rockets, culminating in the enormous Saturn which propelled the Apollo mission to the moon.

An earlier technology that frequently placed different societies in the position of having to make a difficult choice was the gun. In some ways the gun could be said to represent a particularly potent form of the Western inundation of non-Western cultures, which had either to adopt the gun or to perish by it. This was especially true of technologically backward cultures, such as those of Africa or the Americas, for whom the technology that produced the gun was hopelessly unattainable; the episode of the Ghost Dance typifies the frustration of a culture that was faced with a number of new technologies—including the gun —that it could neither fathom nor assimilate.

The situation in Asia was very different. The Arabs, the Indians, and the Chinese represent old civilizations, and the Chinese had actually invented gunpowder and manufactured cannon before the arrival of the Europeans. Others, such as the Ottoman Turks or the Moghuls in India, adopted artillery very rapidly and were soon manufacturing their own. In any case, in Asia, ignorance of firearms by no means implied a lack of other technical skills, so that there were usually no technical impediments to the introduction of the gun. The technological gap (as it would be called today) between Asia and Europe in the fourteenth century was not large, and the adoption of European devices did not make the Ottomans or the Japanese into client states, a condition that characterizes so many less-developed countries today. For all these reasons it is interesting to examine how some of these cultures dealt

---

*A large number of scientists and one hundred V-2 rockets also found their way to the Soviet Union.

with the introduction of the new technology of firearms.

It is generally agreed that the decisive defeat of the Mamelukes by the Ottomans in 1514 was due primarily to the Turks' mastery of the gun. According to David Ayalon, the Mamelukes knew about guns long before the Turks, and were the first Islamic people to use cannon, beginning in 1360, a full sixty years before the Ottoman Turks. But although they had a long experience with guns, the Mamelukes never were able to integrate them into their way of life.

The origin of the Mamelukes is curious. They were of Circassian origin and had been brought to Egypt as slaves from their native Caucasus, a region corresponding roughly to present-day Georgia. They were a warlike people and superb horsemen, and came to dominate the Egyptian society they were intended to serve. They elected the Sultan, staffed the army, and established a self-perpetuating military élite which for almost three hundred years ruled an empire that included Egypt, Syria, and parts of Arabia. Like their European counterparts, the Mameluke knights had an elaborate code of chivalry based largely on horsemanship.

One of the reasons the Mamelukes had been so quick to adopt the cannon—only forty years after it started to be used in Europe—was that their military activities consisted in frequently having to attack, or defend, fortifications. The cannon was such an obvious improvement to the mechanical catapult that the Sultan quickly established a foundry and was turning out artillery in great quantities. While cannons were sometimes portable—being towed to use in a siege—there is no record of their being used on the open battlefield. Here the cavalry charge and the bow and spear remained the principal weapons.

In Europe the cannon was eventually produced in a form small enough to be used by an individual soldier. The weapon was called an arquebus and was a primitive ancestor of the rifle. The arquebus was fired by lighting a match, which in turned exploded the gunpowder, and first appeared in the middle of

the fourteenth century. While they were awkward, crude, and
often misfired, they were much cheaper to manufacture than
cannon, and large numbers of foot soldiers could be equipped
at relatively little expense. The Ottomans were quick to incorporate the weapon into their army, and it was a major factor in
the rapid expansion of their empire. The Mamelukes, on the
other hand, ignored it.

The attitude of the Mameluke knights toward firearms was
one of contempt, not dissimilar to the attitude of British cavalry
officers toward the tank. Horsemanship, as in England, was not
just a skill but a mark of class distinction and moral superiority
—in Egypt only the Mamelukes owned horses—and that was
the problem: to use the arquebus the knights would have to get
off their horses and fight on foot, since the heavy weapon could
not be used in the saddle. This they refused to do. This refusal
(with which they effectively committed military suicide) was
underlined some years later when the arquebus was finally altered into what became known as a horse-pistol—a weapon that
could be fired by a rider. The Mamelukes then showed no
resistance to its use, although it was too late to alter history—
Egypt was already under Ottoman rule. The same pattern of
rejection and then acceptance of the gun is observed by Ayalon
among the nomadic Bedouin, who began to use guns only when
they could be fired from horse- or camelback.

While the Mamelukes continued to reject the arquebus, the
Ottoman Empire continued to grow, finally coming in contact
with the Mameluke kingdom. The Sultan, who was unable to
convince his knights to use guns, formed a regiment of arquebusiers which was composed of black slaves—the untouch-
ables of Mameluke society. It was a short-lived experiment which
he was forced to stop at the insistence of the outraged knights,
who threatened him with insurrection. The idea of arming
slaves offended their military code of honor, and also, one sus-
pects, their social position. When the final confrontation with
the Turks came, it was bows and arrows and chivalry against

powder and bullets, and the Mamelukes were decisively, and horribly, defeated.

The story of the Mamelukes contains many imponderables. What if they had been inventive enough to develop the horse-pistol? What if, like the British aristocracy in the twentieth century, they had been able to preserve horsemanship for fox-hunting and steeple chasing, while adjusting their military tactics to the new infantry weapon? Or what if, like the Ottoman Janissaries, they had had a tradition of infantry archers and were easily able to swap the bow for the gun? There was no technical obstacle that accounts for the Mamelukes' rejection of the gun, only the conditions present within their own society.

If one does not plunge through the door that has been opened by some new device like the arquebus, might one enter the door and then change one's mind and back out? Not long after the Mamelukes lost a kingdom by rejecting the gun, the Japanese used the gun to create one. They resolutely opened that particular door and marched in . . . and, about one hundred years later, gingerly edged out.

When Commodore Perry of the United States navy visited Japan in 1853, he found a society that was technologically advanced in many ways—a culture which, while strange to him, could hardly be called primitive. But there was one field that seemed antiquated—weaponry. Except for some rather obsolete cannons, the Japanese had virtually no knowledge of firearms, and their principal weapons were, by Western standards, medieval: the sword, spear, and bow. Understandably, Perry and subsequent American visitors took this lamentable anachronism to be a sign of uninventiveness, a state of affairs that they rapidly undertook to redress. What they did not know was that the gun had come to Japan about three hundred years before.

The arquebus was first introduced to that country in 1543 by the Portuguese, and the martial Japanese quickly adopted the new weapon and began manufacturing it themselves. Like the

Ottomans and the Mamelukes, they had a fairly advanced
metallurgical industry; Japanese copper was traded as far away
as Europe, while Japanese swords and armor were exported
throughout Asia. Soon the arquebus and small cannon were
integrated into this arms trade.

Guns had come to Japan at a particularly auspicious moment.
Feudal leaders such as Oda Nobunaga and his successor
Toyotomi Hideyoshi were in the process of forcibly unifying the
several hundred semi-independent principalities into one nation, and the gun proved to be a useful tool in this process. This
warlike period of consolidation lasted almost a hundred years,
and the universal use of firearms had a number of important
effects on Japanese society, according to Delmer M. Brown, a
historian of the period. The Japanese army, which had previously consisted largely of individual fighting men, was now composed of interrelated groups of specialists. Gunners, archers,
and swordsmen began fighting as coordinated units, the one
giving way to the other during the course of the battle. The
advantage thus shifted to the army, which had a strong, centralized command, something that definitely favored Nobunaga
against his splintered rivals, and speeded the unification process. The arquebus was most effectively used if the gunners
were located behind breastworks or fortifications and the
enemy was induced to charge. This kind of fighting inevitably
lead to the construction of castles and of castle towns—which
had the indirect effect of stimulating urbanization and promoting commerce and industry within the country.

And the Japanese had no difficulty in assimilating the gun.
Although they used horses, the samurai traditionally fought on
foot, and unlike the Mamelukes, whom the samurai knights in
some ways resembled, they had no compunction about using
firearms. The Japanese also proved to be much more innovative
and flexible as regards military tactics, which they were prepared to alter to suit the new weapon; and while the arquebus
may have originally been a foreign device, the way in which it

was used was uniquely Japanese. They had large regiments of arquebusiers who fired in rank and on command, a tactic Europeans would not discover until some time later. Indeed, at the same time the Japanese were enthusiastically learning to shoot, there was much opposition to the gun in Europe. The Chevalier Bayard, who died in 1524 (of an arquebus ball), so hated firearms that he would hang any captured arquebusier on the spot. It is all the more surprising, therefore, to discover that during the shogunate of Tokugawa Ieyasu, who followed Hideyoshi and established a dynasty that was to rule for more than two hundred years, firearms all but disappeared from use.

Lest the reader jump to any hasty conclusions, there was never any Ban-the-Gun movement in Tokugawa Japan. The repudiation of firearms, which was never total, would be best described as a loss of interest. Small quantities of cannon and arquebuses continued to be manufactured, but as far as the development of the technology was concerned, there was simply stagnation. No attempts were made to improve the matchlock, as the Europeans were to do, although this would have been quite within the capacity of the Japanese craftsmen, who already were acquainted with the flint lighter and could have easily substituted it for the awkward burning match. When Dutch traders presented the shogun with two flintlock pistols in 1636, these improved weapons were apparently treated as curios and no attempt was made to copy them. By then the gun, which had played such an important role in the unification of Japan, was obsolete, not technologically but culturally.

The most striking aspect of this obsolescence was the almost total replacement of the gun as a personal weapon by the sword. This cannot be explained by a simple dislike of the technology, since guns were used and highly prized as hunting weapons. It was their use on the battlefield that was called into question, for aesthetic and moral reasons. To oversimplify the matter, the gun was considered too inelegant a way to kill an enemy.

Miyamoto Musashi, who became known as *"Kensei"* or "sword saint," was one of the most famous samurai of that period. In 1645, a few weeks before his death, he completed a treatise on *Kendo* (the Way of the Sword) which would become a classic. In *A Book of Five Rings* he reflected the attitude of his contemporaries when he differentiated between masters of the long sword, whom he called strategists, and masters of the bow, spear, *and* the gun, who were simply referred to as archers, spearmen, and marksmen. To master the virtue of the long sword, according to Musashi, was "to govern the world and oneself"; the other weapons were only utilitarian "warriors' equipment." Characteristically, the book, which is really a guide to strategy, dealt with that subject almost exclusively in the context of sword-fighting.

For Musashi, as for all samurai, the sword became much more than a weapon. It was a symbol of status—no one else was allowed to wear the long sword—and also, as in other sword societies, a kind of fetish. One has only to think of the dubbing of medieval European knights, or even of the decorative but symbolic daggers issued to soldiers of the Third Reich, to find parallels in other cultures. But more than a fetish, the sword, and sword-play, were for the samurai a kind of religion, and the fencing hall, or *dojo,* was usually located adjacent to a shrine or temple.

The attitude of the samurai to the sword as a "moral weapon" was similar to that of European aristocrats of the nineteenth century, for whom the *arme blanche*—the sword and the lance —were superior weapons, not the least because they were the weapons of gentlemen. "It must be accepted as a principle," proclaimed a 1907 British military manual *(Cavalry Training)* "that the rifle, effective as it is, cannot replace the effect produced by the speed of the horse, the magnetism of the charge, and the terror of cold steel." The same self-justifying sentiment was expressed much earlier by one of the Mameluke generals, who boasted, "They [the Ottomans] have no knowledge of *furūsīya* [the martial arts] and of horsemanship. All they have is arquebusiers and infantrymen. So when we clash with them, we shall give them one push and put them under the hooves of our horses."* The samurai, perhaps lacking the arrogance of the cavalryman, were less self-deluding, but they shared the same belief in the moral superiority of certain weapons.

The Tokugawa period was characterized by a highly centralized political and social system that bore many resemblances to European feudalism. To maintain law and order in the newly unified country, a rigid class system was established which consisted of four categories—samurai, farmers, artisans, and merchants. The military arts underwent a renaissance: new *dojos* were built in the castle towns and fencing occupied the interest of the élite samurai class. The gun did not fit comfortably into this chivalric revival, but its use was also curtailed for another reason. The presence of large numbers of *heimin*—common people—armed with arquebuses posed a serious threat to the stability of the new state, and in 1588, Hideyoshi enacted a law that prohibited peasants from keeping firearms. Later, after the cessation of the war with Korea and China, the functional necessity of guns was greatly reduced, and their use within the country was almost eliminated.

Not that a gunless Japan was such a peaceful place. There is no reason to romanticize Japan's reversion to the sword, as Noel Perrin has done in a recent monograph on the subject. Tokugawa Japan may have been "prosperous and civilized," as he says, but it was so for a relatively small number of people. The two-hundred-and-sixty-year dynasty was marked by over *one thousand* peasant uprisings of one sort or another, usually by landless farmers protesting excessive rents and taxes.† These disturbances were swiftly and harshly quelled, and since the historical record shows that peasants were frequently shot at,

*See David Ayalon.
†See Hugh Borton.

we must assume that some guns were kept in storage for use in such eventualities. While the use of firearms in such instances was relatively rare, it does serve to remind us that the gun was not rejected out of any sentiment of nonviolence, but to preserve a cruel and despotic social structure that favored one particular group. Not surprisingly, the end of feudalism occurred as it had earlier in Europe, when an army of samurai was defeated by an army of common people. Needless to say, the *heimin* used guns.

At this point I should add that there was a similarity between Ranavalona's reaction to foreigners and Japan's during the Tokugawa period. Like Madagascar, Japan was an island state that had had contact with Europe through traders and missionaries, and had expelled both and declared Christianity illegal. Like Ranavalona, the shogun forbade any foreign ships from calling in Japanese ports and moreover prohibited his subjects from traveling abroad. But unlike Madagascar or Burma, Japan remained virtually isolated from the rest of the world for two hundred years.

Yet the rejection of firearms was something quite different from what had occurred among the Boxers or among the Dakota Sioux. By the time of the Tokugawas, the gun had become an indigenous weapon and had been incorporated into Japanese culture in an unambiguous way. Both the weapon and the way it was used were "Made in Japan." The Japanese, unlike the Sioux, were not threatened with extinction—quite the opposite; their attempt to invade Korea and China had very nearly succeeded thanks to their mastery of firearms. The loss of interest in guns was not an attempt to turn back the clock, but rather the putting aside of a technology that was seen as a possible threat to a *newly* established social order. As in the previous examples, the reasons for the choice were not technical. Japan in the seventeenth century was a relatively advanced civilization, not only in mining and metallurgy, but also in agriculture and civil engineering. In some fields, such as paper manufacturing, domestic building, and public sanitation, it was probably the most advanced culture of that time. Thus the setting aside of the gun was not a return to primitivism. The gun had been required for the successful unification of Japan, and it was dispensed with because it was no longer needed, and also because it was no longer wanted.

I am closing with a digression. The theme of this chapter has been that society determines the use of technology—even war technology. While the Mamelukes may have suffered ultimate defeat because they were unable to adopt firearms, one generally feels relieved when a military technology is set aside, for the rejection of a particular method of maiming or killing is not usually a cause for regret. Sometimes, however, the rejection of a military technology seems to represent, on balance, a loss and not a gain. The following curious story is such an example.

The mast atop the Empire State Building is often described as a radio tower, but its original function was quite different. In 1929, the first postwar German rigid airship, the *Graf Zeppelin*, completed a round-the-world flight. The purpose of this highly publicized feat, which was partly sponsored by the newspaper chain of William Randolph Hearst, was frankly propagandizing. Hugo Eckener, director of the Zeppelin Company and captain of its only airship, needed to raise public confidence—and investment capital—in order to establish a commercial airline service between Europe and America.

The year before, the *Graf Zeppelin* had carried twenty paying passengers across the Atlantic, inaugurating the first such commercial service. This proved that transoceanic flight was not reserved for daredevils such as Charles Lindbergh or Amelia Earhart, but could be accomplished safely and comfortably by anyone with the price of a ticket, which in that case had been a steep three thousand dollars one way (this later was reduced to four hundred dollars). The first flight of the *Graf* had been a great public success; the airship had circled Baltimore, New

York, and Washington, and Eckener had survived a Broadway ticker-tape parade and breakfast with President Coolidge.

The subsequent flight around the world had received even more attention, thanks to the Hearst newspapers, and was an even greater success. The twenty-one-thousand-mile journey was completed in three weeks, and the passengers experienced such exotic sights as the Siberian steppes and a Japanese typhoon. There were no technical difficulties, and the great range of the airship required only three refueling stops—in Berlin, Tokyo, and Los Angeles. When Eckener returned to New York —the flight began and ended at the Statue of Liberty—he was met with even more enthusiasm than the year before. Enormous crowds turned out in San Francisco, Los Angeles, and Chicago, and in New York everyone was caught up in Zeppelin fever. Al Smith, who had once run for president and whose construction company was then completing the Empire State Building, announced that he would add an airship mooring mast to the top of the building so that New York would be ready for the coming Age of the Airship.*

The airship that circled the world was named after Count Ferdinand von Zeppelin, whose protégé Eckener had been, and who was the inventor of the rigid airship. Strangely enough, his first ascent in a balloon had been in America, where he was a German observer during the Civil War. After incurring the displeasure of the Kaiser, he was forced to retire from the army and, at the relatively advanced age of fifty-two, set his energy, as well as his personal fortune, to the task of building a dirigible airship. The very first craft he built was a gigantic 416 feet long and flew for only eighteen minutes. That flight occurred in 1900, after ten years of preparation, but it would be some time before a successful airship was finally built. Zeppelin's experiments oscillated between disaster and triumph. Of the seven

---

*Eckener was successful in attracting many American investors; unfortunately for him, the stock-market crash occurred only two months later.

airships that succeeded the first, six were destroyed, usually while the monstrous crafts were being maneuvered out of their hangars. Finally, the Count's perseverance caught the attention of the German public, and the airship, at that time a uniquely German technology, became a *cause célèbre* and a symbol of the technical prowess of the Second Reich. When the *LZ-4* was destroyed at her mooring during a summer storm, public sentiment was so strongly on the side of the obstinate old cavalry general that over six million marks were donated by public subscription.* The government, which until then had not supported his work, could not ignore such an outpouring of popular sympathy—two airships were ordered for the army, and a relenting Kaiser bestowed the Prussian Order of the Black Eagle on their inventor. The future of the airship seemed assured.

Progress was rapid. In 1909, Zeppelin started the world's first commercial airline. Hangars were built in nine of the larger German cities, and in subsequent years thousands of Germans flew in Zeppelins in both comfort and safety. The interior of the vehicle resembled a Pullman railroad car, and the twenty or so passengers were served lunch from a restaurant equipped with a fireless stove that ingeniously used the hot engine exhaust gases for cooking. Travel in an airship was quiet and, with a top speed of fifty miles an hour, sedate.

But the craft was soon to find itself used for a purpose very different from sightseeing. Ever since Zeppelin saw balloons being used by French artillery spotters during the Franco-Prussian War, the military potential of the dirigible had been in the back of his mind, and while looking for government support for his first experiments, he had written to the German army that the airship could be profitably used for "bombardment of enemy fortresses or troop concentrations with projectiles." With the advent of the First World War, the long range of the airship

---

*The public seems always to have had an affection for airships. Twenty years later, Eckener financed three-quarters of the cost of the *Graf Zeppelin* from individual donations; the world flight was paid for in large part by the sale of special stamps to thousands of collectors.

offered the possibility of bombing English cities. Although the
Kaiser was loath to make personal attacks on his royal English
cousins (and expressly forbade any raids on Buckingham Palace), he was less concerned about English commoners. Thus it
was the airship that initiated one of the most hateful aspects of
modern war—the indiscriminate killing of noncombatants.

While the airship was used to bomb Warsaw, Bucharest, and
Paris, as well as purely military objectives, it was England and
especially London that became its main target. Soon the Zeppelin Company was building an average of one airship every two
weeks, and fleets of as many as a dozen airships made hundreds
of raids. These attacks occurred at night, which made them
more or less invulnerable to both airplane attack and the rudimentary antiaircraft defenses of the time. "Zepp nights" came
to be awaited with apprehension by the British public, and for
a while it seemed that the demoralization and destruction the
German generals had hoped for would be a major factor in
winning the war.

This did not happen. For one thing, simply reaching the
target could not always be predicted, since weather forecasting
was erratic and the airships were often blown off course. Navigation technology was also crude, and bombs were frequently
dropped on the wrong targets, causing little damage. Finally,
partway through the war the pendulum of weapon technology,
which had up to then favored the Zeppelins, began to swing.
Mobility was canceled out by a new sort of hitting power in the
form of the incendiary bullet. Phosphorus-coated bullets, which
were not used at the beginning of the war, caused the "enormous bladder of combustible and explosive gas"—as Winston
Churchill called it—to turn into a flying firetrap. Airships began
to go down in flames at an alarming rate.

The Zeppelin builders had few options. They had no substitute for the inflammable hydrogen gas that supported the dirigible, nor any way to increase its speed. The only alternative
was to fly higher than either artillery or airplanes could reach.
By the end of the war, Zeppelins were operating at altitudes

over 20,000 feet, but in the unpressurized cabins, the crews suffered from lack of oxygen and frostbite. Dazed and lightheaded they were barely able to function. Nor was navigation at such high altitudes any easier; one airship, sent to bomb Birmingham, dropped its bombs on a small town one hundred miles away. The vagaries of high-altitude weather also complicated flights, particularly because airships lost much of their power and were unable to resist strong head winds.

The most notable achievement of the airship during the war occurred in 1917, and although that event received less attention than the dramatic bombing raids on London, it demonstrated the remarkable abilities of this device. A specially extended Zeppelin was sent to supply beleaguered colonial troops in German East Africa, a distance of over 3,000 miles from its departure point in Bulgaria. While the military aim was not realized (the Zeppelin was ordered to return only 400 miles short of its destination), the nonstop flight was a feat of aviation that would not be equaled until the *Graf Zeppelin*'s round-the-world journey twelve years later.

Although as a weapon the airship was more or less discredited by the end of the war, the victorious Allies were not taking any chances with the hated "baby-killers," and the Treaty of Versailles forbade the construction of airships altogether. As an added precaution, the entire airship industry was dismantled. The remaining army and navy airships were apportioned to the victors—England, France, and Italy; Japan received not just an airship, but an entire hangar as well. In 1919, when Eckener revived the commercial airline with two civilian airships, they were immediately confiscated by the Allies as belated war reparations, and the airline was ordered to close. The airship, which had been a symbol of Germany's prewar prowess, was now to be a mark of its ignominious defeat, and the Zeppelin Company survived by turning to the manufacture of aluminum kitchen utensils. It would be almost a decade before Eckener would slowly revive the industry and build the *Graf Zeppelin*. *

Eckener's later triumphs seemed to indicate that although finished as a weapon, the airship still had a role to play as civilian transportation, and the mast atop the Empire State Building was witness to that fact. But only Germany had the experience, the technical ability, and the interest to develop airship travel. And Germany finally chose not to develop the airship. Why?

It is popularly assumed that it was the crash of the *Hindenburg*, the successor to the *Graf Zeppelin*, that sealed the fate of the airship, but that is debatable. Until the wreck of the *Hindenburg*, not one civilian passenger had been injured in a Zeppelin (the first airship fatality had occurred in 1912, when a naval Zeppelin crashed into the North Sea). Although thirty-five persons died in the *Hindenburg* crash, including fifteen passengers, it should be remembered that sixty-one persons survived. The freak accident, never properly explained, occurred in spite of many safety precautions that had been incorporated into the new ship, including the use of diesel, rather than gasoline, engines, and the *Hindenburg* had been designed for helium, a nonflammable gas, rather than hydrogen, in anticipation of the day when the United States—the only major source of natural helium—would permit its export. Tragic as the accident was, it does not explain the abandonment of airship travel. When almost fifteen hundred people died aboard the *Titanic* (a real disaster), ocean-going liners were not withdrawn from service. When fifty people died in one of the first serious commercial airplane crashes—that of a DC-6 in Colorado in 1951—safety precautions were reassessed and improved, but no one suggested that air travel be given up altogether. The real reason for the disappearance of the airship lies elsewhere.

In 1935, two years before the crash of the *Hindenburg*, there

---

*Douglas Robinson speculates that had Germany won the war, airship technology and personnel would almost certainly have ensured the rapid proliferation of transoceanic airship services. A still-extant German colonial empire would have made good use of the long-range passenger airship.

was still only one airship in operation, in spite of the success of the transatlantic and round-the-world flights. The *Graf Zeppelin* flew scheduled flights to South America, made a tour of the Mediterranean, and even flew to the Arctic. But funds for expansion were unavailable. The stock-market crash and the Depression had made it impossible for Eckener to raise enough money to establish a regular service between Germany and the Americas, leaving only one other source of funds available—the German government, which by then meant the National Socialist government. Eckener, a popular figure and well-known anti-Nazi, did not expect much help from Hitler's party, but surprisingly, it was made available. A new airship company was formed, with half the shares owned by Lufthansa, the state-controlled airline.

The Nazis had their own reasons for supporting the airship, and these were other than military. Hermann Göring, who was then air minister and had been a flying ace during the First World War, refused even to board a Zeppelin and contemptuously referred to it as a "gas bag"; Hitler, likewise disliked the airship.* It was probably Joseph Goebbels, the minister of propaganda, who first realized the public-relations value of the by now world-famous Zeppelin. With the formation of the new airship company, the Zeppelin became an official extension of the Third Reich. Goebbels personally ordered Eckener to display the swastika on his airships, and after 1935, a twenty-foot-high *hakenkreuz* adorned the tail fin of the *Graf* and of the two subsequent Zeppelins. The airship played an important role in various party rallies and public events: during the Rhineland plebiscite, the *Graf* and the *Hindenburg* were both used to

---

*Walter Dornberger asked Hitler if he had ever been on board an airship, to which the Führer answered, "No. Nor shall I ever get into an airship. The whole thing always seems to me like an inventor who claims to have discovered a cheap new kind of floor covering, which looks marvelous, shines forever, and never wears out. But he adds that there is one disadvantage. It must not be walked on with nailed shoes, and nothing must ever be dropped on it because, unfortunately, it's made of high explosive. No, I shall never get into an airship."

broadcast political speeches through loud-speakers and to drop leaflets, and when the Olympic Games were opened in Berlin, the *Hindenburg*, now increasingly known as the "Nazi ship," flew overhead.

Of course, the Nazis had no real interest in the airship as either a weapon or a commercial technology. It was only a means of "showing the swastika" at home and abroad. As soon as war broke out, Göring ordered the last two remaining Zeppelins to be destroyed, on the pretext that their aluminum frames were needed for plane construction. The giant airship hangar was dynamited and the company disbanded.

So the airship was finally displaced by the airplane; but not in the way one might think. It is easy enough today to see that the plane is enormously faster than the airship and is its inevitable successor, but in the 1930s this was by no means obvious. The first commercial transport plane in the United States was the Boeing 247, introduced in 1933, and while it could fly more than twice as fast as the stately *Hindenburg*, it carried only ten passengers instead of fifty and had a range of less than a thousand miles instead of the airship's eight thousand. As a result of these limitations, when the first transoceanic airplane service was introduced in 1935, it took longer to hop from island to island across the Pacific than it had taken to cross in the *Graf Zeppelin* six years earlier. As for the Atlantic, regular passenger flights did not commence until 1939, and the first nonstop flights did not occur until the mid-1950s. Until that time and the development of long-range airplanes, the airship was a faster, and considerably cheaper, way of crossing oceans.* No, it was not the passenger plane that brought about the demise of the airship.

It was the *war* plane that signaled the end of the airship. The plane had clearly proved itself superior to the slow and bulky

---

*Douglas Robinson quotes F. Willy von Meister, the American representative of the *Zeepelin Reederei*, who stated that, had it not been for political factors, such as the post–First World War dismantling of the airship industry or the American refusal to sell helium to the Nazis, there was no technical reason why the airship could not have survived until 1950.

airship as a weapon, and this lesson was not lost on any government after the war. The fact that airships were popular with the public counted for little. While it is true that the British did attempt to establish an imperial airship service, it was a hurried and ill-conceived effort which resulted in the spectacular crash of the R-101 on its maiden flight to India in 1930. American interest in the airship was strictly military, but after the loss of the *Macon* and the *Akron*, both of which were filled with helium and carried scout planes in their cavernous interiors, airship experiments were discontinued. The Germans, perhaps because of their war experience, never tried to develop military airships after 1918. The Italians and the French, who had pioneered nonrigid and semirigid airships, had only a desultory interest in the rigid airships they acquired as war-reparation payment, and did not build any of their own. The Japanese never even bothered to unpack their German Zeppelin from its crates.

This then was the reason for the disappearance of the airship —its failure as a weapon in a period when weapons were what governments wanted. It was not its technological limitations, or public rejection, or some sort of inevitable "progress" that brought an end to the airship, but rather a choice to pursue one technology rather than another. A disappointed Eckener wrote in his autobiography, "what good is the airship to the contemporary politician or State which is following a policy of ruthless pursuit of power and national safety, when the airship, considered from a military point of view, has become completely worthless? Every penny which a State spends nowadays in promoting aviation is lavished on airplanes, which can be weapons of the greatest value." Dinosaurlike though it may have looked, the rigid airship did not disappear according to any Darwinian law of technological selection. It is ironic that just as the door to the development of the airship was opened by its perceived, and real, ability to wreak violence, so it was finally closed because it was not violent enough.

CHAPTER 8

TECHNOLOGY IS NOT EVERYTHING

No civilization says no to all the new goods, but each one gives them a particular individual significance.

—Fernand Braudel, *On History*

Technology is controlled in three ways, two of which I have already described: the actual design of the device, which is always an attempt to reduce its unpredictability and the choice of whether or not, or when, to use the machine. Although the exercising of choice can be a potent form of controlling technology, as the previous chapter has shown, it is unusual since it tends to be a drastic decision with often unpredictable results. There is no guarantee that rejecting a particular device today will have the desired effect tomorrow. Fortunately, there is a third way to control technology which is much less drastic and more subtle. In fact, it is so obvious that it is often overlooked.

Before describing the third way of controlling the machine, it will be necessary to introduce a concept that the French historian Fernand Braudel has characterized as the difference between civilization, in the singular, and civilizations, in the plural. According to him, *civilization* relates to humanity as a whole. It reflects what could be called "the spirit of the age" or the dominant global culture, which at present is without a doubt the civilization of technical and material progress. But at the same time as one can speak of civilization, one must distinguish particular, individual *civilizations*—those identifiable areas of culture that are scattered in both time and space, and, unlike global civilization, are usually historic phenomena of extremely long duration.

The importance of Braudel's double definition is that it allows us to see that there are really two things occurring. There is the civilization of technology, but there are also individual civilizations, including our own, which confront the global culture. It is thus necessary to distinguish French civilization from technological civilization in general, and to recognize the former as a presence that predates, and will certainly outlast, the Machine Age. In a similar way, we can speak of Indian civilization both before and after British rule, though obviously we can also show that this civilization was deeply affected by its contact with Britain, a country that represented, at the time, the spirit of that age.

While ours may be a civilization that is mainly technological, it is hardly exclusively so, and similarly, the presence of a global technological civilization does not need to preclude the possibility of other, nontechnological civilizations and cultures. The way these various civilizations deal with the technological civilization constitutes the third type of technological control.

Of course, not everyone agrees that there is a dialogue between the predominant technological civilization and the various individual civilizations of the world; according to some critics, it is strictly a one-way conversation. Jacques Ellul goes so far as to call the diffusion of modern technology a "technical invasion" of the technologically less-developed countries. According to him, this transfer of ideas and devices "does not involve the simple addition of new values to old ones. It does not put new wine into old bottles; it does not introduce new content into old forms. The old bottles are all being broken. The old civilizations collapse on contact with the new" *(The Technological Society)*. Ivan Illich has described the same process in even harsher terms, as a kind of plot against cultures that must survive the "machined might of the developed nations" by outwitting them, something Illich feels can be achieved only if the global technological civilization is rejected *(Toward a History of Needs)*. So popular are these gloomy prognostications that they are accepted not only by those who berate the industrialized countries for "imposing" their technology on the rest of the world, but even by advocates of modernization. Thus Peter Drucker, an economist who often refers to the less-developed countries as simply "under-managed," agrees with Ellul's and Illich's underlying assumption when he writes, "The great, perhaps the central, event of our time is the disappearance of all non-Western societies and cultures under the inundation of Western technology."

The problem with what could be called the Great Flood Theory of technological progress is that it ignores the possibility that civilization and particular civilizations can coexist. It mistakenly assumes that one displaces the other, and also, with not a little arrogance, equates technological civilization with Western civilization, putting the West firmly on the winning side. This attitude is similar to that of the European explorers of the sixteenth century who set out with sword and cross to "civilize" the world (and took it for granted that it was *un*civilized). While civilization, whether in the form of making soap or eliminating slavery, did spread, civilization in Japan or in China continued to be an "identifiable area of culture." The same continues to be true today. The Great Flood Theory is much too simplistic an explanation for what is a complex process—not the replacement of one civilization by another, but a confrontation between the global civilization of technology and individual civilizations. The ensuing process of change and adaptation, while often violent and disruptive, is by no means predetermined.

Frequently, the same people who accuse technology of being the great leveler almost in the same breath complain that it has failed because there is too much inequality in the world. This is a telling contradiction. One would expect that a technological inundation would leave the world a more or less consistent place—opulent or miserable, as the case may be—but at least similar. In a flood, after all, everyone gets wet—unless some people know how to build boats, or live on high mountains, or get together to build dykes, or, like Noah, get advance warning. This is exactly what different civilizations have been doing with regard to technology. While the technological gap between Europe and Asia in the fourteenth century was quite small (although it was very large between Europe and the Americas), in the nineteenth and twentieth centuries it has become very wide indeed. Even if there is no straightforward division into rich and poor, as some claim, there is certainly a wide spectrum ranging from very rich to very poor, and different countries are characterized by an extremely uneven distribution of both technology and wealth. Some countries are getting wetter than others. That this is unfair is undeniable, that it is immoral is debatable, but in any case it does point up the fact that technology is not the only factor in the equation. As Braudel observes, by opening up the fan of human possibilities, progress has also widened the range of differences. It is these differences, and especially the different ways in which technology is used, that underscore the heterogeneity of the modern world.

To explain this heterogeneity it is not enough to consider only the tool; one must not ignore the tool-user. The attitude of the tool-user is, in turn, a reflection of his or her civilization and greatly affects the way that the tool is used, not only the mechanics of its use in the narrow functional sense, although even that can vary considerably, but also in the broader, social sense.

Consider the button, a common device that has had an enormous impact on clothing with regard to both appearance and function. Before the button, clothing was held together by sashes or belts, or by some way of folding or wrapping material around the body, or by being loose enough to be pulled over the head. But while loose clothing is comfortable in the tropics, it is less appropriate in temperate climates where snug garments are required for better protection against cold winds, and where outer garments need to be easily and quickly taken off on entering a warmed interior. It should not be a surprise that the button originated in northern Europe, although one might have expected this to have occurred earlier than the thirteenth century.* It took so long to discover the button not because of any technical obstacle, but because of the leap of imagination that was required to conceive of the geometry of the button and the buttonhole. The button did not occur either to the ancient Egyptians and Greeks, who lived in warm climates, or to the Romans, who did not.

When the button finally appeared, it was not an immediate popular success. If one examines the engravings and woodcuts of a German artist such as Albrecht Dürer, who paid a good deal of attention to the detail of costumes, one is immediately struck by the paucity of buttoned garments. Occasionally there appears a buttoned shirt or soutane, but by and large, rich or poor, all the men and women wear belted tunics, loose pullovers, or flowing capes. And Dürer lived about three hundred years *after* the first introduction of this new fastening device.

One reason for slowness in adopting any change in clothing may be, as Braudel suggests, that when society remains more or less stable, everything else stays put *(Capitalism and Material Life 1400–1800)*. Extended periods of stability, such as the European Middle Ages, tend to freeze fashion as much for the rich as for the poor, and it was not until the turbulent seven-

*See White, "The Act of Invention."

teenth century that the button became the main feature of men's, and to a lesser extent of women's, clothing. The coat and vest, both of which rely on buttons to achieve their shape, became popular at this time and formed the basis of a garment which, after various transformations, continues to the present day. After a frenetic period when a gentleman wore literally dozens of buttons, from wrist to elbow and from neck to knee, the button settled into a more utilitarian existence, until only the superfluous buttons on men's jacket sleeves remain to remind us of its jubilee days. Even the military, which once took great stock in displaying a profusion of embossed brass buttons, maintains them only on ceremonial uniforms.

By now the button can be said to be part of world civilization. But how has it affected particular cultures? Frequently, they have shown themselves to be no more hasty in adopting the device than were our medieval ancestors. The Japanese, although they live in a country with cold winters, were ignorant of the device, and seemed reluctant to use it even after its introduction by the early Portuguese explorers. Throughout the Tokugawa period the traditional *kasane,* or loose tunic, was worn with various skirtlike lower garments, all of which were fastened by a sash or belt; women wore kimonos—long gowns held at the waist by an extremely wide sash. It was not until the stability of the Tokugawa regime was terminated by the end of feudalism, and of the country's isolation, that clothing styles began to undergo significant changes. The new conscript army, for instance, wore uniforms with buttons, and buttoned clothing began to be worn increasingly by businessmen and professionals. At the same time—and this reveals much about Japanese culture—the button has never been incorporated into the traditional Japanese costume.

The impact of the button on clothing in India is interesting and seems to support Braudel's suggestion that clothing is a method of communication, not only of status and wealth, but also of values. The fact that Nehru wore buttoned clothing, while Mohandas Gandhi did not, was indicative of the difference in attitude between the two men. Even more striking is the fact that buttons, when they are worn in India today, are worn almost exclusively by men; women, even policewomen, wear saris, which rely on wrapping rather than on any mechanical closing devices. Does this mean that the woman is the custodian of traditional Indian culture? Or does it reflect the fact that in modern India the role of the woman is still, by and large (Prime Minister Indira Gandhi notwithstanding), essentially unchanged?

The creative Chinese were the only civilization outside Europe to have invented something close to the button—the toggle and loop. The toggle was known in Europe but was rarely used on clothing—it was a marine device (hence the naval duffle coat, one of the few Western garments that use toggles). The button is slightly easier to use than the toggle, being less bulky, but although the Chinese probably knew about buttons from their contact with the Portuguese, they did not adopt them in their clothing. Chinese costumes changed little during the Ming and Ch'ing dynasties, a period that lasted over five hundred years, and it was not until the twentieth century and the Chinese Revolution that clothing changed radically. The *po kua,* a long gown for men, and the *chang san,* a slit dress for women, both disappeared. The new mandarins of the People's Republic abandoned the gold-embroidered coats of their predecessors, and instead wore the now well-known dark blue cotton jacket and trousers. But if the so-called Mao jacket is a variation of the traditional *san* and *koo* (jacket and pants), one can search in vain for toggles on the clothing of Communist functionaries. Almost overnight, toggles were replaced by . . . buttons.

Elsewhere, despite the supposed inundation of the world by Western technology, neither the button nor Western dress have made much headway. Asian peasants continue to wear the *dhoti* and the *sarong,* African farmers are enveloped in *djel-*

labahs and *agbadas,* and Latin American *campesinos* wrap themselves in *sarapes* and *ponchos.* It is no coincidence that these costumes (buttonless all) are worn in rural areas that are marked by extreme stability—some would call it stagnation— and the persistence of ancient forms of clothing attests to the immobility of these societies. The point is not that the button is necessarily functionally progressive, but that it often represents progress. It is not necessary to argue for frivolous changes in fashion to recognize that, more often than not, changes in dress reflect important changes in society. New clothes are adopted not necessarily for utilitarian reasons, but as an indication of a new beginning and also as a repudiation of an old passing order, which may be just as important. In this process of repudiation, the button itself can often become a metaphor for change, and thus acquire a significance its forgotten medieval inventor never dreamed of.

The locale for this repudiation of old customs, and old costumes, is almost always the city. It was in the cities of the less-developed countries that buttoned clothing first appeared, and it is in the cities that the universal urban costume—T-shirts and jeans—is found. Indeed, the illustrated T-shirt makes clothing an evident language, whether it proclaims the wearer's allegiance to Mobutu, Muhammad Ali, or Mazda. But above all, the cities demonstrate that in spite of the flood of mopeds, plastic sandals, and transistor radios, the non-Western civilizations are neither prostrate, nor collapsing, nor disappearing.

Every day more than a thousand persons arrive in Bombay or Lagos to live, an immigration that is not due to any natural or political disasters (which, when they occur, only swell the flow), but is a normal fact of life. The immigrants come from villages and hamlets to find employment in the city, or at least to replace the stable poverty of the countryside for the dynamic poverty of the slum, more bearable because it at least contains the promise of change. While the authorities despair, the "exploding cities" grow from two million to five million to ten million and more, without adequate water supply or sewers, without mass transportation or housing or even proper roads. Yet the migration continues, apparently undiscouraged. The largest city in the world is no longer New York or even Tokyo, but Mexico City. The fastest rates of urban growth are no longer in the industrialized cities of Europe, but in the towns of "rural" countries such as Nigeria.

It would be a mistake to suppose that this unprecedented phenomenon is simply a calamity or problem, although it contains elements of both. The farmers and peasants who make the journey to the city in search of jobs do not necessarily travel far in physical terms, but they can traverse centuries of history in one short bus ride. In a matter of hours they leave a preindustrial agrarian culture and arrive in a city that may already have elements of a postindustrial society.

The reasons for the migration are material, certainly. Although some observers have tried to demonstrate that the displaced peasant is no better off in the city slum, the migrants know better than that. The metropolis is no mirage. If life in the city were truly worse than expected, word of this would soon get back to the village, and the flow of people would at least slow down; there is no indication of this happening. But to weigh only the material benefits and costs of leaving the village is to miss the point. The urban migrants are doing something mankind has done for millennia—they are trying something new.

When V. S. Naipaul visited Bombay, he described the slum dwellers as follows: "they saw themselves at the beginning of things: unaccommodated men making a claim on their land for the first time, and out of chaos evolving their own philosophy of community and self-help" *(India: A Wounded Civilization)*. Naipaul saw what most people have missed, that for landless peasants and tenant farmers, trapped in the traditional tyranny of village life, the city can be a gateway, the promise of a new beginning, and their first contact with the global technological civilization. It is no coincidence that in India, as in the Philippines or in Peru, it is the slum dwellers who begin to exercise the political influence which, as peasants, was denied them. It is in the city that they gain access to both the devices and the ideas of the technological civilization.

What is remarkable about the peasant in the city is that he throws off his traditional fatalism and, face to face with a strange and unknown technology, shows himself to be extremely adaptable and inventive, not only to his new surroundings but also to the new tools that suit his needs.

To the frequently scandalized Western observer, the shelter of the urban migrant is a hovel, a shanty or a shack. The neighborhoods are referred to as slums, uncontrolled settlements, squatter settlements (since the builders often do not have legal title to the land), or, more poetically in some countries, *ciudades perdidas*—lost cities. The image of these settlements that is often promoted by international charity organizations is that of hopelessness and despair, of hapless victims ground under the heel of a technological system that they barely understand and whose benefits are forbidden them. Although the last part of this statement may be true given the social inequality that prevails in most of the less-developed countries, the overall impression is misleading. In fact, the urban poor have shown considerable control over their new technological environment, and it is not necessary to denigrate their achievements in order to make the point that assistance is needed.

What is striking about the uncontrolled settlements is precisely that they have been established—and have flourished—without official sanction or support. Electrification and water supply (usually bootlegged from municipal mains) as well as drainage and street layouts are more often than not the work of the poor themselves, sometimes individually, sometimes in groups. Since the building sites are on the least desirable land —marshes and hillsides—they must be excavated or filled in before any construction can begin. Although the houses start as shacks, often little more than some cardboard sheets and left-over plastic, these temporary shelters are soon replaced by more permanent structures which invariably use industrialized building materials such as reinforced concrete, cement blocks, and corrugated iron sheets. Much of this work is substandard, that is to say unofficial, since it is not done by professional build-ers but by the families themselves. But, as the urban planner Tomasz Sudra has observed, it is not the people who build their own houses, which naturally enough reflect their poverty, who constitute a housing problem; paradoxically, it is the authorities who place stumbling blocks in the way of this process who create the problem.

If there is a technical invasion of the less-developed countries, its effects are less visible on the general population than on the bureaucracy. In this instance, it is they who have lost control of technology. They man the ministries of housing—which build little or no housing—and the department of city planning—which cannot plan. Showing none of the pragmatism of the slum dweller, they attempt to put into practice lessons learned in London, Paris, or Prague, trying to build ordered housing estates or tall apartment blocks. Their failed efforts stand empty in Caracas or Bogotá—because no one can afford the rents—surrounded by a sea of the ubiquitous tin-roofed shacks.

Of course, these shacks are the result of improvisation, not design, but it is precisely this that qualifies them as examples of technology under control; it is the user who is manipulating the tool, and not vice versa. I was once invited to give a talk, in Manila, to a group of students in a technical school located in a squatter settlement near the port. I had asked if I could show slides, and Leonard, who was in charge of the school, said he could easily borrow a Kodak projector. Ten minutes before we were to start, we were waiting in the one-room building, and the promised projector was still not delivered. I assumed that we would have to forgo the slides, but I hadn't reckoned on

Leonard. He said he was sure he could make a slide projector —after all, wasn't it just a lens and a light bulb? He started rummaging through the shelves of what appeared to be a pile of scrap but was actually the school's teaching material and soon had found an old lens. Before I had a chance to see just how this improvised device would turn out, however, a more conventional projector suddenly arrived, and the talk began.

For Leonard, as for most of the urban poor, technology is more than simply something to be consumed; more often than not it must first be made to work. As a result, the *significance* of the device is altered. It ceases to be something mysterious or alien and becomes personal and understandable. The attitude toward the machine is also altered; there is less concern about doing something in the approved or "right" way, and more on simply getting it done any way that is possible. This relationship allows the user, metaphorically speaking, to substitute a piece of string for a broken shoelace. It is a state of mind that Americans, who are becoming progressively more intimidated by the machine, are in danger of losing.

Very often, in less-developed countries, technology is used in ways that appear disturbing or incongruous, at least to a Westerner: a television set standing on the dirt floor of a shelter made out of flattened juice tins; an automobile outside a house that has neither a toilet nor running water; a farmer bent double with his hand hoe, and a portable radio hanging from his belt; a saffron-robed Buddhist monk wearing a digital watch; the town market that sells freshly slaughtered goats' heads next to stacks of video cassettes; the hand-carved dugout canoe with a ten-horsepower Evinrude attached to the stern; the wealthy landowner, driving a Range Rover but attired in homespun *khadi*.

Braudel recounts an experience that illustrates this sort of incongruity which occurred while he was traveling by bus across the Algerian desert. The bus, like most modern technology in what was then a French *département*, was certainly foreign, and its operation resembled, one would assume, that of a bus anywhere in France. To Braudel's surprise, and perhaps to the chagrin of some of the passengers, the driver, who was an Arab, would periodically stop the bus, get out, and kneel in the sand to meet his religious obligations. The convergence between the technology of the bus and a particular civilization had produced its own, particular solution.

The bus, which was originally known as the *voiture omnibus,* is a French invention. In America the omnibus was put on tracks—in the Bowery in 1832—and the earliest horse-drawn buses were soon replaced by electrically driven trolleys. Almost every American city had electric trolley cars, but mass transportation was soon threatened by individual automobiles. After the turn of the century, inexpensive automobiles began making their appearance. Even before car ownership became widespread, the automobile competed directly with the bus. Private cars cruised the main trolley lines and for a nickel a jitney—as it was called then—took on passengers. These jitneys became so popular that soon small trucks were being modified with wooden benches, and eventually larger specialized vehicles were built—buses.

A similar process of evolution is taking place in many countries. In Manila, thousands of modified Jeeps (originally left by MacArthur's army), actually known as jitneys, still provide the predominant form of mass transportation for a city of more than five million inhabitants. The Jeeps come no longer from the United States, but from Japan; only the chassis is imported—the bodies are locally made in small workshops out of galvanized tin. They are, with the exception of certain Italian luxury cars, one of the few modern examples of handmade car bodies.

The fact that a vehicle that was developed for military uses has been adapted to public transportation may be surprising, but it is not untypical. When the bicycle came to Asia from Europe, it too underwent a peculiar transformation; it was combined with a Japanese invention—the rickshaw. The bicycle-rickshaw represented an enormous improvement in efficiency and became popular throughout Asia, especially in India. But the evolution of the rickshaw was not finished. In 1946, the Italian Industrie Aeronautica e Mecanica produced one of the world's most successful vehicles for personal transportation—the Vespa motor scooter. Much smaller and cheaper than a motorcycle, but capable of carrying large loads (in Asia I have seen scooters bearing a family of four), the motor scooter has great appeal in the cities of the less-developed countries. In India in the late 1940s, the motor scooter was combined with the bicycle-rickshaw to produce a further hybrid, the motor-rickshaw, which consists of a scooter with the rear wheel replaced by a two-wheeled axle carrying a passenger bench. Fitted with a new differential, but otherwise mechanically unchanged, the motor-rickshaw can carry many times the load of a scooter—up to three or four people in addition to the driver. Thousands of motor-rickshaws can now be seen in most Indian cities, a strange blend of British, Japanese, and Italian technology coupled with Indian ingenuity and driven with Indian abandon.

It is undeniable that poverty has sometimes created the need to improvise ways of using technology. The fact that different civilizations are able to alter machines to suit themselves gives the lie to the idea that these cultures are being destroyed in their meeting with global technological civilization. A lively debate is now under way in Calcutta concerning the introduction of motor-rickshaws, which displace the traditional bicycle-rickshaws and cannot always be afforded by their owners. It is very much the same sort of issue that must have polarized hansom-cab drivers and taxi drivers in American cities in the early 1900s. It is likely that the bicycle-rickshaw will be replaced by the motor-rickshaw in Calcutta, much the same way that the sedan chair, which was carried by two bearers, was replaced by the rickshaw.

The rickshaw is a dramatic example because it involves the

physical adaptation of a device, but there can also be adaptation to the way a device is used. In Canada and the United States, bus travel, like air travel, is characterized by an atmosphere of impersonal formality. The long-distance bus is seen as a kind of large limousine, piloted by a uniformed chauffeur, who is at the same time a kind of captain and a taciturn extension of the machine—we are warned not to speak to him. A determinist might say that this is the technological system imposing its demand for efficiency and uniformity on the human operator as well as on the passengers. Ellul would fulminate against the technological system; Mumford would complain about the inhumanity of bureaucratized travel. But is the impersonality of mass transportation really inevitable? In other words, are there not other ways to use this technology?

When the technology of bus travel "inundates" a country such as Mexico, the results can be very different. The long-distance *camión* certainly superficially resembles its North American counterpart, but the experience of traveling in it does not. Since the driver is not wearing a uniform, he cannot be mistaken for a chauffeur, though his civilian costume does not seem to impair his driving. The impersonality of his "official" position is further eroded by the mementos that decorate the dashboard—pictures, postcards, snapshots—those things that normally surround a person's place of work, whether in the factory or in the office. The mariachi music coming from the portable radio he has propped against the windshield further softens the mechanical environment. The humanization of the machine is also evident in the small but revealing fact that the bus frequently has a name—*Santo Spirito* or *Maria*. Locomotives were once named in America, ships still are; it is a practice that tells much about our attitude toward a particular technology.

Polish buses do not have names, but they have been adapted to meet the requirements of a different culture. I once traveled to Zakopane, in the Tatra mountains, during the holiday season.

The bus was completely full as it left the terminal, and when it was flagged by people along the route, the driver did not stop, not wishing to surpass his legal load limit. After this had happened once or twice, the passengers in the bus started to complain. They clearly did not believe in "leaving the driving to them." Why didn't the bus stop to pick up more passengers? they wanted to know. There was always room for a few more people, and besides, if he didn't stop, those people would have to wait an hour for the next bus. The chiding was friendly but insistent, and after unsuccessfully trying to defend his actions, the driver had to give in. The next time the bus was flagged down he stopped and let on two or three people who squeezed their way in. The rest of the passengers, mollified now, congratulated him. What might have seemed, in another context, to be a mutiny against the authority of the captain-driver, had here been a struggle for consensus. The technology of the bus had been modified to meet this characteristic feature of Polish culture.

There are many such examples. Recent books written about traveling by train in different countries are fascinating to read precisely because trains in different countries *are* different, not mechanically, but in the way they are used. Although the technology of train travel originated in Europe, an Indian train or a Russian train is used in such a way as to be unmistakably Indian or Russian. The point is that technology is not everything. It is a mistake to look at a Mexican or an Indian bus and say, "Look, they are using our technology," or, seeing differences in application, to conclude that it is not being used in the "right" way. This attitude betrays the arrogance and shortsightedness of the originator, who fails to understand that although a technology may at one time have been *ours*, the process of using it, and controlling it, has now made it *theirs*.

The difficulty with belonging to a civilization that has been the source of so many technical devices is that we expect others to use them in the same way we do. We also assume that since our way must be the correct way, and if it is not copied it has somehow been rejected. The most important lesson that can be learned from seeing the different emphases that different civilizations attach to technology is that this process is determined as much by the nature of the tool-user as by the nature of the tool. Moreover, since we are a dynamic society there is no reason why we cannot reconsider some of our own assumptions about tools.

There is evidence that this has already begun to happen. We are learning that we must decide not just what tool to use, but, much more important, how to use it. We can, in the process, find that the machine is more controllable than we have been led to believe. We can have cars without automatically becoming a car culture—nothing stops us from walking, running, or bicycling as well, or from rebuilding the center of our cities to the scale of the pedestrian. There is no reason why supermarkets cannot offer more unprocessed food—as they are doing—and there is no reason why we cannot know what is in those foods that are processed. Who could have foreseen, thirty years ago, that the Air-Conditioned Nightmare would experience a renaissance of vegetable gardening or physical fitness?

This is not to suggest in any way that a return to supposedly happier, pretechnological times is possible, even if it were desirable. Rather, we are discovering that there are more ways of using machines than we had previously imagined, and that control of the machine resides, finally, in ourselves. It is we who have put machines on pedestals and now we complain that they seem to rule. Perhaps it is time to take them down.

CHAPTER 9

MIRROR, MIRROR ON THE WALL

[Technique] truly mirrors man—like man himself it is clever, it represents something intrinsically improbable, it bears a complex, twisted relationship to nature.

—Arnold Gehlen, *Man in the Age of Technology*

his book has dealt extensively with the past, as the reader has by now discovered, but its purpose has been less to review history than to illuminate contemporary attitudes by the light of historical events. The control of technology is not an academic issue. We live, like it or not, in a Machine Age, just as man once lived in a Stone Age. This does not mean that we must become machinelike, or that we shall be governed by our machines, but it does mean that our future, more than before, will be determined to a great extent by the way in which we deal with technology. If, as I have suggested, a number of our assumptions about technology are mistaken, we may find ourselves re-enacting a Ghost Dance of technological revisionism, with ultimately tragic results. If, like William Morris or Henry Thoreau, we embrace the artificiality of avoiding the artificial, we may end by living a romantic, but brief, illusion. If we dig our heels in and resist the machine, letting it act on us—instead of directing it—we will miss the opportunities it offers, and, worse, we will lose the ability to choose.

The economist Paul A. Samuelson once called technical progress a tiger. Part of the difficulty of taming the tiger is that we can't see the animal clearly. It is easy to identify the boldly striped beast in a cage, but in the splotchy light of the jungle its colors become confused with background shadows. So too with technology. It is easy to discuss in isolation, but immersed in the opacity of human culture its outlines frequently become indistinguishable from its surroundings. This is all the more true because we live in such close proximity to all sorts of machines and we tend to see only a part of the whole. Occasionally, one machine will come to the fore—the computer, for instance— but in focusing on one manifestation of technology we lose sight of the overall pattern. Since we lack the historical perspective to observe the pattern of our own technological environment, we have frequently failed to see what should have been obvious: technology is not a thing.

If we visit a museum of anthropology, we may see a glass case full of odd-shaped bits of flint which, we are told, were once ancient tools. But they become technology only when we know what they were used for; a tool, or a machine, is always an object with a purpose. Technology, it is worth reminding ourselves, is not an object, it is always a means to an end, soon to be misused or, worse, abused. The decline of the automobile industry in the United States has been ascribed to a variety of causes, economic as well as technological, but the real problem did not start when oil prices began to rise, or when the Japanese began building small, inexpensive cars. The decline can be traced to the 1950s, when the automobile industry, and the American public, lost sight of the fact that the car was a means to an end and began thinking of it as an object.

At the same time as the French were producing the long-lived Citroën DS19, the Germans the classic Porsche 356, and the Swedes the durable Volvo Amazon, Harley Earl was designing the Buick Le Sabre for General Motors. In this and subsequent cars, Earl introduced such innovations as wraparound windshields, dummy brake vents, sculptural chrome, and the famous tailfin. The point is not that this was a waste of money —during that prosperous period many Americans could afford the purposeless ornamentation—but that in the eyes of the public and of the industry the car was becoming an object divorced from its actual function. This condition has been characterized as the American love affair with the automobile, and indeed it was that. The problem was that while European, and, later, Japanese cars were designed for handling and performance, American machines were getting farther and farther from their original purpose, that of moving people from one place to another. When in the 1970s the public rediscovered the car as transportation, American industry turned out to be poorly placed to respond. Car manufacturers seemed to know more about styling than about automobile technology, more about visual symbols than about safety or dependability.

Surprisingly, a similar distortion is becoming visible in the field of solar energy. Solar devices are seen more and more as desirable objects that confer some kind of special status on the owner. Politicians and corporations have been quick to realize the symbolic nature of solar devices: President Jimmy Carter had a solar heater installed in the stands for his presidential inauguration, and the top of the Citicorp building in New York exhibits a distinctive wedge shape to accommodate solar panels. The fact that in the first case the heater did not function (it was cloudy) and that Citicorp did not actually install any panels (perhaps the shape was enough) seems to matter less than the original intent to demonstrate awareness and concern.

The same symbolic use of solar technology is evidenced in private houses. How else to explain why the building where a family makes its home is referred to as a "solar house" (could there be a propane house, or a coal house?), as if the method of heating somehow determined its very character. Nomenclature is perhaps trivial, but it masks a more important aberration. The goal of a solar heating system is to heat the home in a manner that is not only less expensive, but also more efficient in the use of increasingly scarce natural resources. But when the solar-heated house becomes a desirable object in itself, costly solar panels are installed without any regard for economic viability. This may explain why, so far, solar devices have been used largely by the wealthy.

At the same time as heating energy is being saved, large amounts of copper, glass, and aluminum are being consumed. What is the effect of this additional use of materials? Since relatively few solar-heated houses are being built at the moment, the effect is slight, but as the British author Martin Pawley has pointed out in *Building for Tomorrow,* this will not always be so. Pawley estimates that the use of solar energy to conserve heating fuel has the effect of almost doubling the amount of energy embodied in the materials used for the construction of the house. Should large numbers of solar-heated houses be built, the effect will be not only reduced heating-fuel consumption, but a massive inflationary increase in demand for various building materials as well as for the energy needed to produce them.

The distortion of solar technology has obscured the main issue, which is not to use the sun, but to reduce costs and to conserve energy. It is likely that this can be achieved in quite different ways. William A. Shurcliff, originally a solar advocate, has reluctantly concluded that even the cheapest solar heating system cannot compete economically with conventionally heated buildings that are simply very well insulated. Nevertheless, as long as solar technology is viewed as an object, rather than as a means to an end, such advice will fall on deaf ears.

When a technology is viewed as a means to an end, its appropriate development is much more likely. At the moment, the microcomputer industry is experiencing rapid, prosperous growth, and it is significant that the attraction of personal computers as objects is minimal. They are not manufactured with a choice of colors or styles; models are not changed from year to year. The changes that have occurred have had to do primarily with their purpose, which is to compute. The changes have also been in the direction of increasing their accessibility to the public through simpler operation, easier controls, and more understandable programs. While the early computer "languages" such as FORTRAN required a good deal of time and effort to learn, more recent languages such as BASIC can be used after only a few hours' practice. So far, at least, the computer manufacturers have not forgotten that the reason for buying a computer is not to own the machine but to solve some particular problem, and the real innovation in personal computers has been less in the machines than in the ready-made programs that are available to use with them.

It is revealing to compare the products of this growing industry with those of a stagnating one such as kitchen appliances. The basic configuration of the modern kitchen range was established by Norman Bel Geddes in a design he evolved for the SGE Company in 1932. In fifty years his design has hardly been improved upon, and some models are actually less convenient. While cooking and eating habits have changed, the kitchen-appliance industry has responded with more or with less chrome, with square or with rounded corners, or with tinted rather than clear oven doors. The kitchen range, like the car, is treated as an object that needs to be annually restyled and superficially altered.

The tendency to see technology as an object can make it difficult to see how it can be improved. Railroads, for instance, obviously need to be improved for medium-distance travel—they are both faster and more efficient than cars—but if this is to be done successfully more than a resurrection will be required.

There is nothing final or absolute about the present state of railroad technology, which is the result of a long and sometimes disconnected evolution. The idea of operating vehicles on rails first occurred in German coal mines in 1550 as a way of easing the movement of heavily loaded wagons. By the end of the sixteenth century flanged wheels were in use, although the tracks were of wood and the wagons were pulled by horses. This situation continued for about two hundred years, and it was not until a steam-driven engine was put on the tracks—again in a mine—that the railroad was born.

The modern railroad depended not only on the invention of the steam engine, but also on the development of a method to produce inexpensive rolled-iron rails. The flanged wheel on a steel rail proved to be an effective way of moving coal, but a less efficient way of transporting people. As speeds increased there was a tendency for the relatively light passenger carriage to tip over since the center of gravity of the car was considerably higher than the center of gravity of the wheels. One solution is to adopt a very wide track gauge, which was tried but abandoned as too expensive. The only other ways to keep high-speed trains on the tracks are to make extremely wide radius curves (as the French have done with their recent "Train Grande Vitesse"), or, since that is not always convenient, to make the train as heavy as possible.* This has resulted in passenger trains that are relatively inefficient, and have been so for many years.

If we persist in seeing railroad technology as an object that needs to be "saved" or "revived" it is unlikely that we will be successful. To improve the passenger train means questioning the premise of the flanged wheel—as French engineers did when they developed subway trains that ran on rubber tires, or as Japanese and German designers are presently doing with

---

*Another common device used to permit trains to achieve higher speeds consists in banking the tracks. At very high speeds, the banking becomes so considerable as to be a major inconvenience to the passengers inside. The British have devised a train whose carriages remain horizontal by swiveling on davits, somewhat like a gyroscope. This complicated technology has not, so far, been put into everyday use.

trains that are supported by magnetic levitation—not just building more tracks and rolling stock.

The fact that machines are not considered as objects does not mean that we cannot have affection for them. We should treat machines endearingly because they do something particularly well, not because of some quality that we have managed to separate from what the machine is actually for. There is nothing wrong with forming an attachment to machines, but in doing so we should be aware that we may distort our vision of what technology is really about.

Perhaps we frequently see machines as objects because they characterize the technological environment in much the same way as trees and rocks characterize the natural one. The existence of both a natural and a technological environment side by side may also explain why it often appears as if machines had invaded what was previously an unmechanical world. It is for this reason that so much emphasis is placed on the inventor and on the act of invention. They are imbued with a magical quality, for we assume that it is the act of invention that opens the Pandora's box of diabolical machines. Once again we have reversed the order of things. Technology does not spring from the mind of the solitary inventor, and it does not occur in a vacuum: technology is always the result of technical activity.

It is obvious that technology is the result of technical activity by the inventor, but what may be less apparent, at least at first glance, is that any technological invention is also the product of the overall technical environment of which it is a part. The claw hammer must be anticipated by the activity of carpentry; the plow by that of agriculture. Or, to put it another way, the act of hammering precedes the invention of the hammer, just as the practice of agriculture precedes the plow. This is not to say that the activity will inevitably produce the required device, or that invention is always the result of need. The act of invention is much more haphazard and even more accidental than that, as I have tried to show. But even if need does not, by itself, stimulate invention, one can at least say that without an existing technical milieu, an invention is unlikely to be recognized as useful, or, even if recognized, it is unlikely to be applied.

Inventions rely on earlier discoveries and previously known skills. Even an unprecedented invention such as the flying machine had its roots in the extensive experience of unpowered gliders already extant and in the independent development of the internal combustion engine. It was also no coincidence that the first powered flight was made by Orville Wright, a manufacturer of bicycles.

The invention of a technology does not, however, guarantee its immediate use. Aviation in the United States did not commence on a wide commercial scale until 1926, more than twenty years after the first successful flight at Kitty Hawk. While the Wright brothers were somewhat ahead of their European contemporaries, their counterparts in England, France, and Germany were the first to actually apply this new technology and to promote commercial, as well as military, aviation.

The time lag that occurs between the *invention* of a device and its *application* is a common feature of most technological development. The first bicycle, for instance, was patented in 1818, but the machine did not achieve popular success until more than fifty years later. Television was invented in 1920, but its first commercial application was in 1931, when the Columbia Broadcasting System began the first of a regular schedule of telecasts, and in most of the United States and Europe television was not widespread until after the Second World War.

The distinction between invention and application is an important one. Application depends on many external factors such as public acceptance, economic incentives that make it attractive to pursue the development of a technology, and the general level of technological development that surrounds and reinforces the invention. The popularity, not to mention the comfort, of the bicycle was greatly enhanced by a subsequent invention—the pneumatic tire. The existence of television is due not only to the successful experiments of Vladimir Zworykin, but also to the consumer society that made the rapid dissemination of the new device possible.

The German economist Gerhard Mensch gives an interesting example that illustrates the absence of inevitability in the application of new technological discoveries (*Stalemate in Technology*). The transistor and the holograph were both patented in the same year—1948—but thirty-four years later, while the transistor has developed into a multibillion-dollar industry, the holograph has remained very much on the sidelines. There are no holographic cinemas, no holographic billboards, no holographic teaching aids. It was not so much that holographic technology was not useful, but that, unlike the transistor or later the microprocessor, it did not fit into any established area of technical activity. It has remained what Mensch termed an "unexploited technology."

Mensch's attempt to postulate a causal link between the application of technological inventions and fluctuating economic cycles is much less convincing. According to his theory, application occurs in "spurts" during periods of economic prosperity; between these bouts of innovation are what he calls "technological stalemates." When Mensch published his book in 1979 the Western world was still recovering from the Oil Crisis of six years before, and the economic conditions would have led one to expect a "stalemate" as far as technological innovation was concerned. In fact, while the Oil Crisis may have had a serious negative effect on the American economy, it also promoted a large number of new energy-conserving technologies. So successful was this unexpected reaction that only nine years later petroleum prices actually began to drop, some petroleum producers such as Mexico went into *de facto* bankruptcy, and the seemingly invincible oil cartel, the Organization of Petroleum Exporting Countries, seemed on the verge of collapse. Nor does Mensch's theory explain, as Martin Pawley has pointed out,

why, in 1982 during a major economic recession, we are wit-
nessing what many have called a "Communications Revolution," the result of the massive application of new technology
in the field of telecommunications and computers.

Which all goes to show that while some investment capital
must be available for the application of new technologies, the
relationship between technological innovation and economics
is hardly one of cause and effect. Just as technology is not governed by an internal imperative, neither is it ruled by a narrow
set of economic conditions. This is not so surprising if one considers that the application of technology ultimately involves
society as a whole, and that technology is not just a constraint
on culture, it is itself a part of culture.

It is inaccurate to speak of a "technological invasion" of society, as if machines sprang fully formed from the imagination of
their inventors onto an unsuspecting public. As the gap between invention and application demonstrates, a certain level
of technical activity must be present in society for the successful
application of technology to take place. The manufacture of the
electric car has been feasible for some time—the first vehicle
powered by a battery-charged electric motor was built only
three years after the invention of the electric motor, in 1834—
but we still await the large-scale commercialization of this technology as a passenger car. Sometimes it takes time to recognize
the potential of a technological device. After the Second World
War, the British operated captured Volkswagen automobile
plants in occupied Germany. For a number of years they produced vehicles, but only for military use, and finally ceased
production without any attempt to convert the plants to civilian
use or to transplant the technology of the "Beetle" to Britain.
Another technology acquired by the Allies was the Pier-Farben
coal hydrogenation process which had been developed by the
Germans to produce synthetic fuel from coal. This technology
was likewise ignored, and today the Pier-Farben process is used
by only one country—South Africa.

On the other hand, the success of the microcomputer industry is not just due to the invention of the inexpensive microprocessor chip, but above all to the presence of technically
competent entrepreneurs who, while they did not necessarily
have the resources to invent technology, were better placed
than large, conservative corporations when it came to innovation. The result was that in 1982, the 4.9 billion-dollar market
in personal computers was still dominated by these newcomers
rather than by the larger, established computer manufacturers.

The importance of the pre-existence of technical activity to
the successful application of technology becomes especially
clear if one examines what happens when technology has been
introduced to societies that were largely untechnological. Here
the cart frequently arrived before the horse, and technology
was acquired without the presence of technical activity. The
current difficulties being experienced by almost all less-
developed countries are due in no small part to this condition.

The fashionable euphemism for the difficulty of implanting
technology in untechnological cultures is "technology transfer," but all this really means is that when technology is taken
out of the cultural context that produced it, its application and
use cannot be taken for granted. Technology transfer is sometimes described as a problem of the poor countries trying to
acquire technology from the rich, but even in those less-
developed countries that are wealthy enough to purchase whatever technology they desire, the application of machines in a
technological vacuum has not been without difficulty.

The limited success of technology in the less-developed countries indicates that the presence of machines alone is not
enough to make a society "technological." Conversely, if our
own culture is technological, it is so not because we have been
overcome by technology, but rather because we have organized ourselves in a certain way. While it may be difficult to
accept, the fact is that our technology is a symptom of our
culture, not vice versa. For, as Heidegger reminds us, technol-

ogy is not only a means to an end: technology is a human activity.

Technology begins not with the tool, but with the human imagination, and the acts of imagining, inventing, and using tools and machines are human acts. So, while technology is certainly artificial, it is also eminently natural. Moreover, since technology is a *human* activity, it is thus a part of human culture and hence reflects the human preoccupations of its time.

Inventions and innovations always occur in a social context. Lenses, for example, were known to the Muslims as early as the tenth century, but their first practical use was recorded in Europe four hundred years later. It should not be a surprise that those who lived in a period that promoted literacy, secular literature, and, later, printing, should have found it necessary to invent reading glasses. Three hundred years later, a more militaristic European culture once again used lenses in a new device—the telescope, whose main application was in target spotting for artillery. It was not any technical constraint that accounted for the lag between reading glasses and the telescope, but rather a change in human activities and interests.

Any attempt to control technology must take into account not only its mechanical nature, but its human nature as well. The engineers who designed the automobile assembly plant at Lordstown were very aware of the purpose of their technology —to produce cars as efficiently as possible—but they ignored the fact that assembling cars is also a human activity. Efficiency measured in purely mechanical terms produced a factory environment that was unacceptable to the workers. It is not a question of creating a "technology with a human face" (a catchy but misleading phrase), but rather of recognizing the human component present in all technology.

It is worth bearing the human factor in mind when considering the impact that automation is likely to have on employment in the near future. Adam Osborne, a computer engineer, has estimated that as many as 50 percent of all jobs held in 1978 in the United States could be eliminated in the next twenty-five years as the result of office and factory automation. Such a drastic change—which, should it occur, would truly qualify as a new Industrial Revolution—is by no means preordained. There are many ways in which society could deal with the new technology. Many nine-to-five jobs could be retained as social institutions, inefficient but culturally desirable. The medieval tradition of working at home could be revived, thus further promoting privatization and individualization. Or, with massive "robotization," the leisure society that sociologists have been predicting for the last fifty years could finally come to pass. The inoffensive computer chip could bring about any of these changes, but which one will actually occur will depend as much on how society chooses to organize itself as on the technology alone. Issues such as the redefinition of work in the home (including housework), the relationship between labor and management in the workplace, and adult access to education will have to be re-examined if the right technological choices are to be made.

An earlier communications innovation—the technology of paper-making and movable type—had a momentous effect on life in fifteenth-century Europe. Braudel estimated that during that century, the number of printed books increased from about twenty million to an astonishing two hundred million, with a consequent acceleration in the exchange of information and in the development of ideas *(Capitalism and Material Life 1400–1800)*. The latter had a particularly marked effect on changes in philosophy (humanism), science (the Renaissance), and religion (the Reformation).

The printed book neatly illustrates a number of the points I have been trying to make in this chapter. While it was an object, it was above all a means to an end: the transmission of information. It was also the result of technical activity. Although neither paper-making nor movable type were European inventions—

they had originated in China and Japan—their use in Europe in the early fourteenth century was linked to earlier technical developments. Particularly important were the use of water-power and the knowledge of metallurgy; waterwheels were required for mass producing paper, while metallurgy made possible the rapid proliferation of typesetting (the first type was made by goldsmiths). But the printed book was also the result of another activity (technical in the broadest sense of the word): reading. The development of European paper-making, which preceded the invention of the printing press by more than a hundred years, was a response to the growing demand for books, which, before the introduction of paper, had to be hand-written on expensive parchment manufactured from animal skins. Movable type simply completed the process of making less expensive books available to larger numbers of people.

The printed book also demonstrates the human aspect of technology, for the essence of the book lay not in its printing but in the human activities of writing and reading. The technology of the book also opened possibilities for human insights and understanding that previously would have been impossible. Perhaps the computer will do the same, for it is not just that we are influenced by our tools and machines, but that in using them we are able to rediscover our environment, and ourselves.

Why then do we distrust technology? Why do we still insist on referring to modern technology as inhuman, or at least dehumanizing? Part of the difficulty seems to be that we have a confused attitude toward machines; we form quixotic attachments to old technologies that make it even harder for us to accept new ones. This romantic view generally ignores the disadvantages of old devices and describes previous technologies in idealized and often inaccurate terms. The picturesque medieval hamlet is appealingly portrayed in charming paintings, but the smell, the putrefaction and decay that were a part of that sewerless society are forgotten. Renaissance buildings are admired for their solidity, but their lack of even the most basic comforts goes unremembered. Beautiful, nineteenth-century sailing ships are romanticized, but the suffering and human misery that characterized the lives of their hapless crews are ignored. As a result, it is hardly surprising that we fail to understand why these "wonderful old devices" were replaced by "heartless modern technology."

Not a little of the difficulty that our culture experiences with new technology stems from this romantic posture. No sooner does a new technology come along than we suddenly discover previously unrecognized values in its antecedent. When the typewriter first became popular, it was still considered ill-mannered to use it for personal letters—they had to be written by hand. Today, the word processor is replacing the typewriter, but efficient, automated dot-matrix printers are not used for business letters because the result does not look as if it had been typewritten.

If machines such as old steam engines, hot-air balloons, or horse-drawn carriages are viewed more sentimentally than die-sel generators, wide-body jets, and compact cars, it may be that, having lost their utility, they can now be seen as artistic, rather than scientific, objects. Literature and art have consistently emphasized the duality of the natural and the artificial, but the natural is elusive—as Thoreau found—so it has been necessary to classify older machines as being more "natural" than newer ones. This illogical schism makes it even more difficult to understand and to control new technological developments.

We claim that we are afraid of becoming machinelike, but what if technology is actually humanlike? We believe that mass production goes against "the laws of nature," whereas mass production is precisely how nature reproduces itself, whether it is in the production of seeds by plants or of ova by animals. As we learn more about the biological building blocks of the natural environment, we are coming to realize that the universe is, like a machine, made up of standardized, interchangeable parts.

We think that obsolescence is uniquely the product of technology, but Martin Pawley reminds us that "Short-life products are no more unnatural than short-life insects or fish, and none need be wasteful in an evolutionary sense." Indeed, he goes on to suggest that there is no reason why technological evolution, which thus far has been more or less haphazard, could not be brought under control by a kind of "product eugenics" which would draw on the genetic pool of scientific ideas to form effective chains of reusable products. If this seems farfetched, consider the numerous examples cited previously of technologies that have drawn on earlier, and apparently unrelated devices or have combined known machines in unexpected mutations.

Whether we control technology by directing its evolution, by choosing when and how to use it, or by deciding what significance it should have in our lives, we shall succeed only if we are able to accept what at first appears to be an impossible shift in our point of view: different as people and machines are, they exist not in two different worlds, but at two ends of the same continuum. Just as we have discovered that we are a part of the natural environment, and not just surrounded by it, so also we will find that we are an intimate part of the environment of technology. The auxiliary "organs" that extend our sight, our hearing, and our thinking really are an extension of our physical bodies. When we are able to accept this, we shall discover that the struggle to control technology has all along been a struggle to control ourselves.

BIBLIOGRAPHY

Aronowitz, Stanley. *False Promises: The Shaping of American Working-Class Consciousness.* New York: McGraw-Hill, 1973.

Ashton, T. S. *Industrial Revolution: 1760–1830.* Oxford: Oxford University Press, 1948.

Ayalon, David. *Gunpowder and Firearms in the Mamluk Kingdom.* London: Vallentine, Mitchell, 1956.

Baker, David. *The Rocket: The History and Development of Rocket and Missile Technology.* London: New Cavendish Books, 1978.

Banham, Reyner. *The Architecture of the Well-Tempered Environment.* London: Architectural Press, 1969.

———. *Theory and Design in the First Machine Age.* London: Architectural Press, 1960.

Bauer, P. T. *Equality, the Third World, and Economic Delusion.* Cambridge, Mass.: Harvard University Press, 1981.

Bayer, Herbert, et al. *Bauhaus: 1919–1928.* Boston: Branford, 1959.

Bayley, Stephen. *In Good Shape: Style in Industrial Products 1900–1960.* New York: Van Nostrand, 1979.

Beddall, T. G. "Godin's Familistère," *Architectural Design* (July 1976), Vol. XLVI, 7.

Bell, Daniel. *The Coming of the Post-Industrial Society.* New York: Basic Books, 1973.

Boorstin, Daniel J. *The Republic of Technology: Reflections on Our Future Community.* New York: Harper, 1978.

Borton, Hugh. *Peasant Uprisings in Japan of the Tokugawa Period.* New York: Praeger, 1968.

Braudel, Fernand. *Capitalism and Material Life 1400–1800.* Trans. Miriam Kochan. London: Weidenfeld, 1973.

———. *On History.* Trans. Sarah Matthews. Chicago: University of Chicago Press, 1980.

Brecher, J. *Strike!* San Francisco: Straight Arrow, 1972.

Brown, Delmer M. "The Impact of Firearms on Japanese Warfare, 1543–98," *Far Eastern Quarterly* (May 1948), Vol. VII, 3.

Brown, Frederic J. *Chemical Warfare: A Study in Restraints.* Princeton: Princeton University Press, 1968.

Brown, Mervyn. *Madagascar Rediscovered: A History from Early Times to Independence.* London: Tunnacliffe, 1978.

Burke, James. *Connections.* Boston: Little, Brown, 1978.

Byam, Wally. *Trailer Travel Here and Abroad.* New York: McKay, 1960.

Cipolla, Carlo M. *Guns, Sails and Empires: Technological Innovation and the Early Phases of European Expansion 1400–1700.* New York: Pantheon, 1965.

Cooper, Kent. *Barriers Down: The Story of the News Agency Epoch.* New York: Farrar & Rinehart, 1942.

Davey, Peter, ed. *Arts and Crafts Architecture: The Search for Earthly Paradise.* London: Architectural Press, 1980.

Deighton, Len. *Blitzkrieg: From the Rise of Hitler to the Fall of Dunkirk.* London: Cape, 1979.

Derry, T. K., and Williams, T. I. *A Short History of Technology.* Oxford: Oxford University Press, 1960.

Dornberger, Walter. *V-2.* Trans. James Cleugh and Geoffrey Halliday. New York: Viking, 1955.

Drucker, Peter. *Technology, Management and Society.* New York: Harper, 1970.

Dubois, Pierre. *Sabotage in Industry.* Trans. Rosemary Sheed. Harmondsworth, U.K.: Penguin, 1979.

Eber, Dorothy. *The Computer Centre Party.* Montreal: Tundra, 1969.

Eckener, Hugo. *My Zeppelins.* Trans. Douglas Robinson. New York: Arno, 1980.

Edwards, Richard C. *Contested Terrain: The Transformation of the Workplace in the 20th Century.* New York: Basic Books, 1979.

Ellis, William. *History of Madagascar.* London: Fisher, 1838.

Ellul, Jacques. *The Technological Society.* Trans. John Wilkinson. New York: Vintage, 1964.

———. *The Technological System.* Trans. Joachim Neugroschel. New York: Continuum, 1980.

Emerson, Ralph Waldo. *English Traits.* Cambridge, Mass.: Harvard University Press, 1883.

Engels, Friedrich. *The Condition of the Working Class in England.* Oxford: Blackwell, 1971.

Filene, Edward A. *The Way Out: A Forecast of Coming Changes in American Business and Industry.* Garden City, N.Y.: Doubleday, 1924.

Fitch, James Marston. *American Building 2: The Environmental Forces That Shape It.* New York: Schocken, 1975.

Florman, Samuel C. *Blaming Technology: The Irrational Search for Scapegoats.* New York: St. Martin's, 1981.

Ford, Henry. "Mass Production," *Encyclopaedia Britannica.* Chicago: 1949.

Forslin, Jan, et al. "Automation and Work Organization—A Swedish Experience," from *Automation and Industrial Workers: A Fifteen-Nation Study.* Oxford: Pergamon, 1979.

Franciscono, Marcel. *Walter Gropius and the Creation of the Bauhaus in Weimar: The Ideals and Artistic Theories of Its Founding Years.* Urbana, Ill.: University of Illinois Press, 1971.

Frankel, S. H. *The Economic Impact on Under-developed Societies.* Oxford: Blackwell, 1953.

Freud, Sigmund. *Civilization and Its Discontents.* Trans. Joan Riviere. London: Hogarth, 1963.

Gehlen, Arnold. *Man in the Age of Technology.* Trans. Patricia Lipscomb. New York: Columbia University Press, 1980.

Giedion, Siegfried. *Mechanization Takes Command: A Contribution to Anonymous History.* New York: Norton, 1948.

Gilder, George. *Wealth and Poverty.* New York: Basic Books, 1981.

Gimpel, Jean. *The Medieval Machine: The Industrial Revolution of the Middle Ages.* New York: Holt, Rinehart, 1976.

Gooding, Judson. "Blue-Collar Blues on the Assembly Line," *Fortune* (July 1970).

Hammond, J. L., and Barbara. *The Skilled Labourer, 1760–1832.* London: Longmans, 1919.

———. *The Town Labourer: the new civilization, 1760–1832.* London: Longmans, 1917.

———. *The Village Labourer, 1760–1832.* London: Longmans, 1932.

Handlin, David P. *The American Home: Architecture and Society, 1815–1915.* Boston: Little, Brown, 1979.

Harding, Walter. *The Days of Henry Thoreau.* New York: Knopf, 1966.

Heidegger, Martin. *The Question Concerning Technology and Other Essays.* Trans. William Lovitt. New York: Harper, 1977.

Herbert, Gilbert. *Gropius, Hirsch and the Saga of the Copper Houses.* Publication No. 1, Documentation Unit of Architecture, Haifa: Technion—Israel Institute of Technology, June 1980.

Hildebrand, G. C., and Porter, G. *Cambodia: Starvation and Revolution.* New York: Monthly Review Press, 1976.

Hobsbawm, E. J. *Laboring Men: Studies in the History of Labor.* New York: Basic Books, 1964.

Hobsbawm, E. J., and Rudé, George. *Captain Swing.* New York: Pantheon, 1968.

Hodgkins, Eric, and Magoun, F. Alexander. *Behemoth: The Story of Power.* New York: Junior Literary Guild, 1932.

Hoggart, Richard. *An Idea and Its Servants: UNESCO from Within.* New York: Oxford University Press, 1978.

Howard, Robert. "Brave New Workplace," *Working Papers* (Nov.-Dec. 1980).

Illich, Ivan. *Tools for Conviviality.* New York: Harper, 1973.

———. *Toward a History of Needs.* New York: Pantheon, 1977.

Irving, David. *The Mare's Nest.* Boston: Little, Brown, 1965.

Jaffe, A. J., and Froomkin, Joseph. *Technology and Jobs: Automation in Perspective.* New York: Praeger, 1968.

Jones, Christopher. "In the Land of the Khmer Rouge," *The New York Times Magazine* (Dec. 20, 1981).

Kamarck, Andrew M. *The Tropics and Economic Development: A Provocative Inquiry into the Poverty of Nations.* Baltimore: Johns Hopkins University Press, 1976.

Kasson, John F. *Civilizing the Machine: Technology and Republican Values in America, 1776–1900.* New York: Penguin, 1976.

Kranzberg, Melvin, and Davenport, William H., eds. *Technology and Culture.* New York: Schocken, 1972.

La Barre, Weston. *The Ghost Dance: Origins of Religion.* New York: Dell, 1970.

Latham, Ian, ed. *New Free Style: Arts and Crafts-Art Nouveau-Secession.* London: Rizzoli, 1980.

Lethaby, W. R. *Philip Webb: and his work.* London: Oxford University Press, 1935.

Leys, Simon. *Chinese Shadows.* New York: Viking, 1977.

Lindsay, Jack. *William Morris: His Life and Work.* London: Constable, 1975.

Lukacs, John. *The Passing of the Modern Age.* New York: Harper, 1970.

Lyons, Gene. "Invisible Wars," *Harper's* (Dec. 1981).

Mackail, J. W. *The Life of William Morris.* London: Longmans, 1922.

Macksey, Kenneth. *Guderian: Panzer General.* London: Macdonald and Jane's, 1975.

Marx, Leo. *The Machine in the Garden: Technology and the Pastoral Idea in America.* New York: Oxford University Press, 1964.

Maung, Mya. *Burma and Pakistan: A Comparative Study of Development.* New York: Praeger, 1971.

Mayo, Elton. *The Human Problems of an Industrial Civilization.* New York: Macmillan, 1933.

Mazlish, Bruce. "The Fourth Discontinuity," *Technology and Culture* (Winter 1967), Vol. VIII, 1.

Mensch, Gerhard. *Stalemate in Technology: Innovations Overcome the Depression.* Cambridge, Mass.: Ballinger, 1979.

Mooney, James. "The Ghost Dance Religion," *Fourteenth Annual Report of the Bureau of Ethnology.* Washington, D.C.: Government Printing Office, 1896.

Mooney, Michael M. *The Hindenburg.* New York: Dodd, 1972.

Morison, Elting E. *Men, Machines and Modern Times.* Cambridge, Mass.: MIT Press, 1966.

Mumford, Lewis. *The Myth of the Machine, Vol. 1: Technics and Human Development.* New York: Harcourt, 1967.

——. *The Myth of the Machine, Vol. 2: The Pentagon of Power.* New York: Harcourt, 1970.

―――. *Technics and Civilization.* New York: Harcourt, 1934.

Musashi, Miyamoto. *The Book of Five Rings.* Trans. Victor Harris. Woodstock, N.Y.: Overlook, 1974.

Myrdal, Gunnar. *The Challenge of World Poverty.* New York: Random House, 1970.

Najpaul, V. S. *Among the Believers: An Islamic Journey.* London: Deutsch, 1981.

―――. *India: A Wounded Civilization.* New York: Knopf, 1977.

Neumann, Eckhard. *Bauhaus and Bauhaus People.* New York: Van Nostrand, 1970.

Noble, David. "Social Choice in Machine Design," from *Case Studies on the Labor Process.* A. Zimbalist, ed. New York: Monthly Review Press, 1979.

Oakeshott, Michael. *Rationalism in Politics: and other essays.* New York: Basic Books, 1962.

Orgill, Douglas. *The Tank: Studies in the Development and Use of a Weapon.* London: Heinemann, 1970.

Ortega y Gasset, José. *Revolt of the Masses.* New York: Norton, 1932.

Osborne, Adam. *Running Wild: The Next Industrial Revolution.* Berkeley, Ca.: Osborne/McGraw-Hill, 1979.

Pawley, Martin. *Building for Tomorrow: Putting Waste to Work.* San Francisco: Sierra Club, 1982.

Payne, Lee. *Lighter Than Air: An Illustrated History of the Airship.* New York: Barnes, 1977.

Perrin, Noel. *Giving Up the Gun: Japan's Reversion to the Sword, 1543–1879.* Boulder, Co.: Shambhala, 1980.

Pevsner, Nikolaus. *Pioneers of the Modern Movement: From William Morris to Walter Gropius.* London: Faber, 1936.

Ponchaud, François. *Cambodia: Year Zero.* Trans. Nancy Amphoux. New York: Holt, Rinehart, 1978.

Power, Philip H., and Aber, Elie. "Third World vs. the Media," *The New York Times Magazine* (Sept. 21, 1980).

Prest, J. *Industrial Revolution in Coventry.* London: Oxford University Press, 1960.

Revel, Jean-François. "L'Internationale du mensonge," *L'Express* (March 14, 1981), 1548.

Righter, Rosemary. *Whose News?: Politics, the Press and the Third World.* London: Burnett, 1978.

Roa, Y. V. Lakshmana. "Information FLow from advanced to Developing Countries," from *Getting the Message Across*. Paris: UNESCO Press, 1975.

Robinson, Douglas H. *Giants in the Sky: A History of the Rigid Airship*. Henley-on-Thames, U.K.: Foulis, 1973.

Rosenblum, Mort. "Reporting from the Third World," *Foreign Affairs* (July 1977), Vol. LV, 4.

———. "The Western Wire Services and the Third World," from *The Third World and Press Freedom*. Philip C. Horton, ed. New York: Praeger, 1978.

Rybczynski, Witold. *Paper Heroes: A Review of Appropriate Technology*. Garden City, N.Y.: Anchor, 1980.

Sampson, Anthony. *The Money Lenders: Bankers in a World in Turmoil*. New York: Viking, 1981.

Scoffern, J. *Projectile Weapons of War*. London: Longman, Brown, 1859.

Sethi, S. S. *Kampuchean Tragedy: Maoism in Action*. New Delhi: Kalamkar Prakashaw, 1979.

Shand, Philip Morton. "Type Forms in Great Britain," *Die Form* (Berlin) (Jahrgang 5, 1930).

Shawcross, William. *Side-Show: Kissinger, Nixon and the Destruction of Cambodia*. New York: Simon & Schuster, 1979.

Shepard, Jon M. *Automation and Alienation: A Study of Office and Factory Workers*. Cambridge, Mass.: MIT Press, 1971.

Sheppard, Harold L., and Herrick, Neal Q. *Where Have All the Robots Gone? Worker Dissatisfaction in the 70s*. New York: Free Press, 1972.

Shurcliff, William A. "Superinsulated Houses and Double Envelope Houses." Cambridge, Mass.: Unpublished report, Sept. 9, 1980.

Sibree, James, Jr. *Madagascar and Its People*. London: Religious Tract Society, 1870.

Silverstein, Josef. *Burma: Military Rule and the Politics of Stagnation*. Ithaca, N.Y.: Cornell University Press, 1977.

Simon, Julian L. *The Ultimate Resource*. Princeton, N.J.: Princeton University Press, 1981.

Smith, Anthony. *The Geopolitics of Information*. New York: Oxford University Press, 1980.

Speer, Albert. *Infiltration*. Trans. Joachim Neugroschel. New York: Macmillan, 1981.

Strandh, Sigvard. *A History of the Machine*. Trans. Ann Henning. New York: A & W, 1979.

Stratton, Arthur. *The Great Red Island*. New York: Scribner's, 1964.

Sudra, Tomasz. "The Case of Ismailia—can architect and planner usefully participate in the housing process?" *Open House* (1980), Vol. V, 1.

Taper, Bernard. "The Bittersweet Harvest," *Science 80* (Nov. 1980).

Taylor, L., and Walton, P. "Industrial Sabotage: Motives and Meanings," from *Images of Deviance*. S. Cohen, ed. London: Penguin, 1971.

Thomis, Malcomb I. *The Town Labourer and the Industrial Revolution*. London: Batsford, 1974.

Thompson, E. P. *The Making of the English Working Class*. London: Penguin, 1963.

———. *William Morris: Romantic to Revolutionary*. London: Lawrence & Wishart, 1955.

Thoreau, Henry David. *Walden*. Princeton, N.J.: Princeton University Press, 1971.

Toland, John. *Ships in the Sky: The Story of the Great Dirigibles*. New York: Henry Holt & Co., 1957.

Wain, Barry. "Born-Again Nation," *Wall Street Journal* (Feb. 5, 1981).

Walker, Charles, and Guest, Robert H. *The Man on the Assembly Line*. Cambridge, Mass.: Harvard University Press, 1952.

White, Lynn, Jr. *Medieval Religion and Technology: Collected Essays*. Berkeley, Ca.: University of California Press, 1978.

———. *Medieval Technology and Social Change*. New York: Oxford University Press, 1972.

———. "The Act of Invention: Causes, Contexts, Continuities, and Consequences," *Technology and Culture* (Fall 1962), Vol. III, 4.

Wilcox, Dennis L. *Mass Media in Black Africa: Philosophy and Control*. New York: Praeger, 1975.

Winner, Langdon. *Autonomous Technology: Technics-out-of-Control as a Theme in Political Thought*. Cambridge, Mass.: MIT Press, 1977.

Wingler, Hans Maria, ed. *The Bauhaus*. Cambridge, Mass.: MIT Press, 1969.

Wintringham, Tom. *Weapons and Tactics*. London: Faber, 1943.

Yarrow, M. "The Labor Process in Coal Mining: Struggle for Control," from *Case Studies on the Labor Process*. A. Zimbalist, ed. New York: Monthly Review Press, 1979.

Zimbalist, A. "Technology and the Labor Process," from *Case Studies on the Labor Process*. A. Zimbalist, ed. New York: Monthly Review Press, 1979.

INDEX